Isaac Watts

Doctor Watts's imitation of the Psalms of David

Corrected and enlarged. Fourth Edition

Isaac Watts

Doctor Watts's imitation of the Psalms of David
Corrected and enlarged. Fourth Edition

ISBN/EAN: 9783337101985

Printed in Europe, USA, Canada, Australia, Japan

Cover: Foto ©Lupo / pixelio.de

More available books at **www.hansebooks.com**

Doctor WATTS's
IMITATION
OF THE
PSALMS
OF
DAVID,
CORRECTED AND ENLARGED,
By JOEL BARLOW.
TO WHICH IS ADDED
A COLLECTION OF
HYMNS;

The whole applied to the State of the CHRISTIAN Church in general.

THE FOURTH EDITION.

LUKE XXIV. *All things must be fulfilled which were written in the—PSALMS concerning me.*

AT a Meeting of the General Association of the State of Connecticut in June last, it was thought expedient, that a number of the Psalms in Doctor WATT's version, which are locally appropriated, should be altered and applied to the state of the Christian Church in general, and not to any particular country; and finding some attempts had been made to alter and apply those Psalms to America, or particular parts of America, tending to destroy that uniformity in the use of Psalmony, so desirable in religious assemblies; they appointed the Rev. Messrs. *Timothy Pitkin*, *John Smally* and *Theodore Hinsdale*, a Committee to confer with and apply to Mr. *Joel Barlow*, of Hartford, to make the proposed alteration. These, together with the additions and the collection of Hymns annexed to this Edition, we have carefully examined and approved; and we therefore recommend them to the use of the Church of CHRIST, for the purposes of public worship and private devotion.

TIMOTHY PITKIN, } *Committee of*
JOHN SMALLY, } *General*
THEODORE HINSDALE. } *Association.*

The following Gentlemen, appointed by particular Associations, to examine and revise, concur in the above Recommendation.

NATHAN WILLIAMS,
THOMAS W. BRAY,
NATHAN PERKINS.

January 1, 1785.

PREFACE.

THE reasons for undertaking the Corrections and Additions, contained in this Edition of the Psalms are sufficiently explained in the foregoing Narrative of the General Association's Committee. Yet the difficulty of giving general satisfaction in attempts of this kind, cannot be realized till the experiment be made. Among the many Versions which have been given of these Divine Songs in order to adapt them to the Christian State and Worship, that of DOCTOR WATTS is undoubtedly in many respects to be preferred. His Application of the prophetic passages; his easy and natural explication of parts that are in any measure obscure; his pure and elevated strains of devotion, so pleasing to every pious and attentive Reader, have perhaps never been equalled in our Language: And with respect to his style and manner of versification, they are not only better adapted to the capacities of common assemblies, and the easy solemnity of Church Music, than any other that have yet appeared; but it may be presumed that no Poet after him will succeed in composing devotional songs, without taking his model of style and versification from Doctor Watts. Were it not for his local appropriation of some Psalms, and his omission of a few others, his Version would doubtless have been used for many ages without amendment. But as the author of these corrections is employed, directed and supported by so respectable a Body as the whole Clergy of the State: and as it is an object of great importance that harmony and uniformity should be established as extensively as possible in the use of Psalmody, he has not only avoided all local applications, but has made some slighter corrections in point of elegance, where the rules of grammer, established since the time of Doctor Watts, have made it necessary.

The Psalms considerably altered are the 21st, 60th, 67th, 75th, 124th, 147th; those omitted by Doctor Watts, are the 28th, 43d, 52d, 54th, 59th, 64th, 70th, 79th, 88th, 108th, 137th, 140th.

The Hymns are selected chiefly from Doctor Watts: some are entirely new. It was thought adviseable to bind them in the same volume, that sacramental and other particular occasions, not provided for in the Book of Psalms, might be supplied with suitable songs of devotion.

IMITATION

OF THE

Psalms of David.

PSALM I. Common Metre.
The Way and End of the Righteous and the Wicked.

1. BLEST is the man who shuns the place,
   Where sinners love to meet;
   Who fears to read their wicked ways,
   And hates the scoffer's seat.

2. But in the statutes of the Lord,
   Has plac'd his chief delight;
   By day he reads or hears the word,
   And meditates by night.

3. [He like a plant of generous kind
   By living waters set,
   Safe from the storms and blasting wind,
   Enjoys a peaceful state.]

4. Green as the leaf, and ever fair
   Shall his profession shine;
   While fruits of holiness appear
   Like clusters on the vine.

5. Not so the impious and unjust;
   What vain designs they form!
   Their hopes are blown away like dust,
   Or chaff before the storm.

6. Sinners in judgment shall not stand
   Among the sons of grace,

PSALM I.

When *Christ* the Judge at his right-hand
  Appoints his saints a place.

7. His eye beholds the path they tread,
  His heart approves it well;
But crooked ways of sinners lead
  Down to the gates of hell.

PSALM I. Short Metre.
The Saint happy, the Sinner miserable.

1. THE man is ever blest,
    Who shuns the sinners' ways,
  Among their councils never stands,
    Nor takes the scorner's place.

2. But makes the law of God
    His study and delight,
  Amidst the labours of the day,
    And watches of the night.

3. He like a tree shall thrive,
    With waters near the root;
  Fresh as the leaf his name shall live,
    His works are heavenly fruit.

4. Not so th' ungodly race,
    They no such blessings find:
  Their hopes shall flee like empty chaff
    Before the driving wind.

5. How will they bear to stand
    Before that judgment seat,
  Where all the saints at *Christ's* right hand
    In full assembly meet?

6. He knows and he approves
    The way the righteous go:
  But sinners and their works shall meet
    A dreadful overthrow.

PSALM I. Long Metre.
The Difference between the Righteous and the Wicked.

1. HAPPY the man, whose cautious feet
    Shun the broad way where sinners go,

Who hates the place where Atheists meet,
And fears to talk as scoffers do.

2. He loves t'employ his morning light
Among the statutes of the Lord:
And spends the wakeful hours of night,
With pleasure pond'ring o'er the word.

3. He, like a plant by gentle streams,
Shall flourish in immortal green;
And Heaven will shine with kindest beams,
On every work his hands begin.

4. But sinners find their councils cross'd;
As chaff before the tempest flies;
So shall their hopes be blown and lost,
When the last trumpet shakes the skies.

5. In vain the rebel seeks to stand
In judgment with the pious race;
The dreadful Judge with stern command
Divides him to a different place.

6. " Strait is the Way my saints have trod,
" I blest the path, and drew it plain;
" But you would chuse the crooked road;
" And down it leads to endless pain.

PSALM II. Short Metre.
Translated according to the Divine Pattern.
Acts iv. 24, &c.
Christ *Dying, Rising, Interceding, and Reigning.*

1. [MAKER and sovereign Lord
Of heaven and earth and seas,
Thy providence confirms thy word,
And answers thy decrees.

2. The things so long foretold
By David are fulfill'd;
When *Jews* and *Gentiles* join to slay
Jesus, thine holy Child.]

3. Why did the *Gentiles* rage,
And *Jews* with one accord
Join all their councils to destroy
Th' Anointed of the Lord?

4 Rulers and Kings agree
   To form a vain design;
Against the Lord their powers unite,
   Against his Christ they join.

5. The Lord derides their rage,
   And will support his throne;
He that hath rais'd him from the dead,
   Hath own'd him for his son.

P A U S E.

6. Now he's ascending high,
   To rule the subject earth;
The merit of his blood he pleads,
   And pleads his heavenly birth.

7. Beneath his soveregn sway
   The *Gentile* nations bend;
Far as the world's remotest bounds,
   His Kingdom shall extend.

8. The nations that rebel,
   Must feel his iron rod;
He'll vindicate those honours well
   Which he receiv'd from God.

9. [Be wise, ye rulers, now,
   And worship at his throne;
With trembling joy, ye people bow,
   To God's exalted Son.

10. If once his wrath arise,
   Ye perish on the place;
Then blessed is the soul that flies
   For refuge to his grace.]

P S A L M II. Common Metre.

1. WHY did the nations join to slay
   The Lord's anointed Son?
Why did they cast his laws away,
   And tread his gospel down?

2. The Lord that sits above the skies,
   Derides their rage below,
He speaks with vengeance in his eyes,
   And strikes their spirits through.

3. "I call him my eternal Son,
   "And raise him from the dead ;
   "I make my holy hill his throne,
   "And wide his kingdom spread.

4. "Ask me, my Son, and then enjoy
   "The utmost *heathen* lands ;
   "Thy rod of iron shall destroy
   "The rebel that withstands."

5. Be wise, ye rulers of the earth,
   Obey th' anointed Lord,
   Adore the King of heavenly birth,
   And tremble at his word.

6. With humble love address his throne,
   For if he frown, ye die :
   Those are secure, and those alone
   Who on his grace rely.

PSALM II. Long Metre.

Christ's *Death, Resurrection, and Ascension.*

1. WHY did the *Jews* proclaim their rage ?
   The *Romans* why their swords employ ?
   Against the Lord their powers engage,
   His dear Anointed to destroy ?

2. "Come let us break his bands, they say,
   "This man shall never give us laws ;"
   And thus they cast his yoke away,
   And nail'd the Monarch to the cross.

3. But God, who high in glory reigns,
   Laughs at their pride, their rage controuls ;
   He'll smite their hearts with inward pains,
   And speak in thunder to their souls.

4. "I will maintain the King I made
   "On *Zion's* everlasting hill,
   "My hand shall bring him from the dead,
   "And he shall stand your sovereign still."

5. [His wondrous rising from the earth
   Makes his eternal Godhead known ;
   The Lord declares his heavenly birth :
   "This day have I begot my Son.

6. "Ascend, my Son, to my right-hand,
   "There thou shalt ask, and I bestow
   "The utmost bounds of *heathen* lands ;
   "To thee their suppliant tribes shall bow."]

7. But nations that resist his grace
   Shall fall beneath his lifted rod ;
   His arm shall crush the impious race,
   That dare provoke th' avenging God.

PAUSE.

8. Now ye that sit on earthly thrones,
   Be wise, and serve the Lord, the Lamb ;
   Now to his feet submit your crowns,
   Rejoice and tremble at his name.

9. With humble love address the Son,
   Lest he grow angry, and ye die ;
   His wrath will burn to worlds unknown,
   His love gives life above the sky.

10. His storms shall quell the stubborn foe,
    And sink his honours in the dust :
    Happy the souls, their God that know,
    And make his grace their only trust.

PSALM III. Common Metre.

Doubts and Fears suppressed; or, God our defense from Sin and Satan.

1 MY God, how many are my fears ?
    How fast my foes increase ?
  Conspiring my eternal death,
    They break my present peace.

2 The lying tempter would persuade
    Ther's no releaf in heaven,
  And all my growing sins appear
    Too great to be forgiven.

3 But thou, my glory, and my strength,
    Shalt on the tempter tread,
  Shalt silence all my threatening guilt,
    And raise my drooping head.

4 [I cry'd, and from his holy hill
    He bow'd a listening ear ;

I call'd my Father, and my God,
    And he subdued my fear.

5 He shed soft slumbers on mine eyes,
    In spite of all my foes;
I woke and wonder'd at the grace
    That guarded my repose.]

6 What tho' the hosts of death and hell
    All arm'd against me stood;
Terrors no more shall shake my soul;
    My refuge is my God.

7 Arise, O Lord, fulfill thy grace,
    While I thy glory sing;
My God has broke the serpent's teeth,
    And death has lost his sting.

8 Salvation to the Lord belongs,
    His arm alone can save;
Blessings attend thy people here,
    And reach beyond the grave.

PSALM III. *Ver.* 1, 2, 3, 4, 5. 8. Long Metre.
A Morning Psalm.

1 O Lord, how many are my foes,
    In this weak state of flesh and blood?
My peace they daily discompose,
But my defence and hope is God.

2 Tired with the burdens of the day,
To thee I rais'd an evening cry;
Thou heard'st when I began to pray,
And thine Almighty help was nigh.

3 Supported by thine heavenly aid
I laid me down and slept secure;
Not death should make my heart afraid,
Though I should wake and rise no more.

4 But God sustain'd me all the night;
Salvation doth to God belong:
He rais'd my head to see the light,
And makes his praise my morning song.

PSALM IV. 1, 2, 3, 4 6, 7. Long Metre.

Hearing of Prayer; or God our Portion, and Christ our Hope.

1 O God of grace and righteousness,
   Hear and attend when I complain:
Thou hast enlarg'd me in distress,
Bow down a gracious ear again.

2 Ye sons of men in vain ye try
To turn my glory into shame
How long will scoffers love to lie,
And dare reproach my Saviour's name?

3 Know that the Lord divides his saints
From all the tribes of men beside;
He hears and pities their complaints,
For the dear sake of Christ that died.

4 When our obedient hands have done
A thousand works of righteousness,
We put our trust in God alone,
And glory in his pard'ning grace.

5 Let the unthinking many say,
" *Who will bestow some earthly good?*
But, Lord, thy light and love we pray;
Our souls desire this heavenly food.

6 Then shall my cheerful powers rejoice
At grace divine, and love so great;
Nor will I change my happy choice
For all their wealth and boasted state.

PSALM IV. *Ver.* 3, 4, 5, 8. Com. Metre.
An Evening Hymn.

1 LORD, thou wilt hear me when I pray;
   I am for ever thine;
I fear before thee all the day,
   Nor would I dare to sin.

2 And while I rest my weary head,
   From cares and business free,
'Tis sweet conversing on my bed,
   With my own heart and thee.

3 I pay this evening sacrifice;
　　And when my work is done,
Great God, my faith and hope relies
　　Upon thy grace alone.

4 Thus with my thoughts compos'd to peace,
　　I'll give mine eyes to sleep:
Thy hand in safety keeps my days,
　　And will my slumbers keep.

PSALM V. Common Metre.
For the Lord's Day Morning.

1 LORD, in the morning thou shalt hear
　　My voice ascending high;
To thee will I direct my prayer,
　　To thee lift up mine eye.

2 Up to the hills where Christ is gone
　　To plead for all his saints,
Presenting at his Father's throne
　　Our songs and our complaints.

3. Thou art a God, before whose sight
　　The wicked shall not stand;
Sinners shall ne'er be thy delight,
　　Nor dwell at thy right hand.

4 But to thy house will I resort,
　　To taste thy mercies there;
I will frequent thine holy court,
　　And worship in thy fear.

5 O may thy spirit guide my feet,
　　In ways of righteousness.
Make every path of duty strait,
　　And plain before my face.

PAUSE.

6 My watchful enemies combine
　　To tempt my feet astray;
They flatter with a base design,
　　To make my soul their prey.

7 Lord, crush the serpent in the dust,
　　And all his plots destroy;
While those that in thy mercy trust,
　　For ever shout for joy.

8 The men that love and fear thy name,
   Shall see their hopes fulfill'd;
The mighty God will compass them
   With favour as a shield.

PSALM VI. Common Metre.

Complaint in sickness; or, diseases healed.

1 IN anger, Lord, do not chastise,
     Withdraw the dreadful storm;
  Nor let thine awful wrath arise
     Against a feeble worm.

2 My soul bow'd down with heavy cares,
     My flesh with pain oppress'd;
  My couch is witness to my tears,
     My tears forbid my rest.

3 Sorrow and grief wear out my days;
     I waste the night with cries,
  And count the minutes as they pass,
     'Till the slow morning rise.

4 Shall I be still tormented more?
     My eyes consum'd with grief:
  How long, my GOD, how long, before
     Thine hand afford relief.

5 He hears his mourning children speak,
     He pities all our groans;
  He saves us for his mercy's sake,
     And heals our broken bones.

6 The virtue of his sovereign word,
     Restores our fainting breath;
  For silent graves praise not the Lord,
     Nor is he known in death.

PSALM VI. Long Metre.

Temptations in Sickness overcome.

1 LORD, I can suffer thy rebukes,
     When thou with kindness dost chastise;
  But thy fierce wrath I cannot bear,
     O let it not against me rise!

B

2 Pity my languishing estate,
   And ease the sorrows that I feel;
   The wounds thine heavy hand hath made,
   O let thy gentler touches heal!

3 See how in sighs I pass my days,
   And waste in groans the weary night:
   My bed is water'd with my tears;
   My grief consumes, and dims my sight.

4 Look how the powers of nature mourn!
   How long, Almighty God, how long?
   When shall thine hour of grace return?
   When shall I make thy grace my song?

5 I feel my flesh so near the grave,
   My thoughts are tempted to despair:
   But graves can never praise the Lord,
   For all is dust and silence there.

6 Depart, ye tempters, from my soul.
   And all despairing thoughts depart;
   My God, who hears my humble moan,
   Will ease my flesh, and chear my heart.

PSALM VII. Common Metre.

God's care of his People, and punishment of Persecutors.

1 MY trust is in my heavenly Friend,
      My hope in thee, my God:
   Rise and my helpless life defend,
      From those that seek my blood.

2 With insolence and fury they
      My soul in pieces tear,
   As hungry lions rend the prey,
      When no deliverer's near.

3 If e'er my pride provok'd them first,
      Or once abused my foe,
   Then let them tread my life to dust,
      And lay my honour low.

4 If there be malice found in me,
      I know thy piercing eyes;
   I should not dare appeal to thee,
      Nor ask my God to rise.

5 Arise, my God, lift up thy hand,
   Their pride and power controul?
Awake to judgment, and command
   Deliverance for my soul.

PAUSE.

6 Let sinners and their wicked rage
   Be humbled to the dust:
Shall not the God of truth engage
   To vindicate the just?

7 He knows the heart, he tries the reins,
   He will defend th' upright:
His sharpest arrows he ordains
   Against the sons of spite.

8 Tho' leagu'd in guile their malice spread,
   A snare before my way;
Their mischiefs on their impious head,
   His vengeance shall repay.

9 That cruel persecuting race
   Must feel his dreadful sword;
Awake my soul, and praise the grace
   And justice of the LORD.

PSALM VIII. Short Metre.

God's sovereignty and goodness; and Man's dominion over the creatures.

1 O LORD, our heavenly King,
   Thy name is all divine;
Thy glories round the earth are spread,
   And o'er the heavens they shine.

2 When to thy works on high
   I raise my wondering eyes,
And see the moon, complete in light
   Adorn the darksome skies.

3 When I survey the stars
   And all their shining forms,
LORD, what is man, that worthless thing,
   A-kin to dust and worms?

4 LORD, what is worthless man,
   That thou should'st love him so?

PSALM VIII.

Next to thine angels is he plac'd,
  And lord of all below:

5 Thine honours crown his head,
    While beasts like slaves obey,
  And birds that cut the air with wings,
    And fish that cleave the sea.

6 How rich thy bounties are!
    And wondrous are thy ways:
  Of dust and worms thy power can frame
    A monument of praise.

7 [From mouths of feeble babes
    And fucklings, thou canst draw
  Surprising honours to thy name!
    And strike the world with awe.

8 O Lord, our heavenly King,
    Thy name is all divine;
  Thy glories round the earth are spread,
    And o'er the heavens they shine.]

PSALM VIII. Common Metre.

Christ's condescension and glorification; or, God made man.

1 O LORD, our Lord, how wondrous great
    Is thine exalted name!
  The glories of thy heavenly state
    Let men and babes proclaim,

2 When I behold the works on high,
    The moon that rules the night,
  And shining stars that grace the sky,
    Those moving worlds of light.

3 Lord, what is man, or all his race,
    Who dwells so far below,
  That thou should'st visit him with grace,
    And love his nature so?

4 That thine eternal Son should bear
    To take a mortal form,
  Made lower than his angels are,
    To save a dying worm?

PSALM VIII.

[5 Yet while he liv'd on earth unknown,
  And men would not adore,
Behold obedient nature own,
  His Godhead and his power.

6 The waves lay spread beneath his feet;
  And fish at his command,
Bring their large shoals to *Peter*'s net,
  Bring tribute to his hand.

7 These smaller glories of the Son,
  Shone through the fleshly cloud;
Now we behold him on his throne,
  And men confess him God.

8 Let him with majesty be crown'd,
  Who bow'd his head do death;
And his eternal honours found,
  From all things that have breath.

9 *Jesus*, our Lord, how wondrous great
  Is thine exalted name!
The glories of thy heavenly state
  Let the whole earth proclaim.

PSALM VIII. *Ver.* 1, 2, *Paraphrased*.

First Part. Long Metre.

The Hosanna *of the children; or, infants praising* God

1 ALMIGHTY Ruler of the skies,
  Thro' the wide earth thy name is spread,
And thine eternal glorious rise
  O'er all the heavens thy hands have made.

2 To thee the voices of the young
  Their sounding notes of honour raise;
And babes, with uninstructed tongue,
  Declare the wonders of thy praise.

3 Thy power assists their tender age
  To bring proud rebels to the ground,
To still the bold blasphemer's rage,
  And all their policies confound.

4 Children amidst thy temple throng
  To see their great Redeemer's face;
  The *Son of David*, is their song,
  And loud *Hosannas* fill the place.

5 The frowning scribes and angry priests
  In vain their impious cavils bring;
  Revenge sits silent in their breasts,
  While *Jewish* babes proclaim their King.

PSALM VIII. Ver. 3, &c. Paraphrased.
Second Part. Long Metre.

Adam and Christ, *Lords of the Old and New Creation.*

1 LORD, what was man, when made at first,
    Adam, the offspring of the dust,
  That thou should'st set him and his race,
  But just below an angel's place?

2 That thou should'st raise his nature so,
  And make him lord of all below;
  Make every beast and bird submit,
  And lay the fishes at his feet?

3 But O! what brighter glories wait,
  To crown the second *Adam*'s state?
  What honours shall thy Son adorn;
  Who condescended to be born?

4 See him below his angels made!
  Behold him number'd with the dead,
  To save a ruin'd world from sin;
  But he shall reign with power divine.

5 The world to come, redeem'd from all
    The miseries that attend the fall,
  New made, and glorious, shall submit
    At our exalted Saviour's feet.

PSALM IX. *First Metre.*

Wrath and Mercy from the Judgment Seat.

1 WITH my whole heart I'll raise my song,
      Thy wonders I'll proclaim,
  Thou sovereign judge of right and wrong
      Wilt put thy foes to shame.

2 I'll sing thy majesty and grace;
   My God prepares his throne
To judge the world in righteousness,
   And make his vengeance known.

3 Then shall the Lord a refuge prove
   For all the poor opprest;
To save the people of his love,
   And give the weary rest.

4 The men that know thy name will trust
   In thy abundant grace;
For thou hast ne'er forsook the just,
   Who humbly seek thy face.

5 Sing praises to the righteous Lord,
   Who dwells on *Zion*'s Hill,
Who executes his threat'ning word,
   Whose works his grace fulfil.

PSALM IX. Ver. 12. Second Part.
The Wisdom and Equity of Providence.

1 WHEN the great Judge, supreme and just,
      Shall once enquire for blood;
The humble souls that mourn in dust,
   Shall find a faithful God.

2 He from the dreadful gates of death
   Does his own children raise:
In *Zion*'s gates, with cheerful breath,
   They sing their Father's praise.

3 His foes shall fall, with heedless feet,
   Into the pit they made;
And sinners perish in the net
   That their own hands have spread.

4 Thus by thy judgments, mighty God,
   Are thy deep councils known:
When men of mischief are destroyed,
   In snares that were their own.

PAUSE.

5 The wicked shall sink down to hell;
   Thy wrath devour the lands
That dare forget thee, or rebel
   Against thy known commands.

6 Though saints to sore distress are brought,
    And wait, and long complain,
  Their cries shall never be forgot,
    Nor shall their hopes be vain.

7 [Rise, great Redeemer, from thy seat,
    To judge and save the poor;
  Let nations tremble at thy feet,
    And man prevail no more.

8 Thy thunder shall affright the proud,
    And put their hearts to pain,
  Make them confess that thou art GOD,
    And they but feeble men.]

PSALM X. Common Metre.

Prayer heard, and saints saved; or, pride, atheism, and oppression punished.

For a humiliation day.

1 WHY doth the Lord depart so far?
    And why conceal his face,
  When great calamities appear,
    And times of deep distress?

2 Lord, shall the wicked still deride
    Thy justice and thy laws?
  Shall they advance their heads in pride,
    And slight the righteous cause.

3 They cast thy judgments from their sight,
    And then insult the poor,
  They boast in their exalted height,
    That they shall fall no more.

4 Arise, O God, lift up thine hand,
    Attend our humble cry;
  No enemy shall dare to stand,
    When God ascends on high.

PAUSE.

5 Why do the men of malice rage,
    And say with foolish pride,
  The God of heaven will ne'er engage
    To fight on Zion's side.

6 But thou forever art our Lord ;
  And powerful is thine hand,
As when the Heathens felt thy sword,
  And perish'd from thy land.

7 Thou wilt prepare our hearts to pray,
  And cause thine ear to hear ;
Accept the vows thy children pay,
  And free thy saints from fear.

8 Proud tyrants shall no more oppress,
  No more despise the just ;
And mighty sinners shall confess,
  They are but earth and dust.

PSALM XI. Long Metre.
God loves the righteous, and hates the wicked.

1 MY refuge is the God of love ;
    Why do my foes insult and cry,
  Fly like a timerous trembling dove,
  To distant woods or mountains fly ?

2 If government be once destroy'd,
  (That firm foundation of our peace)
  And violence make justice void,
  Where shall the righteous seek redress ?

3 The Lord in heaven has fix'd his throne,
  His eye surveys the world below ;
  To him all mortal things are known ;
  His eye-lids search our spirits through.

4 If he afflicts his saints so far,
  To prove their love, and try their grace,
  What may the bold transgressors fear ?
  His soul abhors their wicked ways.

5 On impious wretches he shall rain
  Sulpherous flames of wasting death,
  Such as he kindled on the plain
  Of *Sodom*, with his angry breath.

6 The righteous Lord loves righteous souls,
  Whose thoughts and actions are sincere,
  And with a gracious eye beholds
  The men that his own image bear.

PSALM XII. Long Metre.

The Saint's Safety and Hope in evil Times: Or, Sins of the Tongue complained of, viz. Blasphemy, Falshood, &c.

1. ALMIGHTY God, appear and save !
   For vice and vanity prevail;
   The godly perish in the grave,
   The just depart, the faithful fail.

2. The whole discourse when crouds are met,
   Is fill'd with trifles loose and vain;
   Their lips are flattery and deceit,
   And their proud language is profane.

3. But lips that with deceit abound,
   Shall not maintain their triumph long:
   The God of vengeance will confound
   The flattering and blaspheming tongue.

4. *Yet shall our words be free, they cry,
   Our tongues shall be controul'd by none:
   Where is the Lord will ask us why?
   Or say our lips are not our own?*

5. The Lord who sees the poor opprest,
   And hears the oppressor's haughty strain,
   Will rise to give his children rest,
   Nor shall they trust his word in vain.

6. Thy word, O Lord, though often try'd,
   Void of deceit shall still appear;
   Not silver, seven times purify'd
   From dross and mixture, shines so clear.

7. Thy grace shall in the darkest hour
   Defend from danger and surprise;
   Tho' when the vilest men have power,
   On every side oppressors rise.

PSALM XII. Common Metre.

Complaint of a general Corruption of Manners: or, The Promise and Signs of Christ's coming to Judgment.

1. HELP, Lord, for men of virtue fail,
   Religion looses ground !

The sons of violence prevail,
  And treacheries abound;

2. Their oaths and promises they break,
  Yet act the flatterer's part;
With fair deceitful lips they speak,
  And with a double heart.

3 If we reprove some hateful lie,
  They scorn our faithful word:
" *Are not our lips our own,*" they cry,
  " *And who shall be our Lord?*"

4 Scoffers appear on every side,
  Where a vile race of men
Is rais'd to seats of power and pride,
  And bears the sword in vain.

PAUSE.

5 Lord, when iniquities abound,
  And blasphemy grows bold,
When faith is rarely to be found,
  And love is waxing cold:

6 Is not thy chariot hasting on?
  Hast thou not given the sign?
May we not trust and live upon
  A promise so divine?

7 " Yes, saith the Lord, now will I rise,
  " And make th' oppressors flee;
" I shall appear to their surprise,
  " And set my servants free."

8 Thy word, like silver seven times try'd,
  Through ages shall endure:
The men that in thy truth confide,
  Shall find thy promise sure.

PSALM XIII. Common Metre.

Complaint under the Temptation of the Devil.

1 HOW long wilt thou conceal thy face?
  My God, how long delay?
When shall I feel those heavenly rays
  That chase my fears away?

PSALM XIV.

2 How long shall my poor labouring soul
  wrestle and toil in vain?
Thy word can all my foes controul.
  And ease my raging pain.

3 See how the Prince of darkness tries
  All his malicious arts;
He spreads a mist around my eyes,
  And throws his fiery darts.

4 Be thou my Sun, and thou my shield,
  My soul in safety keep;
Make haste before mine eyes are seal'd
  In death's eternal sleep.

5 How would the tempter boast aloud,
  Should I become his prey!
Behold the sons of hell grow proud,
  To see thy long delay.

6 But they shall fly at thy rebuke,
  And *Satan* hide his head;
He knows the terrors of thy look,
  And hears thy voice with dread.

7 Thou wilt display that sovereign grace
  Whence all my comforts spring:
I shall employ my lips in praise,
  And thy salvation sing.

PSALM XIV. *First Part.* Com. Metre.
By Nature all Men are Sinners.

1 FOOLS in their hearts believe and say,
    "That all religion's vain,
  "There is no God that reigns on high,
  "Or minds th' affairs of men."

2 From thoughts so dreadful and profane
    Corrupt discourse proceeds;
  And in their impious hands are found
    Abominable deeds.

3 The Lord, from his celestial throne
    Look'd down on things below,
  To find the man that sought his grace,
    Or did his justice know.

4 By nature all are gone astray,
　　Their practice all the same;
　There's none that fears his Maker's hand,
　　There's none that loves his name.

5 Their tongues are us'd to speak deceit,
　　Their slanders never cease;
　How swift to mischief are their feet;
　　Nor know the paths of peace.

6 Such seeds of sin (that bitter root)
　　In every heart are found;
　Nor can they bear diviner fruit,
　　'Till grace refine the ground.

PSALM XIV. *Second Part.* Com. Metre.
The Folly of Persecutors.

1 ARE sinners now so senseless grown
　　That they the saints devour?
　And never worship at thy throne,
　　Nor fear thine awful power?

2 Great God, appear to their surprise,
　　Reveal thy dreadful name;
　Let them no more thy wrath despise,
　　Nor turn our hopes to shame.

3 Dost thou not dwell among the just?
　　And yet our foes deride,
　That we should make thy name our trust:
　　Great God, confound their pride.

4 Oh that the joyful day were come
　　To finish our distress!
　When God shall bring his children home,
　　Our songs shall never cease.

PSALM XV. Common Metre.
Character of a Saint; or, a Citizen of Zion; or the Qualifications of a Christian.

1 WHO shall inhabit in thy hill,
　　O God of holiness?
　Whom will the Lord admit to dwell
　　So near his throne of grace?

C

2 The man that walks in pious ways,
    And works with righteous hands;
That trusts his Maker's promis'd grace,
    And follows his commands.

3 He speaks the meaning of his heart,
    Nor slanders with his tongue;
Will scarce believe an ill report,
    Nor do his neighbour wrong.

4 The wealthy sinner he contemns,
    Loves all that fear the Lord:
And tho' to his own hurt he swears,
    Still he performs his word.

5 His hands disdain a golden bribe,
    And never wrong the poor;
This man shall dwell with God on earth,
    And find his heaven secure.

PSALM XV. Long Metre.

Religion and Justice, Goodness and Truth; or, Duties to God and Man; or, the Qualifications of a Christian.

1 WHO shall ascend thy heavenly place,
    Great God, and dwell before thy face?
The man that minds religion now,
And humbly walks with God below:

2 Whose hands are pure, whose heart is clean;
Whose lips still speak the thing they mean;
No slanders dwell upon his tongue;
He hates to do his neighbour wrong.

3 [Scarce will he trust an ill report,
Or vent it to his neighbour's hurt:
Sinners of state he can despise,
But saints are honour'd in his eyes.]

4 [Firm to his word he ever stood,
And always makes his promise good,
Nor dares to change the thing he swears,
Whatever pain or loss he bears.]

5 [He never deals in bribing gold,
And mourns that justice should be sold:

While others scorn and wrong the poor,
Sweet charity attends his door.]

6 He loves his enemies, and prays
For those that curse him to his face;
And doth to all men still the same
That he would hope or wish from them.

7 Yet, when his holiest works are done,
His soul depends on grace alone:
This is the man thy face shall see,
And dwell forever, Lord, with thee.

PSALM XVI. *First Part.* Long Metre.

*Confession of our poverty; and, Saints the best Company;
or, Good Works profit Men, not God.*

1 PRESERVE me, Lord, in time of need,
   For succour to thy throne I flee,
But have no merits there to plead;
My goodness cannot reach to thee.

2 Oft have my heart and tongue confest
How empty and how poor I am;
My praise can never make thee blest,
Nor add new glories to thy name.

3 Yet, Lord, thy saints on earth may reap
Some profit by the good we do;
These are the company I keep,
These are the choicest friends I know.

4 Let others chuse the sons of mirth
To give a relish to their wine?
I love the men of heavenly birth,
Whose thoughts and language are divine.

PSALM XVI. *Second Part.* Long Metre.

Christ's Allsufficiency.

1 HOW fast their guilt and sorrows rise,
   Who haste to seek some idol god!
I will not taste their sacrifice,
Their offerings of forbidden blood.

2 My God provides a richer cup,
And nobler food to live upon;

He for my life has offer'd up
Jesus, his best beloved Son.

3 His love is my perpetual feast;
By day his counsels guide me right;
And be his name forever blest,
Who gives me sweet advice by night.

4 I set him still before mine eyes;
At my right hand he stands prepar'd
To keep my soul from all surprise,
And be my everlasting guard.

PSALM XVI. *Third Part.* Long Metre.

Courage in Death, and Hope of the Resurrection.

1 WHEN God is nigh, my faith is strong,
His arm is my almighty prop:
Be glad my heart, rejoice my tongue,
My dying flesh shall rest in hope.

2 Though in the dust I lay my head,
Yet, gracious God, thou wilt not leave
My soul forever with the dead,
Nor lose thy children in the grave.

3 My flesh shall thy first call obey,
Shake off the dust, and rise on high;
Then shalt thou lead the wondrous way
Up to the throne above the sky.

4 There streams of endless pleasure flow;
And full discoveries of thy grace
(Which we but tasted here below)
Spread heavenly joys through all the place.

PSALM XVI. 1--8. *First Part.* Com. Metre.

Support and Counsel from God without Merit.

1 SAVE me, O Lord, from every foe;
In thee my trust I place,
Though all the good that I can do
Can ne'er deserve thy grace:

2 Yet if my God prolong my breath,
The saints may still rejoice,

PSALM XVI.

  The saints, the glory of the earth,
   The people of my choice.

3 Let heathens to their idols haste,
  And worship wood or stone;
But my delightful lot is cast
  Where the true God is known.

4 His hand provides my constant food,
  He fills my daily cup;
Much am I pleas'd with present good,
  But more rejoice in hope.

5 God is my portion and my joy;
  His counsels are my light:
He gives me sweet advice by day,
  And gentle hints by night.

6 My soul would all her thoughts approve
  To his all-seeing eye;
Not death nor hell my hope shall move
  While such a friend is nigh.

PSALM XVI. *Second Part.* Common Metre.
The Death and Resurrection of Christ.

1 " I SET the Lord before my face,
 " He bears my courage up:
" My heart, my tongue their joys express,
 " My flesh shall rest in hope.

2 " My spirit, Lord, thou wilt not leave
 " Where souls departed are;
" Nor quit my body to the grave
 " To see corruption there.

3 " Thou wilt reveal the path of life,
 " And raise me to thy throne:
" Thy courts immortal pleasure give
 " Thy presence joys unknown."

4 [Thus in the name of Christ the Lord,
 The holy *David* sung,
And Providence fulfils the word
 Of his prophetic tongue.

5 Jesus, whom every saint adores,
    Was crucify'd and slain;
 Behold the tomb its prey restores,
    Behold he lives again.

6 When shall my feet arise and stand
    On heaven's eternal hills?
 There sits the Son at God's right hand,
    And there the Father smiles.]

PSALM XVII. Ver. 13, &c. Short Metre.

Portion of Saints and Sinners; or Hope and Despair in Death.

1 ARISE, my gracious God,
    And make the wicked flee;
 They are but thy chastning rod
    To drive thy saints to thee.

2 Behold the sinner dies,
    His haughty words are vain;
 Here in this life his pleasure lies,
    And all beyond is pain.

3 Then let his pride advance,
    And boast of all his store;
 The Lord is my inheritance,
    My soul can wish no more.

4 I shall behold the face
    Of my forgiving God;
 And stand complete in righteousness,
    Wash'd in my Saviour's blood.

5 There's a new heaven begun
    When I awake from Death,
 Drest in a likeness of thy Son,
    And draw immortal breath.

PSALM XVII. Long Metre.

The Sinner's Portion and Saint's Hope; or, the Heaven of separate Souls, and the Resurrection.

1 LORD, I am thine; but thou wilt prove
    My faith, my patience, and my love;
 When men of spite against me join,
    They are the sword, the hand is thine.

2 Their hope and portion lie below;
'Tis all the happiness they know,
'Tis all they seek; they take their shares;
And leave the rest among their heirs.

3 What sinners value, I resign;
Lord, 'tis enough that thou art mine:
I shall behold thy blissful face,
And stand complete in righteousness.

4 His life's a dream, an empty show;
But the bright world, to which I go,
Hath joys substantial and sincere;
When shall I wake and find me there?

5 O glorious hour! O blest abode!
I shall be near, and like my God?
And flesh and sin no more controul
The sacred pleasures of the soul.

6 My flesh shall slumber in the ground,
Till the last trumpet's joyful sound:
Then burst the chains with sweet surprise,
And in my Saviour's image rise.

PSALM XVIII. *First Part.* Long Metre.
Ver. 1—9, 15—18.
Deliverance from Despair; or, Temptation overcome.

1 THEE will I love, O Lord, my strength,
My rock, my tower, my high defence;
Thy mighty arm shall be my trust,
For I have found salvation thence.

2 Death, and the terrors of the grave,
Stood round me with their dismal shade;
While floods of high temptation rose,
And made my sinking soul afraid.

3 I saw the opening gates of hell,
With endless pains and sorrows there,
(Which none but they that feel can tell)
While I was hurry'd to despair.

4 In my distress I call'd my God,
When I could scarce believe him mine;
He bow'd his ear to my complaint;
And prov'd his saving grace divine.

PSALM XVIII.

5 [With speed he flew to my relief,
As on a cherub's wing he rode;
Awful, and bright as lightening, shone
The face of my deliverer God.

6 Temptations fled to his rebuke,
The blast of his Almighty breath
He sent salvation from on high,
And drew me from the deeps of death.]

7 Great were my fears, my foes were great,
Much was their strength, and more their rage;
But Christ, my Lord, is conqueror still
In all the wars the proud can wage.

8 My song forever shall record
That terrible, that joyful hour;
And give the glory to the Lord
Due to his mercy and his power.

PSALM XVIII.
Second Part. Ver. 20.—26. *Long Metre.*
Sincerity proved and rewarded.

1 LORD, thou hast seen my soul sincere,
Hast made thy truth and love appear:
Before mine eyes I set thy laws,
And thou hast own'd my righteous cause.

2 Since I have learn'd thy holy ways,
I've walk'd upright before thy face:
Or if my feet did e'er depart,
Thy love reclaim'd my wandering heart.

3 What sore temptations broke my rest!
What wars and strugglings in my breast!
But through thy grace that reigns within,
I guard against my darling sin.

4 That sin that close besets me still,
That works and strives against my will;
When shall thy spirit's sovereign power
Destroy it, that it rise no more.

5 With an impartial hand, the Lord
Deals out to mortals their reward:
The kind and faithful souls shall find
A God as faithful and as kind.

And men that love revenge shall know,
  God hath an arm of vengeance too:
The just and pure shall ever say,
  Thou art more pure, more just than they.

PSALM XVIII. Third Part. Long Metre.
Ver. 30, 31, 34, 35, 36, &c.

1 JUST are thy ways, and true thy word,
    Great Rock of my secure abode:
  Who is a God beside the Lord?
    Or where's a refuge like our God?

2 'Tis he that girds me with his might,
    Gives me his holy sword to wield;
  And while with sin and hell I fight,
    Spreads his salvation for my shield.

3 He lives, and blessings crown his reign,
    The God of my salvation lives,
  The dark designs of hell are vain;
    While heavenly peace my Father gives.

4 Before the scoffers of the age,
    I will exalt my Father's name,
  Nor tremble at their mighty rage,
    But meet reproach, and bear the shame.

5 To *David* and his royal seed
    Thy grace forever shall extend;
  Thy love to saints, in *Christ* their head,
    Knows not a limit, nor an end.

PSALM XVIII. First Part. Common Metre.
Victory and Triumph over Temporal Enemies.

1 WE love thee, Lord, and we adore,
    Now is thine arm reveal'd;
  Thou art our strength, our heavenly tower,
    Our bulwark and our shield.

2 We fly to our eternal Rock,
    And find a sure defence;
  His holy name our lips invoke,
    And draw salvation thence.

3 When God our leader shines in arms,
    What mortal heart can bear

The thunder of his loud alarms?
　　The lightning of his spear?

4 He rides upon the winged wind,
　　And angels in array
In millions wait to know his mind,
　　And swift as flames obey.

5 He speaks, and at his fierce rebuke
　　Whole armies are dismay'd;
His voice, his frown, his angry look
　　Strikes all their courage dead.

6 He forms our generals for the field,
　　With all their dreadful skill;
Gives them his awful sword to wield,
　　And makes their hearts of steel.

7 Oft has the Lord whole nations blest
　　For his own church's sake;
The powers that give his people rest,
　　Shall of his care partake.

PSALM XVIII. *Second Part.* Com. Metre.
The Conqueror's Song.

1 TO thine almighty arm we owe
　　The triumphs of the day;
Thy terrors, Lord, confound the foe,
　　And melt their strength away.

2 'Tis by thy aid our troops prevail,
　　And break united powers,
Or burn their boasted fleets, or scale
　　The proudest of their towers.

3 How have we chas'd them through the field,
　　And trod them to the ground,
While thy salvation was our shield,
　　But they no shelter found!

4 In vain to idol saints they cry,
　　And perish in their blood;
Where is a rock so great, so high,
　　So powerful as our God?

5 The God of *Israel* ever lives:
　　His name be ever blest;

'Tis his own arm the victory gives,
 And gives his people rest.

PSALM XIX. *First Part.* Short Metre.
The Book of Nature and Scripture.
For a Lord's Day Morning.

1 BEHOLD the lofty sky
  Declares its maker God,
And all the starry works on high
  Proclaim his power abroad.

2 The darkness and the light,
  Still keep their course the same;
While night to day and day to night
  Divinely teach his name.

3 In every different land
  Their general voice is known;
They shew the wonders of his hand,
  And orders of his throne.

4 Ye christian lands, rejoice,
  Here he reveals his word;
We are not left to nature's voice
  To bid us know the Lord.

5 His statutes and commands
  Are set before our eyes,
He puts his gospel in our hands,
  Where our salvation lies.

6 His laws are just and pure,
  His truth without deceit,
His promises forever sure,
  And his rewards are great.

7 [Not honey to the taste
  Affords so much delight;
Nor gold that has the furnace pass'd
  So much allures the sight.

8 While of thy works I sing,
  Thy glory to proclaim,
Accept the praise, my God, my King,
  In my Redeemer's name.]

PSALM XIX, Short Metre.

God's Word most excellent; or, Sincerity and Watchfulness.

For a Lord's Day Morning.

1 BEHOLD the morning sun
  Begins his glorious way:
His beams through all the nations run,
  And life and light convey.

2 But where the gospel comes
  It spreads diviner light,
It calls dead sinners from their tombs,
  And gives the blind their sight.

3 How perfect is thy word!
  And all thy judgments just,
Forever sure thy promise, Lord,
  And men securely trust.

4 My gracious God, how plain
  Are thy directions given!
Oh may I never read in vain,
  But find the path to heaven!

PAUSE.

5 I heard thy word with love,
  And I would fain obey:
Send thy good spirit from above
  To guide me lest I stray,

6 Oh who can ever find
  The errors of his ways?
Yet with a bold presumptuous mind
  I would not dare transgress.

7 Warn me of every sin,
  Forgive my secret faults,
And cleanse this guilty soul of mine,
  Whose crimes exceed my thoughts.

8 While with my heart and tongue
  I spread thy praise abroad;
Accept the worship and the song,
  My Saviour and my God.

PSALM XIX. Long Metre,

The Books of Nature, and Scripture compared; or the Glory and Success of the Gospel.

1 THE heavens declare thy glory, Lord,
   In every star thy goodness shines;
   But when our eyes behold thy word,
   We read thy name in fairer lines.

2 The rolling sun, the changing light,
   And nights and days thy power confess;
   But the blest volume thou hast writ,
   Reveals thy justice and thy grace.

3 Sun, moon and stars convey thy praise
   Round the whole earth, and never stand;
   So when thy truth began it's race,
   It touch'd and glanc'd on every land.

4 Nor shall thy spreading gospel rest
   Till through the world thy truth has run;
   Till *Christ* has all the nations blest,
   That see the light or feel the sun.

5 Great Sun of Righteousness, arise,
   Bless the dark world with heavenly light;
   Thy gospel makes the simple wise,
   Thy laws are pure, thy judgments right.

6 Thy noblest wonders here we view,
   In souls renew'd and sins forgiven,
   Lord, cleanse my sins, may soul renew,
   And make thy word my guide to heaven.

PSALM XIX. To the Tune of the 113th Psalm.

The Book of Nature and Scripture.

1 GREAT God, the heaven's well order'd frame
   Declares the glories of thy name:
   There thy rich works of wonder shine;
   A thousand starry beauties there,
   A thousand radiant marks appear
   Of boundless power, and skill divine.

2 From night to day, from day to night,
The dawning and the dying light,
   Lectures of heavenly wisdom read:
With silent eloquence they raise
Our thoughts to our Creator's praise,
   And neither sound nor language need.

3 Yet their divine instructions run
Far as the journies of the sun,
   And every nation knows their voice:
The sun, like some young bridegroom drest,
Breaks from the chambers of the east,
   Rolls round, and makes the earth rejoice.

4 Where e'er he spreads his beams abroad,
He smiles, and speaks his maker God:
   All nature joins to shew thy praise:
Thus God in every creature shines;
Fair is the book of nature's lines,
   But fairer is the book of grace.

PAUSE.

5 I love the volumes of thy word;
What light and joy those leaves afford,
   To souls benighted and distrest!
Thy precepts guide my doubtful way,
Thy fear forbids my feet to stray,
   Thy promise leads my heart to rest.

6 From the discoveries of thy law
The perfect rules of life I draw:
   These are my study and delight;
Not honey so invites the taste,
Nor gold that hath the furnace past
   Appears so pleasing to the sight.

7 Thy threatenings wake my slumbering eyes,
And warn me where my dangers lies;
   But 'tis thy blessed gospel, Lord,
That makes my guilty conscience clean,
Converts my soul, subdues my sin,
   And gives a free, but large reward.

8 Who knows the errors of his thoughts?
My God, forgive my secret faults,
   And from presumptuous sins restrain;

Accept my poor attempts of praise,
That I have read thy book of grace
And book of nature not in vain.

PSALM XX.

Prayer and Hope of Victory.

For a Day of Prayer in Time of War.

1 NOW may the God of power and grace
Attend his people's humble cry !
Jehovah hears when *Israel* prays,
And brings deliverance from on high.

2 The name of *Jacob*'s God defends,
When bucklers fail and brazen walls ;
He from his sanctuary sends
Succour and strength when *Zion* calls.

3 Well he remembers all our sighs,
His love exceeds our best deserts ;
His love accepts the sacrifice
Of humble groans and broken hearts.

4 In this salvation is our hope,
And in the name of *Israel*'s God.
Our troops shall lift their banners up,
Our navies spread their flags abroad.

5 Some trust in horses train'd for war,
And some of chariots make their boasts
Our surest expectations are
From thee, the Lord of heavenly hosts.

6 [O may the memory of thy name
Inspire our armies for the fight !
Our foes shall fall and die with shame,
Or quit the field with coward flight.]

7 Now save us, Lord, from slavish fear,
Now let our hopes be firm and strong,
Till thy salvation shall appear,
And joy and triumph raise the song,

PSALM XXI. Common Metre.

National Bleſſings acknowledged.

1 IN thee, great God, with ſongs of praiſe,
  Our favour'd realms rejoice;
And, bleſt with thy ſalvation, raiſe
  To heaven their cheerful voice.

2 Thy ſure defence, through nations round,
  Hath ſpread our riſing name,
And all our feeble efforts crown'd
  With freedom and with fame.

3 In deep diſtreſs our injur'd land
  Implor'd thy power to ſave;
For life we pray'd; thy bounteous hand
  The timely bleſſing gave.

4 Thy mighty arm, eternal Power,
  Oppos'd their deadly aim,
In mercy ſwept them from our ſhore,
  And ſpread their ſails with ſhame.

5 On thee, in want, in woe or pain,
  Our hearts alone rely;
Our rights thy mercy will maintain,
  And all our wants ſupply.

6 Thus, Lord, thy wondrous power declare,
  And ſtill exalt thy fame;
While we glad ſongs of praiſe prepare,
  For thine Almighty name.

PSALM XXI. 1——9. Long Metre.

Chriſt exalted to the Kingdom.

1 DAVID rejoic'd in God his ſtrength,
   Rais'd to the throne by ſpecial grace.
But *Chriſt* the ſon appears at length,
  Fulfils the triumph and the praiſe.

2 How great the bleſt *Meſſiah*'s joy
  In the ſalvation of thy hand!
Lord, thou haſt rais'd his kingdom high,
  And given the world to his command.

3 Thy goodness grants whate'er he will,
   Nor doth the least request with-hold:
   Blessings of love prevent him still,
   And crowns of glory, not of gold.

4 Honour and majesty divine
   Around his sacred temples shine:
   Blest with the favour of thy face,
   And length of everlasting days.

5 Thine hand shall find out all his foes:
   And as a firey oven glows
   With raging heat and living coals,
   So shall thy wrath devour their souls.

PSALM XXII. 1—16 *First Part.* Com. Metre.
The Sufferings and Death of Christ.

1 WHY has my God my soul forsook,
     Nor will a smile afford?
  (Thus *David* once in anguish spoke,
     And thus our dying Lord.)

2 Though 'tis thy chief delight to dwell
     Among thy praising saints,
  Yet thou canst hear our groan as well,
     And pity our complaints.

3 Our fathers trusted in thy name,
     And great deliverance found:
  But I'm a worm despis'd of men,
     And trodden to the ground.

4 With shaking head they pass me by,
     And laugh my soul to scorn:
  In vain he trusts in God, they cry,
     Neglected and forlorn.

5 But thou art he, who form'd my flesh,
     By thine Almighty word;
  And since I hung upon the breast
     My hope is in the Lord.

6 Why will my father hide his face
     When foes stand threatening round
  In the dark hour of deep distress,
     And not an helper found?

PAUSE.

7 Behold thy darling left among
  The cruel and the proud,
 By foes encompass'd fierce and strong,
  As lions roaring loud

8 From earth and hell my sorrows meet,
  To multiply the smart;
 They nail my hands, they pierce my feet,
  And try to vex my heart.

9 Yet if thy sovereign hand let loose
  The rage of earth and hell,
 Why will my heavenly Father bruise
  The son he loves so well?

10 My God, if possible it be,
  With-hold this bitter cup;
 But I resign my will to thee,
  And drink the sorrows up.

11 My heart dissolves with pangs unknown,
  In groans I waste my breath;
 Thy heavy hand has brought me down,
  Low as the dust of death.

12 Father, I give my spirt up.
  And trust it in thy hand;
 My dying flesh shall rest in hope,
  And rise at thy command.

PSALM XXII. 20, 21, 27—31. *Second Part.*
  Common Metre.

1 " NOW from the roaring lion's rage,
   " O Lord, protect thy Son,
  " Nor leave thy darling to engage
   " The powers of hell alone."

2 Thus did our suffering Saviour pray
   With mighty cries and tears,
  God heard him in that dreadful day,
   And chas'd away his fears.

3 Great was the victory of his death
   His throne exalted high;
  And all the kindreds of the earth
   Shall worship or shall die.

PSALM XXII.

4 A numerous offspring must arise
  From his expiring groans;
They shall be reckon'd in his eyes
  For daughters and for sons.

5 The meek and humble souls shall see
  His table richly spread;
And all that seek the Lord shall be
  With joys immortal fed.

6 The isles shall know the righteousness
  Of our incarnate God,
And nations yet unborn profess
  Salvation in his blood.

PSALM XXII. Long Metre.

Christ's Sufferings and Exaltation.

1 NOW let our mournful songs record
    The dying sorrows of our Lord,
  When he complain'd in tears and blood,
  As one forsaken of his God.

2 The *Jews* behold him thus forlorn,
  And shake their heads and laugh in scorn;
  " He rescued others from the grave,
  " Now let him try himself to save.

3 " This is the man did once pretend
  " God was his father and his friend;
  " If God the blessed lov'd him so,
  " Why doth he fail to help him now?

4 Oh savage people! cruel priests!
  How they stood round like raging beasts;
  Like lions gaping to devour,
  When God had left him in their power.

5 They wound his head, his hands, his feet,
  Till streams of blood each other meet;
  By lot his garments they divide,
  And mock the pangs in which he died.

6 But God his father heard his cry;
  Rais'd from the dead he reigns on high;
  The nations learn his righteousness,
  And humble sinners taste his grace.

PSALM XXIII. Long Metre.
God our Shepherd.

1 MY shepherd is the living Lord,
　　Now shall my wants be well supply'd:
His providence and holy word
Become my safety and my guide.

2 In pastures where salvation grows
He makes me feed, he makes me rest,
There living water gently flows,
And all the food divinely blest.

3 My wandering feet his ways mistake,
But he restores my soul to peace,
And leads me for his mercy's sake,
In the fair paths of righteousness.

4 Though I walk through the gloomy vale,
Where death and all its terrors are,
My heart and hope shall never fail,
For God, my shepherd's with me there.

5 Amidst the darkness and the deeps
Thou art my comfort, thou my stay;
Thy staff supports my feeble steps,
Thy rod directs my doubtful way.

6 The sons of earth and sons of hell
Gaze at thy goodness, and repine
To see my table spread so well
With living bread and cheerful wine.

7 [How I rejoice, when on my head
Thy Spirit condescends to rest!
'Tis a divine anointing shed,
Like oil of gladness at a feast.

8 Surely the mercies of the Lord
Attend his houshold all their days:
There will I dwell to hear his word,
To seek his face, and sing his praise.]

PSALM XXIII. Common Metre.

1 MY Shepherd will supply my need,
　　Jehovah is his name;
In pastures fresh he makes me feed,
Beside the living stream.

PSALM XXIII.

2 He brings my wandering spirit back
    When I forsake his ways,
And leads me for his mercy's sake
    In paths of truth and grace.

3 When I walk through the shades of death,
    Thy presence is my stay;
One word of thy supporting breath
    Drives all my fears away.

4 Thy hand in sight of all my foes
    Doth still my table spread;
My cup with blessings overflows,
    Thine oil anoints my head.

5 The sure provisions of my God
    Attend me all my days:
Oh may thy house be mine abode,
    And all my work be praise!

6 There would I find a settled rest,
    (While others go and come)
No more a stranger or a guest,
    But like a child at home.

PSALM XXIII. Short Metre.

1 THE Lord my shepherd is,
    I shall be well supply'd;
Since he is mine and I am his,
    What can I want beside?

2 He leads me to the place,
    Where heavenly pasture grows,
Where living waters gently pass,
    And full salvation flows.

3 If e'er I go astray,
    He doth my soul reclaim,
And guides me in his own right way,
    For his most holy name.

4 While he affords his aid,
    I cannot yield to fear;
Tho' I should walk thro' death's dark shade,
    My shepherd's with me there.

5 Amid surrounding foes
  Thou dost my table spread,
My cup with blessings overflows,
  And joy exalts my head.
6 The bounties of thy love
  Shall crown my following days;
Nor from thy house will I remove,
  Nor cease to speak thy praise.

PSALM XXIV. Common Metre.
Dwelling with God.

1 THE earth forever is the Lord's
    With *Adam*'s numerous race;
  He rais'd its arches o'er the floods,
    And built it on the seas.
2 But who among the sons of men
    May visit thine abode?
  He that has hands from mischief clean,
    Whose heart is right with God.
3 This is the man may rise and take
    The blessings of his grace;
  This is the lot of those that seek
    The God of *Jacob*'s face.
4 Now let our soul's immortal powers,
    To meet the Lord prepare,
  Lift up their everlasting doors,
    The king of glory's near.
5 The king of glory! Who can tell
    The wonders of his might?
  He rules the nations; but to dwell
    With saints is his delight.

PSALM XXIV. Long Metre.
Saints dwell in Heaven; or, Christ's Ascention.

1 THIS spacious earth is all the Lord's,
    And men and worms, and beasts and birds;
  He rais'd the building on the seas,
  And gave it for their dwelling-place.
2 But there's a brighter world on high,
  Thy palace, Lord, above the sky;

PSALM XXV.

Who shall ascend that blest abode,
And dwell so near his Maker God?

3 He that abhors and fears to sin,
Whose heart is pure, whose hands are clean,
Him shall the Lord, the Saviour bless,
And clothe his soul with righteousness.

4 These are the men, the pious race,
That seek the God of *Jacob*'s face;
These shall enjoy the blissful sight
And dwell in everlasting light.

PAUSE.

5 Rejoice, ye shining worlds on high,
Behold the King of glory nigh;
Who can this King of glory be?
The mighty Lord, the Saviour's he.

6 Ye heavenly gates, your leaves display,
To make the Lord, the Saviour way:
Laden with spoils from earth and hell,
The Conqueror comes with God to dwell.

7 Rais'd from the dead in royal state,
He opens heaven's eternal gate,
To give his saints a blest abode,
Near their Redeemer and their God.

PSALM XXV. 1—11. *First Part.*
Waiting for Pardon and Direction.

1 I LIFT my soul to God,
 My trust is in his name;
Let not my foes that seek my blood
 Still triumph in my shame.

2 Sin and the powers of hell
 Persuade me to despair;
Lord, make me know thy covenant well,
 That I may 'scape the snare.

3 From gleams of dawning light
 Till evening shades arise,
For thy salvation, Lord, I wait,
 With ever-longing eyes.

4 Remember all thy grace,
 And lead me in thy truth;

> Forgive the sins of riper days,
> And follies of my youth.

5 The Lord is just and kind,
> The meek shall learn his ways,
> And every humble sinner find
> The methods of his grace.

6 For his own goodness sake
> He saves my soul from shame;
> He pardons (tho' my guilt be great)
> Thro' my Redeemer's name.

PSALM XXV. 12, 14, 10, 13, Second Part.
Short Metre. *Divine Instruction.*

1 WHERE shall the man be found,
> That fears t' offend his God,
> That loves the gospel's joyful sound,
> And trembles at the rod?

2 The Lord shall make him known
> The secrets of his heart,
> The wonders of his covenant show,
> And all his love impart.

3 The dealings of his power
> Are truth and mercy still,
> With such as keep his covenant sure,
> And love to do his will.

4 Their souls shall dwell at ease
> Before their Maker's face,
> Their seed shall taste the promises
> In their extensive grace,

PSALM XXV. 15—22. Third Part.
Short Metre.

Distress of soul; or, Backsliding and Desertion.

1 MINE eyes and my desire
> Are ever to the Lord;
> I love to plead his promis'd grace
> And rest upon his word.

2 Turn, turn thee to my soul,
   Bring thy salvation near;
When will thy hand assist my feet
   To 'scape the deadly snare?

3 When shall the sovereign grace
   Of my forgiving God
Restore me from those dangerous ways
   My wandering feet have trod?

4 The tumult of my thoughts
   Doth but enlarge my woe;
My spirit languishes, my heart
   Is desolate and low.

5 With every morning light
   My sorrow new begins;
Look on my anguish and my pain,
   And pardon all my sins.

PAUSE.

6 Behold the hosts of hell,
   How cruel is their hate!
Against my life they rise, and join
   Their fury with deceit.

7 Oh keep my soul from death,
   Nor put my hope to shame,
For I have plac'd my only trust
   In my Redeemer's name.

8 With humble faith I wait
   To see thy face again;
Of *Israel* it shall ne'er be said,
   He sought the Lord in vain.

PSALM XXVI. Long Metre.
Self-Examination; or, Evidences of Grace.

1 JUDGE me, O Lord, and prove my ways,
   And try my reins, and try my heart;
My faith upon thy promise stays,
Nor from thy law my feet depart.

2 I hate to walk, I hate to sit
   With men of vanity and lies;
The scoffer and the hypocrite
   Are the abhorrence of mine eyes.

E

PSALM XXVII.

3 Amongst thy saints will I appear
Array'd in robes of innocence;
But when I stand before thy bar,
The blood of *Christ* is my defence.

4 I love thy habitation, Lord,
The temple where thine honours dwell;
There shall I hear thy holy word,
And there thy works of wonder tell.

5 Let not my soul be join'd at last
With men of treachery and blood,
Since I my days on earth have past
Among the saints, and near my God.

PSALM XXVII. 1—6. *First Part.*
The Church is our Delight and Safety.

1 THE Lord of glory is my light,
  And my salvation too;
God is my strength; nor will I fear
  What all my foes can do.

2 One Privilege my heart desires;
  Oh grant me mine abode
Among the churches of thy saints,
  The temples of my God.

3 There shall I offer my requests
  And see thy beauty still;
Shall hear thy messages of love,
  And there enquire thy will.

4 When troubles rise and storms appear,
  There may his children hide;
God has a strong pavilion, where
  He makes my soul abide.

5 Now shall my head be lifted high
  Above my foes around,
And songs of joy and victory
  Within thy temple found.

PSALM XXVII. 8, 9. 13, 14. *Second Part.*
Common Metre.   *Prayer and Hope.*

1 SOON as I heard my Father say,
  "*Ye children, seek my grace,*"

My heart reply'd without delay,
"*I'll seek my Father's face.*"

2 Let not thy face be hid from me,
Nor frown my soul away;
God of my life, I fly to thee
In a distressing day.

3 Should friends and kindred near and dear
Leave me to want or die,
My God will make my life his care,
And all my need supply.

4 My fainting flesh had died with grief,
Had not my soul believ'd,
To see thy grace provide relief,
Nor was my hope deceiv'd.

5 Wait on the Lord, ye trembling saints,
And keep your courage up;
He'll raise your spirit when it faints,
And far exceed your hope.

PSALM XXVIII. Long Metre.
God the Refuge of the Afflicted.

1 TO thee, O Lord, I raise my cries;
My fervent prayer in mercy hear;
For ruin waits my trembling soul,
If thou refuse a gracious ear.

2 When suppliant tow'rd thy holy hill,
I lift my mournful hands to pray,
Afford thy grace, nor drive me still,
With impious hypocrites away.

3 To sons of falsehood, that despise
The works and wonders of thy reign,
Thy vengeance gives the due reward,
And sinks their souls to endless pain.

4 But, ever blessed be the Lord,
Whose mercy hears my mournful voice,
My heart, that trusted in his word,
In his salvation shall rejoice.

5 Let every saint in sore distress,
  By faith approach his Saviour God;
  Then grant, O Lord, thy pardoning grace,
  And feed thy church with heavenly food.

PSALM XXIX. Long Metre.
Storm and Thunder.

1 GIVE to the Lord, ye sons of fame,
    Give to the Lord renown and power,
  Ascribe due honours to his name,
  And his eternal might adore.

2 The Lord proclaims his power aloud
  Thro' every ocean, every land;
  His voice divides the watery cloud,
  And lightnings blaze at his command.

3 He speaks, and tempest, hail and wind,
  Lay the wide forest bare around;
  The fearful hart, and frighted hind,
  Leap at the terror of the sound.

4 To *Lebanon* he turns his voice,
  And lo, the stately cedars break;
  The mountains tremble at the noise,
  The vallies roar, the deserts quake.

5 The Lord sits sovereign on the flood,
  The Thunderer reigns forever king;
  But makes his church his blest abode,
  Where we his awful glories sing.

6 In gentler language, there the Lord
  The counsel of his grace imparts;
  Amidst the raging storm, his word
  Speaks peace and courage to our hearts.

PSALM XXX. First Part. Long Metre.
Sickness healed, and Sorrows removed.

1 I Will extol thee, Lord, on high,
    At thy command diseases fly:
  Who but a God can speak and save
  From the dark borders of the grave?

2 Sing to the Lord, ye saints, and prove
  How large his grace, how kind his love,

Let all your powers rejoice, and trace
The wondrous records of his grace.

3 His anger but a moment stays;
His love is life and length of days:
Tho' grief and tears the night employ,
The morning-star restores the joy.

Psalm XXX. ver. 6. Second Part. Long Metre.

Health, Sickness and Recovery.

1 FIRM was my health, my day was bright,
And I presum'd 'twould ne'er be night;
Fondly I said within my heart,
" *Pleasure and peace shall ne'er depart.*"

2 But I forget thine arm was strong
Which made my mountain stand so long;
Soon as thy face began to hide,
My health was gone, my comforts di'd.

3 I cried aloud to thee my God:
" What can'st thou profit by my blood?
" Deep in the dust can I declare
" Thy truth, or sing thy goodness there?

4 " Hear me, O God of Grace, I said,
" And bring me from among the dead:"
" Thy word rebuk'd the pains I felt,
Thy pardoning love remov'd my guilt.

5 My groans, and tears, and forms of woe,
Are turn'd to joy and praises now;
I throw my sackcloth on the ground,
And ease and gladness gird me round.

6 My tongue, the glory of my frame,
Shall ne'er be silent of thy name;
Thy praise shall sound thro' earth and heaven,
For sickness heal'd, and sins forgiven.

Psalm XXXI. 5, 13—21, 22, 23, First Part. Common Metre.

Deliverance from Death.

1 TO thee, O God of truth and love
My spirit I commit;

Thou hast redeem'd my soul from death,
  And sav'd me from the pit.

2 Despair and comfort, hope and fear
    Maintain'd a doubtful strife;
  While sorrow, pain, and sin conspir'd
    To take away my life.

3 "My time is in thy hand, I cried,
    "Though I draw near the dust:"
  Thou art the refuge where I hide,
    The God in whom I trust.

4 Oh make thy reconciled face
    Upon thy servant shine,
  And save me from thy mercy's sake,
    For I'm entirely thine.

            PAUSE.
5 'Twas in my haste, my spirit said,
    "I must despair and die,
  "I am cut off before thine eyes;"
    But thou hast heard my cry.

6 Thy goodness how divinely free!
    How sweet thy smiling face,
  To those that fear thy majesty,
    And trust thy promis'd grace.

7 Oh love the Lord, all ye his saints,
    And sing his praises loud;
  He'll bend his ear to your complaints,
    And recompence the proud.

PSALM XXXI. 7—33, 11—21. *Second Part,*
          Common Metre.
    Deliverance from Slander and Reproach.

1 MY heart rejoices in thy name,
      My God, my heavenly trust;
  Thou hast preserv'd my face from shame,
    Mine honour from the dust.

2 "My life is spent with grief, I cried,
    "My years consum'd in groans,
  "My strength decays, mine eyes are dried,
    "And sorrow wastes my bones."

3 Among mine enemies my name
   A proverb vile was grown,
 While to my neighbours I became
   Forgotten and unknown.

4 Slander and fear on every side,
   Seiz'd and befet me round,
 I to thy throne of grace applied,
   And speedy rescue found.

PAUSE.

5 How great deliverance thou hast wrought
   Before the sons of men!
 The lying lips to silence brought,
   And made their boasting vain!

6 Thy children from the strife of tongues
   Shall thy pavilion hide,
 Guard them from infamy and wrongs,
   And crush the sons of pride.

7 Within thy secret presence, Lord,
   Let me forever dwell;
 No fenced city wall'd and barr'd
   Secures a faint so well.

PSALM XXXII. Short Metre.
Forgiveness of Sins upon Confession.

1 OH blessed souls are they
    Whose sins are cover'd o'er!
  Divinely blest to whom the Lord
    Imputes their guilt no more.

2 They mourn their follies past,
    And keep their hearts with care;
  Their lips and lives without deceit
    Shall prove their faith sincere.

3 While I conceal'd my guilt,
    I felt the festering wound,
  Till I confess'd my sins to thee,
    And ready pardon found.

4 Let sinners learn to pray,
    Let saints keep near the throne;
  Our help in times of deep distress,
    Is found in God alone.

PSALM XXXII. Common Metre.
Free Pardon and sincere Obedience; or, Confession and Forgiveness.

1 HOW blest the man to whom his God
  No more imputes his sin,
But wash'd in the Redeemer's blood
  Hath made his garments clean!

2 And blest beyond expression he,
  Whose debts are thus discharg'd;
While from the guilty bondage free
  He feels his soul enlarg'd.

3 His spirit hates deceit and lies,
  His words are all sincere:
He guards his heart, he guards his eyes,
  To keep his conscience clear.

4 While I my inward guilt suppreft,
  No quiet could I find;
Thy wrath lay burning in my breast,
  And rack'd my tortur'd mind.

5 Then I confess'd my troubled thoughts,
  My secret sins reveal'd,
Thy pardoning grace forgave my faults,
  Thy grace my pardon seal'd.

6 This shall invite thy saints to pray;
  When like a raging flood
Temptations rise, our strength and stay
  Is a forgiving God.

PSALM XXXII. *First Part.* Long Metre.
Repentance and free Pardon; or, Justification and Sanctification.

1 BLEST is the man, forever blest,
  Whose guilt is pardon'd by his God,
Whose sins with sorrow are confess'd
  And cover'd with his Saviour's blood.

2 Before his judgment seat the Lord
  Nor more permits his crimes to rise;
He pleads no merit of reward.
  And not on works but grace relies.

3 From guile his heart and lips are free,
 His humble joy, his holy fear,
With deep repentance well agree,
 And join to prove his faith sincere.

4 How glorious is that righteousness
 That hides and cancels all his sins!
While a bright evidence of grace
 Through all his life appears and shines.

PSALM XXXII. *Second Part.* Long Metre.
A guilty Conscience eased by Confession and Pardon.

1 WHILE I keep silence and conceal
 My heavy guilt within my heart,
What torments doth my conscience feel!
What agonies of inward smart!

2 I spread my sins before the Lord,
And all my secret faults confess;
Thy gospel speaks a pardoning word,
Thine holy spirit seals the grace.

3 For this shall every humble soul
Make swift addresses to thy seat:
When floods of huge temptations roll,
There shall they find a blest retreat.

4 How safe beneath thy wings I lie,
When days grow dark, and storms appear?
And when I walk, thy watchful eye,
Shall guide me safe from every snare.

PSALM XXXIII. *First Part.* Com. Metre.
Works of Creation and Providence.

1 REJOICE, ye righteous in the Lord,
 This work belongs to you:
Sing of his name, his ways, his word,
 How holy, just and true!

2 His mercy and his righteousness
 Let heaven and earth proclaim;
His works of nature and of grace
 Reveal his wondrous name.

3 His word, with energy divine,
 Those heavenly arches spread,

    Bade starry hosts around them shine,
        And light the heavens prevade.

4 He taught the swelling waves to flow
      To their appointed deep;
    Bade raging seas their limits know,
      And still their station keep.

5 Ye tenants of the spacious earth,
      With fear before him stand;
    He spake, and nature took its birth,
      And rests on his command.

9 He scorns the angry nations' rage,
      And breaks their vain designs?
    His counsel stands through every age,
      And in full glory shines.

PSALM XXXIII. *Second Part. Com. Metre.*

Creatures vain, and God All sufficient.

1 BLEST is the nation, where the Lord
      Hath fix'd his gracious throne?
    Where he reveals his heavenly word,
      And calls their tribes his own.

2 His eye, with infinite survey,
      Does the whole world behold;
    He form'd us all of equal clay,
      And knows our feeble mould.

3 Kings are not rescued by the force
      Of armies from the grave;
    Nor speed nor courage of an horse
      Can his bold rider save.

4 Vain is the strength of beasts or men,
      Nor springs our safety thence;
    But holy souls from God obtain
      A strong and sure defence.

5 God is their fear, and God their trust:
      When plagues or famine spread,
    His watchful eye secures the just,
      Among ten thousand dead.

6 Lord let our hearts in thee rejoice,
      And bless us from thy throne;

For we have made thy word our choice,
  And trust thy grace alone.

PSALM XXXIII. As the 113th Psalm. *First Part.*
  Works of Creation and Providence.

1 YE holy souls in God rejoice,
    Your Maker's praise becomes your voice,
  Great is your theme, your songs be new;
  Sing of his name, his word, his ways,
  His works of nature and of grace,
    How wise and holy, just and true!

2 Behold, to earth's remotest ends,
  His goodness flows, his truth extends;
    His power the heavenly arches spread;
  His word, with energy divine,
  Bade starry hosts around them shine,
    And light the circling heavens pervade.

3 His hand collects the flowing seas;
  Those watry treasures know their place,
    And fill the store-house of the deep:
  He spake, and gave all nature birth;
  And fires, and seas, and heaven and earth
    His everlasting orders keep.

4 Let mortals tremble and adore
  A God of such resistless power,
    Nor dare indulge their feeble rage:
  Vain are your thoughts, and weak your hands,
  But his eternal counsel stands,
    And rules the world from age to age.

PSALM XXXIII. As the 113th Psalm. *Second Part.*
  Creatures vain, and God All-sufficient.

1 OH happy nation, where the Lord
    Reveals the treasure of his word,
    And builds his church, his earthly throne!
  His eye the heathen world surveys,
  He form'd their hearts, he knows their ways,
    But God their maker is unknown.

2 Let kings rely upon their host,
  And of his strength the champion boast,
    In vain they boast, in vain rely;

    In vain we trust the brutal force,
      Or speed or courage of an horse,
        To guard his rider, or to fly.

3 The arm of our almighty Lord,
   Doth more secure defence afford,
     When deaths or dangers threatening stand,
   Thy watchful eye preserves the just,
   Who make thy name their fear and trust,
     When wars and famine waste the land.

4 In sickness or the bloody field,
   Our great physician and our shield,
     Shall send salvation from his throne;
   We wait to see thy goodness shine;
   Let us rejoice in help divine,
     For all our hope is God alone.

PSALM XXXIV. *First Part.* Long Metre.

God's Care of the Saints; or, Deliverance by Prayer.

1 LORD, I will bless thee all my days,
    Thy praise shall dwell upon my tongue:
My soul shall glory in thy grace,
While saints rejoice to hear the song.

2 Come, magnify the Lord with me,
   Let every heart exalt his name;
I sought th' eternal God, and he
Has not expos'd my hope to shame.

3 I told him all my secret grief,
   My secret groaning reach'd his ears;
He gave my inward pains relief,
And calm'd the tumult of my fears.

4 To him the poor lift up their eyes,
   With heavenly joy their faces shine,
A beam of mercy from the skies
Fills them with light and love divine.

5 His holy angels pitch their tents
   Around the men that serve the Lord;
Oh fear and love him, all his saints,
Taste of his grace and trust his word.

6 The wild young lions, pinch'd with pain
   And hunger, roar through all the wood;
   But none shall seek the Lord in vain,
   Nor want supplies of real good.

PSALM XXXIV. 11—22. Second Part.
Long Metre.
Religious Education; or, Instructions of Piety.

1 CHILDREN, in years and knowledge young,
   Your parents' hope, your parents' joy,
   Attend the counsels of my tongue,
   Let pious thoughts your minds employ.

2 If you desire a length of days,
   And peace to crown your mortal state,
   Restrain your feet from impious ways,
   Your lips from slander and deceit.

3 The eyes of God regard his saints,
   His ears are open to their cries;
   He sets his frowning face against
   The sons of violence and lies.

4 To humble souls and broken hearts
   God with his grace is ever nigh;
   Pardon and hope his love imparts
   When men in deep contrition lie.

5 He tells their tears, he counts their groans,
   His son redeems their souls from death;
   His spirit heals their broken bones,
   His praise employs their tuneful breath.

PSALM XXXIV. 1—10. First Part.
Common Metre.
Prayer and Praise for eminent Deliverance.

1 I'LL bless the Lord from day to day;
   How good are all his ways!
   Ye humble souls that use to pray,
   Come, help my lips to praise.

2 Sing to the honour of his name,
   How a poor sufferer cried,

F

Nor was his hope expos'd to shame,
Nor was his suit denied.

3 When threatening sorrows round me stood,
And endless fears arose,
Like the loud billows of a flood,
Redoubling all my woes.

4 I told the Lord my sore distress,
With heavy groans and tears;
He gave my sharpest torments ease,
And silenc'd all my fears.

PAUSE.

5 [Oh sinners, come and taste his love,
Come, learn his pleasant ways,
And let your own experience prove
The sweetness of his grace.

6 He bids his angels pitch their tents
Round where his children dwell;
What ills their heavenly care prevents
No earthly tongue can tell.]

7 [Oh love the Lord, ye saints of his;
His eye regards the just,
How richly bless'd their portion is,
Who make the Lord their trust!

8 Young lions pinch'd with hunger roar,
And famish in the wood:
But God supplies his holy poor
With every needful good.]

PSALM XXXIV. 11—22. Second Part.
Common Metre.

Exhortation to Peace and Holiness.

1 COME children, learn to fear the Lord,
And that your days be long,
Let not a false or spiteful word
Be found upon your tongue.

2 Depart from mischief, practice love,
Pursue the works of peace;
So shall the Lord your ways approve,
And set your souls at ease.

3 His eyes awake to guard the just,
   His ears attend their cry;
  When broken spirits dwell in dust,
   The God of grace is nigh.

4 What tho' the sorrows here they taste
   Are sharp and tedious too,
  The Lord who saves them all at last,
   Is their supporter now.

5 Evil shall smite the wicked dead;
   But God secures his own,
  Prevents the mischief when they slide,
   Or heals the broken bone.

6 When desolation like a flood
   O'er the proud sinner rolls,
  Saints find a refuge in their God,
   For he redeem'd their souls.

PSALM XXXV. ver. 12, 13, 14.
Love to Enemies; or, the Love of Christ to Sinners typified in David.

1 BEHOLD the love, the generous love
   That holy *David* shows;
  Behold his kind compassion move
   For his afflicted foes.

2 When they are sick, his soul complains,
   And seems to feel the smart;
  The spirit of the gospel reigns,
   And melts his pious heart.

3 How did his flowing tears condole
   As for a brother dead!
  And fasting mortified his soul,
   While for their life he pray'd.

4 They groan'd, and curs'd him on their bed,
   Yet still he pleads and mourns;
  And double blessings on his head
   The righteous God returns.

5 Oh glorious type of heavenly grace!
   Thus *Christ* the Lord appears;
  While sinners curse, the Saviour prays,
   And pities them with tears.

6 He, the true *David*, *Israel's* king,
　Blest and belov'd of God,
To save us rebels dead in sin,
　Paid his own dearest blood.

PSALM XXXVI. 5—9. Long Metre.
*The Perfections and Providence of God; or, General
Providence and Special Grace.*

1 HIGH in the heavens, eternal God,
　Thy goodness in full glory shines;
Thy truth shall break through every cloud
That veils and darkens thy designs.

2 Forever firm thy justice stands,
As mountains their foundations keep;
Wise are the wonders of thy hands,
Thy judgments are a mighty deep.

3 Thy providence is kind and large,
Both man and beast thy bounty share;
The whole creation is thy charge,
But saints are thy peculiar care.

4 My God, how excellent thy grace!
Whence all our hope and comfort springs,
The sons of *Adam* in distress
Fly to the shadow of thy wings.

5 From the provisions of thy house
We shall be fed with sweet repast;
There mercy like a river flows,
And brings salvation to our taste.

6 Life, like a fountain rich and free,
Springs from the presence of my Lord;
And in thy light our souls shall see
The glories promis'd in thy word.

PSALM XXXVI. 1, 2, 5, 6, 7, 9. Com. Metre.
*Practical Atheism exposed, or, the Being and Attributes
of God asserted.*

1 WHILE men grow bold in wicked ways,
　And yet a God they own,
My heart within me often says,
" Their thoughts believe there's none.

2 Their thoughts and ways at once declare
  (Whate'er their lips profess)
 God hath no wrath for them to fear,
  Nor will they seek his grace.

3 What strange self-flattery blinds their eyes!
  But there's a hastening hour,
 When they shall see with sore surprise
  The terrors of thy power.

4 Thy justice shall maintain its throne,
  Though mountains melt away;
 Thy judgments are a world unknown,
  A deep, unfathom'd sea.

5 Above these heaven's created rounds,
  Thy mercies, Lord, extend;
 Thy truth out-lives the narrow bounds,
  Where time and nature end.

6 Safety to man thy goodness brings,
  Nor overlooks the beast;
 Beneath the shadow of thy wings
  Thy children chuse to rest.

7 [From thee, when creature-streams run low,
  And mortal comforts die,
 Perpetual springs of life shall flow,
  And raise our pleasures high.

8 Though all created light decay,
  And death close up our eyes,
 Thy presence makes eternal day
  Where clouds can never rise.

PSALM XXXVI. 1—7. Short Metre.
The Wickedness of Man, and the Majesty of God; or Practical Atheism exposed.

1 WHEN man grows bold in sin,
   My heart within me cries.
 " He hath no faith of God within,
 " Nor fear before his eyes.

2 [He walks a while conceal'd
   In a self-flattering dream,

F 2

Till his dark crimes at once reveal'd,
    Expose his hateful name.]

3 His heart is false and foul,
    His words are smooth and fair;
Wisdom is banish'd from his soul,
    And leaves no goodness there.

4 He plots upon his bed
    New mischief to fulfil;
He sets his heart, and hand, and head
    To practise all that's ill.

5 But ther's a dreadful God,
    Tho' men renounce his fear;
His justice, hid behind the cloud,
    Shall one great day appear.

6 His truth transcends the sky,
    In heaven his mercies dwell;
Deep as the sea his judgments lie,
    " His anger burns to hell.

7 How excellent his love,
    Whence all our safety spaings!
Oh never let my soul remove
    From underneath his wings.

PSALM XXXVII. 1—15. *First Part.*
The Cure of Envy, Fretfulness and Unbelief; or, the Rewards of the Righteous and the Wicked.

1 WHY should I vex my soul, and fret
    To see the wicked rise?
Or envy sinners waxing great,
    By violence and lies?

2 As flowery geass cut down at noon,
    Before the evening fades,
So shall their glories vanish soon,
    In everlasting shades.

3 Then let me make the Lord my truth,
    And practise all that's good;
So shall I dwell among the just,
    And He provide me food.

4 I to my God my ways commit,
    And cheerful wait his will;

Thy hand, which guides my doubtful feet,
  Shall my desires fulfil.

5 Mine innocence shalt thou display,
  And make thy judgments known,
Fair as the light of dawning day,
  And glorious as the noon.

6 The meek at last the earth possess,
  And are the heirs of heaven;
True riches, with abundant peace,
  To humble souls are given.

PAUSE.

7 Rest in the Lord, and keep his way,
  Nor let your anger rise;
Though providence should long delay,
  To punish haughty vice.

8 Let sinners join to break your peace,
  And plot, and rage, and foam;
The Lord derides them, for he sees
  Their day of vengeance come.

9 They have drawn out the threatening sword,
  Have bent the murderous bow,
To slay the men that fear the Lord,
  And bring the righteous low.

10 My God shall break the bows, and burn
  Their persecuting darts,
Shall their own swords against them turn,
  And pierce their stubborn hearts.

PSALM XXXVII. 16, 21, 26—31. *Second Part.*
Charity to the Poor; or, Religion in Words and Deeds.

1 WHY do the wealthy wicked boast,
    And grow profanely bold?
  The meanest portion of the just,
    Excels the sinner's gold.

2 The wicked borrows of his friends,
    But ne'er designs to pay:
  The saint is merciful and lends,
    Nor turns the poor away.

3 His arms with liberal heart he gives
    Amongst the sons of need;

  His memory to long ages lives,
   And bleſſed is his ſeed.
4 His lips abhor to talk profane,
  To ſlander or defraud;
  His ready tongue declares to men
   What he has learn'd of God.
5 The law and goſpel of the Lord
  Deep in his heart abide;
  Led by the ſpirit and the word
   His feet ſhall never ſlide.
6 When ſinners fall, the righteous ſtand,
  Preſerv'd from every ſnare;
  They ſhall poſſeſs the promis'd land,
   And dwell forever there.

PSALM XXXVII. ver. 23—37. *Third Part.*
The Way and End of the Righteous and the Wicked.

1 MY God, the ſteps of pious men
  Are order'd by thy will:
  Though they ſhould fall, they riſe again,
   Thy hand ſupports them ſtill.
2 The Lord delights to ſee their ways,
  Their virtue he approves:
  He'll ne'er deprive them of his grace,
   Nor leave the men he loves.
3 The heavenly heritage is theirs,
  Their portion and their home;
  He feaſts them now, and makes them heirs
   Of bleſſings long to come.
4 Wait on the Lord, ye ſons of men,
  Nor fear when tyrants frown:
  Ye ſhall confeſs their pride was vain,
   When juſtice caſts them down.

    PAUSE.

5 The haughty ſinner have I ſeen,
  Not fearing man nor God,
  Like a tall bay-tree fair and green,
   Spreading his arms abroad:
6 And lo, he vaniſh'd from the ground,
  Deſtroy'd by hands unſeen;

Nor root, nor branch, nor leaf was found
  Where all that pride had been.

7 But mark the man of righteousness,
  His several steps attend;
True pleasure runs thro' all his ways,
  And peaceful is his end.

PSALM XXXVIII. Common Metre.
Guilt of Conscience and Relief; or, Repentance and Prayer for Pardon and Health.

1 AMIDST thy wrath remember love;
    Restore thy servant, Lord,
  Nor let a Father's chastening prove
    Like an avenger's sword.

2 Thine arrows stick within my heart,
    My flesh is sorely prest;
  Between the sorrow and the smart
    My spirit finds no rest.

3 My sins a heavy load appear,
    And o'er my head are gone;
  Too heavy they for me to bear,
    Too hard for me t' atone.

4 My thoughts are like a troubled sea,
    That sinks my comforts down;
  And I go mourning all the day
    Beneath my father's frown.

5 Lord I am weaken'd and dismay'd,
    None of my powers are whole:
  My wounds with piercing anguish bleed,
    The anguish of my soul.

6 All my desires to thee are known,
    Thine eye counts every tear,
  And every sigh and every groan
    Is notic'd by thine ear.

7 Thou art my God, my only hope:
    My God will hear my cry,
  My God will bear my spirit up
    When Satan bids me die.

8 My foes rejoice whene'er I slide,
    To see my virtue fail;

      They raise their pleasure and their pride,
        When'er their wiles prevail.

9 But I'll confess my guilty ways,
    And grieve for all my sin;
  I'll mourn how weak the seeds of grace,
    And beg support divine.

10 My God, forgive my follies past,
    And be forever nigh;
  O Lord of my salvation haste,
    Before thy servant die.

PSALM XXXIX. 1, 2, 3. *First Part.* Com. Metre.
Watchfulness over the Tongue; or, Prudence and Zeal.

1 THUS I resolv'd before the Lord,
     "Now will I watch my tongue,
  "Lest I let slip one sinful word,
    "Or do my neighbour wrong."

2 Whene'er constrain'd a while to stay
    With men of lives profane,
  I'll set a double guard that day,
    Nor let my talk be vain.

3 I'll scarce allow my lips to speak
    The pious thoughts I feel,
  Lest scoffers should th' occasion take
    To mock my holy zeal.

4 Yet if some proper hour appear,
    I'll not be over-aw'd,
  But let the scoffing sinners hear
    That we can speak for God.

PSALM XXXIX. 4, 5, 6, 7. *Second Part.*
The Vanity of Man as Mortal.

1 TEACH me the measure of my days,
    Thou maker of my frame;
  I would survey life's narrow space,
    And learn how frail I am.

2 A span is all that we can boast,
    An inch or two of time:
  Man is but vanity and dust
    In all his flower and prime.

3 See the vain race of mortals move
   Like shadows o'er the plain;
  They rage and strive, desire and love,
   But all the noise is vain.

4 Some walk in honour's gaudy show,
   Some dig for golden ore,
  They toil for heirs, they know not who,
   And strait are seen no more.

5 What should I wish or wait for then
   From creatures earth and dust?
  They make our expectations vain,
   And disappoint our trust.

6 Now I forbid my carnal hope,
   My fond desires recall;
  I give my mortal interest up,
   And make my God my all.

PSALM XXXIX. *Ver.* 9—13. *Third Part.*
Sick-Bed Devotion; or, pleading without Repining.

1 GOD of my life, look gently down,
   Behold the pains I feel;
  But I am dumb before thy throne,
   Nor dare dispute thy will.

2 Diseases are thy servants Lord,
   They come at thy command;
  I'll not attempt a murmuring word,
   Against thy chastening hand.

3 Yet I may plead with humble cries,
   Remove thy sharp rebukes:
  My strength consumes, my spirit dies,
   Through thy repeated strokes.

4 Crush'd as a moth beneath thy hand,
   We moulder to the dust;
  Our feeble powers can ne'er withstand,
   And all our beauty's lost.

5 I'm but a stranger here below,
   As all my fathers were;
  May I be well prepar'd to go,
   When I thy summons hear!

6 But if my life be spar'd a while
    Before my last remove,
Thy praise shall be my business still,
    And I'll declare thy love.

PSALM XL. *ver.* 1, 2, 3, 5, 17. *First Part.*
Common Metre.
A Song of Deliverance from great Distress.

1 I Waited patient for the Lord,
    He bow'd to hear my cry;
He saw me resting on his word,
    And brought salvation nigh.

2 He rais'd me from a horrid pit,
    Where mourning long I lay,
And from my bonds releas'd my feet,
    Deep bonds of miry clay

3 Firm on a rock he made me stand,
    And taught my cheerful tonge
To praise the wonders of his hand,
    In a new thankful song.

4 I'll spread his works of grace abroad;
    The saints with joy shall hear,
And sinners learn to make my God
    Their only hope and fear.

5 How many are thy thoughts of love;
    Thy mercies, Lord, how great!
We have not words nor hours enough
    Their numbers to repeat.

6 When I'm afflicted, poor and low,
    And light and peace depart,
My God beholds my heavy woe,
    And bears me on his heart.

PSALM XL. 6—9 *Second Part.* Com. Metre.
The Incarnation and Sacrifice of Christ.

1 THUS saith the Lord, "your work is vain,
    " Give your burnt-offerings o'er,
" In dying goats and bullocks slain
    " My soul delights no more."

2 Then spake the Saviour, " Lo, I'm here,
    " My God, to do thy will;

PSALM XL.

"Whate'er thy sacred books declare
  "Thy servant shall fulfil.
"Thy law is ever in my sight,
  "I keep it near my heart;
"Mine eyes are open'd with delight
  "To what thy lips impart."

And see the blest Redeemer comes,
  Th' eternal Son appears,
And at th' appointed time assumes
  The body God prepares.

Much he reveal'd his Father's grace,
  And much his truth he shew'd,
And preach'd the way of righteousness
  Where great assemblies stood.

His Father's honour touch'd his heart,
  He pity'd sinners' cries,
And to fulfil a Saviour's part
  Was made a sacrifice.

PAUSE.

No blood of beasts on altars shed
  Could wash the conscience clean,
But the rich sacrifice he paid
  Atones for all our sin.

Then was the great salvation spread,
  And satan's kingdom shook;
Thus by the woman's promis'd seed
  The serpent's head was broke.

PSALM XL. 5—10. Long Metre.

Christ our Sacrifice.

THE wonders, Lord, thy love has wrought,
  Exceed our praise, surmount our thought;
Should I attempt the long detail,
My speech would faint, my numbers fail.

No blood of beasts on altars spilt,
Can cleanse the souls of men from guilt;
But thou hast set before our eyes
An all sufficient sacrifice.

3 Lo thine eternal Son appears,
   To thy defigns he bows his ears;
 Affumes a body well prepar'd,
 And well performs a work fo hard.

4 " Behold I come (the Saviour cries,
 " With love and duty in his eyes,)
 " I come to bear the heavy load
 " Of fins, and do thy will, my God.

5 " 'Tis written in thy great decree,
 " 'Tis in thy book foretold of me,
 " I muft fulfil the Saviour's part,
 " And lo! thy law is in my heart.

6 " I'll magnify thy holy law,
 " And rebels to obedience draw,
 " When on my crofs I'm lifted high,
 " Or to my crown above the fky.

7 " The Spirit fhall defcend and fhow
 " What thou haft done and what I do;
 " The wondering world fhall learn thy grace,
 " And all creation tune thy praife."

PSALM XLI. 1, 2, 3.
Charity to the Poor; or, Pity to the Afflicted.

1 BLEST is the man, whofe breaft can move,
   And melt with pity to 'the poor,
 Whofe foul by fympathizing love,
 Feels what his fellow-faints endure.

2 His heart contrives for their relief,
 More good than his own hands can do;
 He in the time of general grief
 Shall find the Lord has mercy too.

3 His foul fhall live fecure on earth,
 With fecret bleffings on his head,
 When drouth, and peftilence, and death,
 Around him multiply their dead.

4 Or if he languifh on his couch
 God will pronounce his fins forgiven,
 Will fave him with a healing touch,
 Or take his willing foul to heaven.

PSALM XLII. 1—9. *First Part.*
Desertion and hope; or, Complaint of Absence from public Worship.

1 WITH earnest longings of the mind,
   My God, to thee I look;
So pants the hunted heart to find,
   And taste the cooling brook.

2 When shall I see thy courts of grace,
   And meet my God again?
So long an absence from thy face
   My heart endures with pain.

3 Temptations vex my weary soul,
   And tears are my repast;
The foe insults without controul,
   "And where's your God at last?"

4 'Tis with a mournful pleasure now
   I think on ancient days:
Then to thy house did numbers go,
   And all our work was praise.

5 But why, my soul, sink down so far
   Beneath this heavy load?
My spirit, why indulge despair,
   And sin against my God?

6 Hope in the Lord, whose mighty hand
   Can all thy woes remove;
For I shall yet before him stand,
   And sing restoring love.

PSALM XLII. 6—11. *Second Part.*
Melancholy Thoughts Reproved; or, Hope in Affliction.

1 MY spirit sinks within me, Lord.
   But I will call thy name to mind,
And times of past distress record,
When I have found my God was kind.

2 Huge troubles with tumultuous noise
   Swell like a sea, and round me spread;
The rising waves drown all my joys,
And roll tremendous o'er my head.

3 Yet will the Lord command his love,
   When I address his throne by day,

Nor in the night his grace remove;
The night shall hear me sing and pray.

4 I'll cast myself before his feet,
And say, " my God, my heavenly rock,
" Why doth thy love so long forget
" The soul that groans beneath thy stroke?"

5 I'll chide my heart that sinks so low,
Why should my soul indulge her grief;
Hope in the Lord, and praise him too;
He is my rest, my sure relief.

6 My God, my most exceeding joy,
Thy light and truth shall guide me still;
Thy word shall thy best thoughts employ,
And lead me to thine heavenly hill.

PSALM XLIII. Common Metre.

Safety in Divine Protection.

1 JUDGE me, O God, and plead my cause,
  Against a sinful race;
From vile oppression and deceit
  Secure me by thy grace.

2 On thee my stedfast hope depends,
  And am I left to mourn?
To sink in sorrows, and in vain
  Implore thy kind return?

3 Oh send thy light to guide my feet,
  And bid thy truth appear,
Conduct me to thy holy hill,
  To taste thy mercies there.

4 Then to thy altar, oh my God,
  My joyful feet shall rise,
And my triumphant songs shall praise
  The God that rules the skies.

5 Sink not, my soul, beneath thy fear,
  Nor yield to weak despair;
For I shall live to praise the Lord,
  And bless his guardian care.

PSALM XLIV. ver. 1, 2, 3, 8, 15, 26.

The Church's Complaint in Perfecution.

1 LORD, we have heard thy works of old,
   Thy works of power and grace,
When to our ears our fathers told,
   The wonders of their days.

2 They saw thy beauteous churches rife,
   The spreading gospel run;
While light and glory from the skies
   Through all their temples shone.

3 In God they boasted all the day,
   And in a cheerful throng
Did thousands meet to praise and pray,
   And grace was all their song.

4 But now our souls are seiz'd with shame,
   Confusion fills our face,
To hear the enemy blaspheme,
   And fools reproach thy grace.

5 Yet have we not forgot our God,
   Nor falsely dealt with heaven,
Nor have our steps declin'd the road
   Of duty thou hast given.

6 Though dragons all around us roar
   With their destructive breath,
And thine own hand has bruis'd us sore,
   Hard by the gates of death.

PAUSE.

7 We are expos'd all day to die,
   As martyrs for thy name;
As sheep for slaughter bound we lie,
   And wait the kindling flame.

8 Awake, arise, almighty Lord,
   Why sleeps thy wonted grace?
Why should we seem like men abhor'd,
   Or banish'd from thy face?

9 Wilt thou forever cast us off,
   And still neglect our cries?

Forever hide thine heavenly love
    From our afflicted eyes?

10 Down to the dust our soul is bow'd,
    And dies upon the ground;
  Rise for our help, rebuke the proud,
    And all their powers confound.

11 Redeem us from perpetual shame,
    Our Saviour and our God;
  We plead the honours of thy name,
    The merits of thy blood.

PSALM XLV. Short Metre.

The Glory of Christ. The Success of the Gospel, and the Gentile Church.

1 MY Saviour and my King,
    Thy beauties are divine;
  Thy lips with blessings overflow,
    And every grace is thine.

2 Now make thy glory known,
    Gird on thy dreadful sword;
  And rise in majesty to spread
    The conquests of thy word.

3 Strike through thy stubborn foes,
    Or make their hearts obey,
  While justice, meekness, grace and truth
    Attend thy glorious way.

4 Thy laws, O God, are right,
    Thy throne shall ever stand;
  And thy victorious gospel prove
    A sceptre in thy hand.

5 [Thy Father and thy God
    Hath without measure shed
  His spirit like a grateful oil
    T' anoint thy sacred head.]

6 [Behold at thy right hand
    The *Gentile* church is seen,
  A beauteous bride in rich attire,
    And princes guard the Queen.

7 Fair bride, receive his love,
    Forget thy father's house;
Forsake thy gods, thy idol gods,
    And pay the Lord thy vows.

8 Oh let thy God and King
    Thy sweetest thoughts employ;
Thy children shall his honour sing,
    And taste the heavenly joy.

PSALM XLV. Common Metre.
The personal Glories and Government of Christ.

1 I'LL speak the honours of my King,
    His form divinely fair;
None of the sons of mortal race
    May with the Lord compare.

2 Sweet is thy speech, and heavenly grace
    Upon thy lips is shed;
Thy God with blessings infinite
    Hath crown'd thy sacred head.

3 Gird on thy sword, victorious Prince,
    Ride with majestic sway;
Thy terror shall strike through thy foes,
    And make the world obey.

4 Thy throne, O God, forever stands.
    Thy word of grace shall prove.
A peaceful sceptre in thy hands,
    To rule thy saints by love.

5 Justice and truth attend thee still,
    But mercy is thy choice:
And God, thy God, thy soul shall fill
    With most peculiar joys.

PSALM XLV. First Part. Long Metre.
The Glory of Christ, and Power of his Gospel.

1 NOW be my heart inspir'd to sing
    The glories of my Saviour King,
Jesus the Lord; how heavenly fair
His form! how bright his beauties are!

2 O'er all the sons of human race
He shines with far superior grace,

Love from his lips divinely flows,
And blessings all his state compose.

3 Dress thee in arms, most mighty Lord,
Gird on the terror of thy sword,
In majesty and glory ride
With truth and meekness at thy side.

4 Thine anger, like a pointed dart,
Shall pierce the foes of stubborn heart;
Or words of mercy kind and sweet
Shall melt the rebels at thy feet.

5 Thy throne, O God, forever stands,
Grace is the sceptre in thy hands;
Thy laws and works are just and right,
But grace and justice thy delight.

6 God thine own God has richly shed
His oil of gladness on thy head;
And with his sacred spirit bless'd
His first born Son above the rest.

PSALM XLV. *Second Part.* Long Metre
Christ and his Church; or, the Mystical Marriage.

1 THE King of saints, how fair his face,
Adorn'd with majesty and grace!
He comes with blessings from above,
And wins the nations to his love.

2 At his right hand our eyes behold
The queen array'd in purest gold;
The world admires her heavenly dress;
Her robes of joy and righteousness.

3 He forms her beauties like his own,
He calls and seats her near his throne;
Fair stranger, let thine heart forget
The idols of thy native state.

4 So shall the king the more rejoice
In thee the favourite of his choice;
Let him be lov'd, and yet ador'd
For he's thy Maker and thy Lord.

5 Oh happy hour, when thou shall rise
To his fair palace in the skies,

And all thy sons, (a numerous train)
Each like a prince in glory reign.

6 Let endless honours crown his head;
Let every age his praises spread;
While we with cheerful songs approve
The condescention of his love.

PSALM XLVI. First Part.
The Church's Safety and Triumph among national Desolations.

1 GOD is the refuge of his saints,
   When storms of sharp distress invade;
Ere we can offer our complaints,
Behold him present with his aid.

2 Let mountains from their seats be hurl'd
Down to the deep, and buried there,
Convulsions shake the solid world,
Our faith shall never yield to fear.

3 Loud may the troubled ocean roar,
In sacred peace our souls abide,
While every nation, every shore
Trembles, and dreads the swelling tide.

4 There is a stream, whose gentle flow
Supplies the city of our God!
Life, love and joy still gliding through
And watering our divine abode.

5 That sacred stream, thine holy word,
Supports our faith, our fear controuls,
Sweet peace thy promises afford,
And give new strength to fainting souls.

6 *Sion* enjoys her Monarch's love,
Secure against a threatening hour;
Nor can her firm foundation move,
Built on his truth, and arm'd with power.

PSALM XLVI. Second Part.
God fights for his Church.

1 LET *Sion* in her King rejoice,
    Tho' tyrants rage, and kingdoms rise;
He utters his almighty voice,
The nations melt, the tumult dies.

2 The Lord of old for *Jacob* fought,
And *Jacob's* God is still our aid;
Behold the works his hand has wrought,
What desolutions he has made.

3 From sea to sea, through all the shores
He makes the noise of battle cease;
When from on high his thunder roars,
He awes the trembling world to peace.

4 He breaks the bow, he cuts the spear,
Chariots he burns with heavenly flame;
Let earth in silent wonder hear
The sound and glory of his name.

5 " Be still, and learn that I am God,
" I reign exalted o'er the lands,
" I will be known and fear'd abroad,
" But still my throne in *Sion* stands."

6 O Lord of hosts, almighty King,
While we so near thy presence dwell,
Our faith shall sit secure, and sing,
Nor fear the raging powers of hell.

PSALM XLVII.
Christ ascending and Reigning.

1. OH for a shout of sacred joy
    To God the sovereign King!
Let every land their tongues employ,
   And hymns of tryumph sing.

2 *Jesus* our God ascends on high;
   His heavenly guards around
Attend him rising thro' the sky,
   With trumpet's joyful sound.

3 While angels shout and praise their King,
   Let mortals learn their strains;
Let all the earth his honours sing;
   O'er all the earth he reigns

4 Rehearse his praise with awe profound,
   Let knowledge guide the song;
Nor mock him with a solemn sound
   Upon a thoughtless tongue.

5 In *Israel* stood his antient throne,
    He lov'd that chosen race;
But now he calls the world his own,
    And heathens taste his grace.

6 The Gentile nations are the Lord's,
    There *Abraham's* God is known;
While powers and princes, shields and swords
    Submit before his throne.

PSALM XLVIII. 1—8. *First Part.*
The Church is the Honour and Safety of a Nation.

1 [GREAT is the Lord our God,
    And let his praise be great;
He makes his churches his abode,
    His most delightful seat.

2 These temples of his grace,
    How beautiful they stand?
The honours of our native place,
    And bulwarks of our land.]

3 In *Sion* God is known
    A refuge in distress;
How bright has his salvation shone;
    How fair his heavenly grace?

4 When kings against her join'd,
    And saw the Lord was there,
In wild confusion of the mind
    They fled with hasty fear.

5 When navies tall and proud
    Attempt to spoil our peace,
He sends his tempest roaring loud,
    And sinks them in the seas.

6 Oft have our fathers told,
    Our eyes have often seen,
How well our God secures the fold
    Where his own flocks have been.

7 In every new distress
    We'll to his house repair,
Recal to mind his wondrous grace,
    And seek deliverance there.

PSALM XLVIII. 10—14. *Second Part.*

The Beauty of the Church; or, Gospel Worship and Order.

1 FAR as thy name is known
  The world declares thy praise;
Thy saints, O Lord, before thy throne
  Their songs of honour raise.

2 With joy thy people stand
  On *Sion*'s chosen hill,
Proclaim the wonders of thy hand,
  And counsels of thy will.

3 Let strangers walk around
  The city where we dwell,
Compass and view thine holy ground,
  And mark the building well.

4 The orders of thy house,
  The worship of thy court,
The cheerful songs, the solemn vows,
  And make a fair report.

5 How decent and how wise!
  How glorious to behold!
Beyond the pomp that charms the eyes,
  And rites adorn'd with gold.

6 The God we worship now
  Will guide us till we die;
Will be our God while here below,
  And ours above the sky.

PSALM XLIX. 6—14. *First Part.* Com. Metre.

Pride and Death; or, the Vanity of Life and Riches.

1 WHY doth the man of riches grow
  To insolence and pride,
To see his wealth and honours flow
  With every rising tide.

2 [Why doth he treat the poor with scorn,
  Made of the self-same clay,
And boast as though his flesh was born
  Of better dust than they?]

3 Not all his treasures can procure
   His soul a short reprieve,
Redeem from death one guilty hour,
   Or make his brother live.

4 Eternal life can ne'er be sold,
   The ransom is too high;
Justice will ne'er be brib'd with gold,
   That man may never die.

5 He sees the brutish and the wise,
   The timorous and the brave
Quit their possessions, close their eyes,
   And hasten to the grave.

6 Yet 'tis his inward thought and pride,
   " My house shall ever stand;
" And that my name may long abide
   " I'll give it to my land."

7 Vain are his thoughts, his hopes are lost,
   How soon his memory dies!
His name is buried in the dust,
   Where his own body lies.

PAUSE.

8 This is the folly of their way
   And yet their sons are vain
Approve the words their fathers say,
   And act their works again.

9 Men void of wisdom and of grace,
   Tho' honour raise them high,
Live like a beast, a thoughtless race,
   And like the beast they die.

10 [Laid in the grave like silly sheep,
   Death triumphs o'er them there.
Till the last trumpet breaks their sleep,
   And wakes them in despair.]

PSALM XLIX. ver. 14—15. *Second Part.*
       Common Metre.

Death and the Resurrection.

1 YE sons of pride, that hate the just,
   And trample on the poor,

When death has brought you down to dust
Your pomp shall raise no more.

2 The last great day shall change the scene;
When will that hour appear?
When shall the just revive, and reign
O'er all that scorn'd them here?

3 God will my naked soul receive,
Call'd from the world away,
And break the prison of the grave,
To raise my mouldering clay.

4 Heaven is my everlasting home,
Th' inheritance is sure;
Let men of pride their rage resume,
But I'll repine no more.

PSALM XLIX. Long Metre.
The rich sinner's Death, and the Saint's Resurrection.

1 WHY do the proud insult the poor,
And boast the large estates they have!
How vain are riches to secure
Their haughty owners from the grave!

2 They can't redeem an hour from death
With all the wealth in which they trust;
Nor give a dying brother breath,
When God commands him down to dust.

3 There the dark earth and dismal shade
Shall clasp their naked bodies round;
That flesh so delicately fed
Lies cold and moulders in the ground.

4 Like thoughtless sheep the sinner dies,
And leaves his glories in the tomb;
The saints shall in the morning rise,
And hear the oppressor's awful doom.

5 His honours perish in the dust,
And pomp and beauty, birth and blood;
That glorious day exalts the just
To full dominion o'er the proud.

6 My Saviour shall my life restore,
And raise me from my dark abode;

My flesh and soul shall part no more,
　　But dwell forever near my God.

PSALM L. ver. 1—6. *First Part.* Common Metre.

The last Judgment ; or, the Saints rewarded.

1 THE Lord, the Judge, before his throne,
　　Bids the whole earth draw nigh,
The nations near the rising sun,
　　And near the *Western* sky.

2 No more shall bold blasphemers say,
　　" *Judgment will ne'er begin ;*"
No more abuse his long delay
　　To impudence and sin.

3 Thron'd on a cloud our God shall come,
　　Bright flames prepare his way,
Thunder and darkness, fire and storm
　　Lead on the dreadful day.

4 Heaven from above his call shall hear,
　　Attending Angels come,
And earth and hell shall know, and fear
　　His justice and their doom.

5 " But gather all my saints (he cries)
　　" That made their peace with God,
　" By the Redeemer's sacrifice,
　　" And seal'd it with his blood.

6 " Their faith and works, brought fourth to light,
　　" Shall make the world confess
　" My sentence of reward is right,
　　'" And heaven adore my grace."

PSALM L. ver. 10, 11, 14, 15, 23. *Second Part.*
Common Metre.

Obedience is better than Sacrifice.

1 THUS saith the Lord, " the spacious fields
　　" And flocks and herds are mine,
" O'er all the cattle of the hills
　　" I claim a right divine.

2 " I ask no sheep for sacrifice,
　　" Nor bullocks burnt with fire ;

"To hope and love, to pray and praise;
"Is all that I require.

3 "Invoke my name when trouble's near,
"My hand shall set thee free;
"Then shall thy thankful lips declare
"The honour due to me.

4 "The man that offers humble praise,
"Declares my glory best;
"And those that tread my holy ways,
"Shall my salvation taste."

PSALM L. *ver.* 1, 5, 8, 16, 21, 22. *Third Part.*
Common Metre.

The Judgment of Hypocrites.

1 WHEN *Christ* to judgment shall descend,
And saints surround their Lord,
He calls the nations to attend,
And hear his awful word.

2 "Not for the want of bullocks slain
"Will I the world reprove;
"Altars and rites, and forms are vain
"Without the fire of love.

3 "And what have hypocrites to do
"To bring their sacrifice?
"They call my statutes just and true,
"But deal in theft and lies.

4 "Could you expect to 'scape my sight,
"And sin without controul?
"But I shall bring your crimes to light,
"With anguish in your soul."

5 Consider, ye, that slight the Lord,
Before his wrath appear;
If once you fall beneath his sword,
There's no deliverer there.

PSALM L. Long Metre.
Hypocrisy exposed.

1 THE Lord, the Judge his churches warns,
Let hypocrites attend and fear,

PSALM L.

Who place their hope in rites and forms,
But make not faith nor love their care.

2 Vile wretches dare rehearse his name
With lips of falsehood and deceit;
A friend or brother they defame,
And sooth and flatter those they hate.

3 They watch to do their neighbours wrong,
Yet dare to seek their Maker's face;
They take his covenant on their tongue,
But break his laws, abuse his grace.

4 To heaven they lift their hands unclean,
Defil'd with lust, defil'd with blood;
By night they practise every sin,
By day their mouths draw near to God.

5 And while his judgments long delay,
They grow secure and sin the more;
They think he sleeps as well as they,
And put far off the dreadful hour.

6 Oh dreadful hour! when God draws near,
And sets their crimes before their eyes!
His wrath their guilty souls shall tear,
And no deliverer dare to rise.

PSALM L. To a new Tune.

The last Judgment.

THE Lord, the sovereign sends his summons forth,
  Calls the *south* nations, and awakes the *north*;
From *East* to *West* the founding orders spread
Thro' distant worlds and regions of the dead;
No more shall atheists mock his long delay;
His vengeance sleeps no more; behold the day.

2 Behold the Judge descends; his guards are nigh,
Tempest and fire attend him down the sky;
Heaven, earth and hell, draw near: let all things come
To hear his justice and the sinners' doom;
But gather first my saints (the Judge commands)
Bring them, ye angels, from their distant lands.

3 Behold my covenant stands forever good,
　Seal'd by th' eternal sacrifice in blood,
　And sign'd with all their names; the *Greek* the *Jew*
　That paid the ancient worshiper the new,
　There's no distinction here, prepare their thrones,
　And near me seat my favourites and my sons.

4 I, their almighty Saviour and their God,
　I am their Judge; Ye heavens proclaim abroad
　My just, eternal sentence, and declare
　Those awful truths, that sinners dread to hear;
　Sinners in *Zion*, tremble and retire;
　I doom the painted hypocrit to fire.

5 Not for the want of goats or bullocks slain
　Do I condemn thee; bulls and goats are vain,
　Without the flame of love; in vain the store
　Of brutal offerings that were mine before;
　Mine are the tamer beasts and savage breed,
　Flocks, herds, and fields, and forests where they feed.

6 If I were hungry, would I ask thee food?
　When did I thirst, or taste the victim's blood?
　Can I be flatter'd with thy cringing bows,
　Thy solem chatterings and fantastic vows?
　Are my eyes charm'd thy vestments to behold,
　Glaring in gems, and gay, in woven gold?

7 Unthinking wretch! how could'st thou hope to please
　A God, a spirit, with such toys as these?
　While with my grace and statues on thy tongue
　Thou lov'st deceit, and dost thy brother wrong;
　In vain to pious forms thy zeal pretends,
　Thieves and adulterers are thy chosen friends.

8 Silent I waited with long-suffering love,
　But didst thou hope that I should ne'er reprove?
　And cherish such an impious thought within,
　That God the righteous would indulge thy sin?
　Behold my terrors now; my thunders roll,
　And thy own crimes affright thy guilty soul.

9 Sinners, awake betimes; ye fools, be wise;
　Awake before this dreadful morning rise;
　Change your vain thoughts, your sinful works amend;
　Fly to the Saviour, make the Judge your friend;
　Lest like a lion his last vengeance tear
　Your trembling souls, and no deliverer near.

PSALM L. To the old proper Tune.

The last Judgment.

1 THE God of glory sends his summons forth,
　　Calls the *south* nations and awakes the *north*:
From *east* to *west* the sovereign orders spread,
Thro' distant worlds and regions of the dead.
The trumpt sounds; hell trembles, heaven rejoices
Lift up your heads, ye saints, with cheerful voices.

2 No more shall atheists mock his long delay:
　His vengeance sleeps no more: behold the day:
　Behold the Judge descends; his guards are nigh;
　Tempest and fire attend him down the sky.
When God appears, all nature shall adore him;
While sinners tremble, saints rejoice before him.

3 " Heaven, earth, and hell, draw near: let all things
　" To hear my justice and the sinner's doom; [come
　" But gather first my saints; the Judge commands;
　" Bring them, ye angels, from their distant lands.
When Christ returns, wake every cheerful passion;
And shout, ye saints; he comes for your salvation.

4 " Behold my covenant stands forever good,
　" Seal'd by th' eternal sacrifice in blood.
　" And sign'd with all their names; *the Greek the Jews.*
　" That paid the ancient worship or the new.
There's no distinction here; join all your voices,
And raise your heads, ye saints, for heaven rejoices.

5 " Here (saith the Lord) ye angels spread their thrones
　" And near me set my favourites and my sons.
　" Come, my redeem'd possess the joys prepar'd
　" Ere time began, 'tis your divine reward.
When Christ returns, wake every cheerful passion;
And shout, ye saints, he comes for your salvation.

PAUSE the First.

6 " I am the Saviour, I th' almighty God,
　" The sovereign Judge: ye heavens proclaim abroad
　" My just eternal sentence, and declare
　" Those awful truths, that sinners dread to hear.
When God appears all nature shall adore him;
While sinners tremble, saints rejoice before him.

7 " Stand forth, thou bold blasphemer, and profane,
  " Now feel my wrath, nor call my threatnings vain;
  " Thou hypocrite once drest in saint's attire,
  " I doom the painted hypocrite to fire.
Judgment proceeds ; hell trembles ; heaven rejoices ;
Lift up your heads, ye saints, with cheerful voices.

8 " Not for the want of goats, or bullocks slain
  " Do I condemn thee ; bulls and goats are vain
  " Without the flames of love ; in vain the store
  " Of brutal offerings that were mine before.
Earth is the Lord's, all nature shall adore him ;
While sinners tremble, saints rejoice before him.

9 " If I were hungry, would I ask thee food ?
  " When did I thirst or drink thy bullock's blood?
  " Mine are the tamer beasts and savage breed,
  " Flocks, herds, and fields, and forests where they
All is the Lord's he rules the wide creation ; [feed.
Gives sinners vengeance, and the saints salvation.

10 " Can I be flatter'd with thy cringing bows,
   " Thy solemn chattering and fantastic vows ?
   " Are my eyes charm'd thy vestments to behold
   " Glaring in gems, and gay in woven gold ?
God is the judge of hearts, no fair disguises
Can screen the guilty when his vengeance rises.

      P A U S E the Second.   [please
11 " Unthinking wretch ! how coul'd thou hope to
   " A God, a spirit, with such toys as these ?
   " While with my grace and statues on thy tongue
   " Thou lov'st deceit, and dost thy brother wrong.
Judgment proceeds ; hell trembles ; heaven rejoices ;
Lift up your heads, ye saints, with cheerful voices.

12 " In vain to pious forms thy zeal pretends ;
   " Thieves and adulterers are thy chosen friends ;
   " While the false flatterer at mine altar waits,
   " His harden'd soul divine instruction hates.
God is the judge of hearts, no fair disguises
Can screen the guilty when his vengeance rises.

13 " Silent I waited with long-suffering love ;
   " But didst thou hope that I should ne'er reprove ?
   " And cherish such an impious thought within,

"That the All-Holy would indulge thy sin?
See God appears, all nations join t' adore him;
Judgment proceeds, and sinners fall before him.

14 " Behold my terrors now, my thunder roll,
   " And thy own crimes affright thy guilty soul;
   " Now like a lion shall my vengeance tear
   " Thy bleeding heart, and no deliverer near.
Judgment concludes; hell trembles; heaven rejoices;
Lift up your heads, ye saints, with cheerful voices.

Epiphonema.

15 " Sinners, awake betimes; ye souls be wise;
   " Awake before this dreadful morning rise: [amend,
   " Change your vain thoughts, your sinful works
   " Fly to the Saviour, make the Judge your friend.
Then join, ye saints, wake every cheerful passion;
When Christ returns, he comes for your salvation.

PSALM LI. *First Part.* Long Metre.
A Penitent pleading for Pardon.

1 SHEW pity, Lord, O Lord, forgive,
   Let a repenting rebel live;
   Are not thy mercies large and free?
   May not a sinner trust in thee?

2 My crimes are great, but can't surpass
   The power and glory of thy grace:
   Great God, thy nature hath no bound,
   So let thy pardoning love be found?

3 Oh wash my soul from every sin,
   And make my guilty conscience clean;
   Here on my heart the burden lies,
   And past offences pain mine eyes.

4 My lips with shame my sins confess
   Against thy law, against thy grace;
   Lord, should thy judgment grow severe,
   I am condemn'd but thou art clear.

5 Should sudden vengeance seize my breath,
   I must pronounce thee just in death;
   And if my soul were sent to hell,
   Thy righteous law approves it well.

6 Yet save a trembling sinner, Lord,
   Whose hope, still hovering round thy word,

Would light on some sweet promise there,
Some sure support against despair.

PSALM LI. Second Part. Long Metre.

Original and actual Sin confessed.

1 LORD, I am vile, conceiv'd in sin,
And born unholy and unclean;
Sprung from the man whose guilty fall
Corrupts the race, and taints us all.

2 Soon as we draw our infant breath,
The seeds of sin grow up for death;
The law demands a perfect heart;
But we'er defil'd in every part.

3 [Great God, create my heart a-new,
And form my spirit pure and true;
Oh make me wise betimes to spy
My danger and my remedy.]

4 Behold I fall before thy face;
My only refuge is thy grace;
No outward forms can make me clean;
The leprosy lies deep within.

5 No bleeding bird, nor bleeding beast,
Nor hysop-branch, nor sprinkling priest,
Nor running brook, nor flood, nor sea,
Can wash the dismal stain away.

6 *Jesus*, my God, thy blood alone
Hath power sufficient to attone;
Thy blood can make me white as snow;
No *Jewish* types could cleanse me so.

7 While guilt disturbs and breaks my peace,
Nor flesh nor soul hath rest or ease;
Lord, let me hear thy pardoning voice,
And make my broken heart rejoice.

PSALM LI. Third Part. Long Metre.

The Backslider restored; or, Repentance and Faith in the Blood of Christ.

1 O Thou that hear'st when sinners cry,
Though all my crimes before thee lie.

  Behold them not with angry look,
  But blot their memory from thy book.

2 Create my nature pure within,
 And form my soul averse to sin;
 Let thy good spirit ne'er depart,
 Nor hide thy presence from my heart.

3 I cannot live without thy light,
 Cast out and banish'd from thy sight:
 Thine holy joys, my God, restore,
 And guard me, that I fall no more.

4 Though I have griev'd thy spirit, Lord,
 Thy help and comfort still afford,
 And let a wretch come near thy throne,
 To plead the merits of thy Son.

5 A broken heart, my God, my King,
 Is all the sacrifice I bring;
 The God of grace will ne'er despise
 A broken heart for sacrifice.

6 My soul lies humbled in the dust,
 And owns thy dreadful sentence just;
 Look down, O Lord, with pitying eye,
 And save the soul condemn'd to die.

7 Then will I teach the world thy ways;
 Sinners shall learn thy sovereign grace;
 I'll lead them to my Saviour's blood,
 And they shall praise a pardoning God.

8 O may thy love inspire my tongue!
 Salvation shall be all my song;
 And all my powers shall join to bless
 The Lord my strength and righteousness.

PSALM LI. 3—13, *First Part*. Common Metre.
Original and actual Sin confessed and pardoned.

LORD, I would spread my sore distress
 And guilt before thine eyes;
Against thy laws, against thy grace,
 How high my crimes arise!

Should'st thou condemn my soul to hell,
 And crush my flesh to dust,

Heaven would approve thy vengeance well,
　　And earth must own it just.

3 I from the stock of *Adam* came,
　　Unholy and unclean;
　All my original is shame,
　　And all my nature sin.

4 Born in a world of guilt, I drew
　　Contagion with my breath;
　And as my days advanc'd, I grew
　　A juster prey for death.

5 Cleanse me, O Lord, and cheer my soul
　　With thy forgiving love;
　O make my broken spirit whole,
　　And bid my pains remove.

6 Let not thy spirit e'er depart,
　　Nor drive me from thy face;
　Create a-new my vicious heart,
　　And fill it with thy grace.

7 Then will I make thy mercy known
　　Before the sons of men;
　Backsliders shall address thy throne,
　　And turn to God again.

PSALM LI. 14—17. *Second Part.* Com. Metre.
Repentance and Faith in the Blood of Christ.

1 O GOD of mercy, hear my call,
　　My loads of guilt remove,
　Break down this separating wall
　　That bars me from thy love.

2 Give me the presence of thy grace,
　　Then my rejoicing tongue
　Shall speak aloud thy righteousness,
　　And make thy praise my song.

3 No blood of goats nor heifer slain
　　For sin could e'er atone;
　The death of Christ shall still remain
　　Sufficient and alone.

4 A soul opprest with sin's desert
　　My God will ne'er despise;

A Humble groan, a broken heart,
   Is our best sacrifice.

PSALM LII. Common Metre.
The Disappointment of the Wicked.

1 WHY should the mighty make their boast,
     And heavenly grace despise?
In their own arm they put their trust,
   And fill their mouth with lies.

2 But God in vengeance shall destroy,
     And drive them from his face;
No more shall they his church annoy,
     Nor find on earth a place.

3 But like a cultur'd olive grove,
     Dress'd in immortal green,
Thy children, blooming in thy love,
     Amid thy courts are seen.

4 On thine eternal grace, O Lord,
     Thy saints shall rest secure,
And all, who trust thy holy word,
     Shall find salvation sure.

PSALM LII. Long Metre.
The Folly of Self-Dependence.

1 WHY should the haughty hero boast
     His vengeful arm, his warlike host?
While blood defiles his cruel hand,
And desolation wastes the land.

2 He joys to hear the captive's cry,
The widow's groan, the orphan's sigh;
And when the wearied sword would spare,
His falsehood spreads the fatal snare.

3 He triumphs in the deeds of wrong,
And arms with rage his impious tongue;
With pride proclaims his dreadful power,
And bids the trembling world adore.

4 But God beholds and with a frown,
   Cast to the dust his honours down;

  The righteous freed, their hopes recal,
  And hail the proud oppressor's fall.

5 How low th' insulting tyrant lies,
  Who dar'd th' eternal Power despise;
  And vainly deem'd with envious joy,
  His arm almighty to destroy.

6 We praise the Lord, who heard our cries,
  And sent salvation from the skies;
  The saints, who saw our mournful days,
  Shall join our greatful songs of praise.

PSALM LIII. 4—6.
Victory and Deliverance from Persecution.

1 ARE all the foes of *Sion* fools
  Who thus destroy her saints?
 Do they not know her Saviour rules,
  And pities her complaints?

2 They shall be siez'd with sad surprise;
  For God's avenging arm
 Shall crush the hand that dares arise,
  To do his children harm.

3 In vain the sons of *satan* boast
  Of armies in array;
 When God has first despis'd their host,
  They fall an easy prey.

4 Oh for a word from *Sion*'s King,
  Her captives to restore!
 Thy joyful saints thy praise shall sing
  And *Israel* weep no more.

PSALM LIV. Common Metre.

1 BEHOLD us Lord, and let our cry
  Before thy throne ascend,
 Cast thou on us a pitying eye,
  And still our lives defend.

2 For slaughtering foes insult us round,
  Oppressive, proud and vain,
 They cast thy temples to the ground,
  And all our rites profane.

3 Yet thy forgiving grace we trust,
  And in thy power rejoice;

PSALM LV.

Thine arm shall crush our foes to dust,
 Thy praise inspire our voice.

4 Be thou with those whose friendly hand
 Upheld us in distress,
Extend thy truth through every land,
 And still thy people bless.

PSALM LV. 1—8, 16, 17, 18, 22. Com. Metre.
Support for the afflicted and tempted Soul.

1 O GOD, my refuge, hear my cries,
  Behold my flowing tears,
 For earth and hell my hurt devise,
  And triumph in my fears.

2 Their rage is level'd at my life,
  My soul with guilt they load,
 And fill my thoughts with inward strife,
  To shake my hope in God.

3 What inward pains my heart-strings wound,
  I groan with every breath;
 Horror and fear beset me round
  Amongst the shades of death.

4 O were I like a feather'd dove,
  And innocence had wings;
 I'd fly, and make a long remove
  From all these restless things.

5 Let me to some wild desert go,
  And find a peaceful home,
 Where storms of malice never blow,
  Temptations never come.

6 Vain hopes, and vain inventions all
  To 'scape the rage of hell!
 The mighty God, on whom I call,
  Can save me here as well.

PAUSE.

7 By morning light I'll seek his face,
  At noon repeat my cry,
 The night shall hear me ask his grace,
  Nor will he long deny.

8 God shall preserve my soul from fear,
  Or shield me when afraid;

Ten thousand angels must appear
If he commands their aid.

9 I cast my burdens on the Lord,
The Lord sustains them all;
My courage rests upon his word,
That saints shall never fall.

10 My highest hopes shall not be vain,
My lips shall spread his praise;
While cruel and deceitful men,
Scarce live out half their days.

PSALM LV. 15, 16, 17, 19, 22. Short Metre.

1 LET sinners take their course,
And chuse the road to death;
But in the worship of my God
I'll spend my daily breath.

2 My thoughts address his throne,
When morning brings the light;
I seek his blessing every noon,
And pay my vows at night.

3 Thou wilt regard my cries,
O my eternal God,
While sinners perish in surprise
Beneath thine angry rod.

4 Because they dwell at ease,
And no sad changes feel.
They neither fear nor trust thy name,
Nor learn to do thy will.

5 But I with all my cares,
Will lean upon the Lord;
I'll cast my burdens on his arm,
And rest upon his word.

6 His arm shall well sustain
The children of his love;
The ground on which their safety stands,
No earthly power can move.

PSALM LVI.

Deliverance from Oppression and Falshood; or, God's Care of his People in answer to Faith and Prayer.

1 O Thou, whose justice reigns on high,
   And makes th' oppressor cease,
  Behold how envious sinners try
   To vex and break my peace.

2 The sons of violence and lies
   Join to devour me, Lord;
  But as my hourly dangers rise,
   My refuge is thy word.

3 In God most holy, just, and true,
   I have repos'd my trust;
  Nor will I fear what flesh can do,
   The offspring of the dust.

4 They wrest my words to mischief still,
   Charge me with unknown faults;
  For mischiefs all their counsels fill,
   And malice all their thoughts.

5 Shall they escape without thy frown?
   Must their devices stand?
  O cast the haughty sinner down,
   And let him know thy hand!

PAUSE.

6 God sees the sorrows of his saints,
   Their groans affect his ears;
  Thy mercy counts my just complaints,
   And numbers all my tears.

7 When to thy throne I raise my cry
   The wicked fear and flee;
  So swift is prayer to reach the sky,
   So near is God to me.

8 In thee, most holy, just, and true,
   I have repos'd my trust;
  Nor will I fear what man can do,
   The offspring of the dust.

9 Thy solemn vows are on me, Lord,
   Thou shalt receive my praise;

I'll sing, *how faithful is thy word!*
How righteous all thy ways!

10 Thou hast secur'd my soul from death,
Oh set thy prisoner free,
That heart and hand, and life and breath
May be employ'd for thee.

PSALM LVII.
Praise for Protection; Grace and Truth.

1 MY God, in whom are all the springs,
Of boundless love and grace unknown,
Hide me beneath thy spreading wings,
Till the dark cloud is overblown.

2 Up to the heavens I send my cry,
The Lord will my desires perform;
He sends his angel from the sky,
And saves me from the threatening storm.

3 Be thou exalted, O my God,
Above the heavens, where angels dwell;
Thy power on earth be known abroad,
And land to land thy wonders tell.

4 My heart is fix'd; my song shall raise
Immortal honours to thy name;
Awake, my tongue, to sound his praise,
My tongue, the glory of my frame.

5 High o'er the earth his mercy reigns,
And reaches to the utmost sky;
His truth to endless years remains,
When lower worlds dissolve and die.

6 Be thou exalted, O my God,
Above the heavens, where angels dwell;
Thy power on earth be known abroad,
And land to land thy wonders tell.

PSALM LVIII. As the 113th Psalm.
Warning to Magistrates.

1 JUDGES, who rule the world by laws,
Will ye despise the righteous cause,
When vile oppression wastes the land?
Dare ye condemn the righteous poor,

PSALM LIX.

　　And let rich sinners 'scape secure,
　　　While gold and greatness bribe your hand?

2 Have ye forgot, or never knew
　　That God will judge the judges too?
　　　High in the heavens his justice reigns;
　　Yet you invade the rights of God;
　　And send your bold decrees abroad
　　　To bind the conscience in your chains.

3 A poison'd arrow is your tongue,
　　The arrow sharp, the poison strong,
　　　And death attends where e'er it wounds;
　　You hear no counsels, cries or tears;
　　So the deaf adder stops her ears!
　　　Against the power of charming sounds.

4 Break out their teeth, eternal God;
　　Those teeth of lions dy'd in blood;
　　　And crush the serpents in the dust:
　　As empty chaff when whirlwinds rise,
　　Before the sweeping tempest flies,
　　　So let their hopes and names be lost.

5 Th' Almighty thunders from the sky,
　　Their grandeur melts, their titles die,
　　　As hills of snow dissolve and run,
　　Or snails that perish in their slime,
　　Or births that come before their time,
　　　Vain births that never see the sun.

6 Thus shall the vengeance of the Lord
　　Safety and joy to saints afford;
　　　And all that hear shall join and say,
　　" Sure there's a God that rules on high,
　　" A God that hears his children cry,
　　　" And will their suffering well repay."

PSALM LIX. Short Metre.
Prayer for National Deliverance.

FROM foes, that round us rise,
　　O God of heaven, defend,
Who brave the vengeance of the skies,
　　And with thy saints contend.

2 Behold, from diſtant ſhores,
   And deſert wilds they come,
Combine for blood their barbarous force,
   And through thy cities roam.

3 Beneath the ſilent ſhade,
   Their ſecret plots they lay,
Our peaceful walls by night invade,
   And waſte the fields by day.

4 And will the God of grace,
   Regardleſs of our pain,
Permit ſecure that impious race,
   To riot in their reign?

5 In vain their ſecret guile,
   Or open force they prove,
His eye can pierce the deepeſt veil,
   His hand their ſtrength remove.

6 Yet ſave them, Lord, from death,
   Leſt we forget their doom;
But drive them with thine angry breath,
   Through diſtant lands to roam.

7 Then ſhall our grateful voice
   Proclaim our guardian God;
The nations round the earth rejoice,
   And ſound the praiſe abroad.

PSALM LX. Common Metre.

Looking to God in the Diſtreſs of War.

1 LORD, thou haſt ſcourg'd our guilty land,
   Behold thy people mourn;
Shall vengeance ever guide thy hand?
   And mercy ne'er return?

2 Beneath the terrors of thine eye,
   Earth's haughty towers delay;
Thy frowning mantle ſpreads thy ſky,
   And mortals melt away.

3 Our Sion trembles at thy ſtroke,
   And dreads thy lifted hand!
Oh, heal the people thou haſt broke,
   And ſave the ſinking land.

4 Exalt thy banner in the field,
  For those that fear thy name;
From barbarous hosts our nation shield,
  And put our foes to shame.

5 Attend our armies to the fight,
  And be their guardian God;
In vain shall numerous powers unite,
  Against thy lifted rod.

6 Our troops, beneath thy guiding hand,
  Shall gain a glad renown:
'Tis God who makes the feeble stand,
  And treads the mighty down.

PSALM LXI. 1—6.

Safety in God.

1 WHEN overwhelm'd with grief,
    My heart within me dies:
  Helpless and far from all relief
    To heaven I lift mine eyes.

2 O lead me to the rock
    That's high above my head,
  And make the covert of thy wings
    My shelter and my shade.

3 Within thy presence, Lord,
    Forever I'll abide;
  Thou art the tower of my defence,
    The refuge where I hide.

4 Thou givest me the lot
    Of those that fear thy name;
  If endless life be their reward,
    I shall possess the same.

PSALM LXII. 5—12.

No Trust in the Creatures; or, Faith in divine Grace and Power.

MY spirit looks to God alone;
  My rock and refuge is his throne;
In all my fears, in all my straits,
My soul on his salvation waits.

Trust him, ye saints, in all your ways,
Pour out your hearts before his face;

When helpers fail, and foes invade,
　　　God is our all-sufficient aid.

3　False are the men of high degree,
　　The baser sort are vanity;
　　Laid in the balance both appear
　　Light as a puff of empty air.

4　Make not increasing gold your trust,
　　Nor set your hearts on glittering dust;
　　Why will you grasp the fleeting smoke,
　　And not believe what God has spoke?

5　Once has his awful voice declar'd,
　　Once and again my ears have heard,
　　" All power is his eternal due;"
　　He must be fear'd and trusted too.

6　For sovereign power reigns not alone,
　　Grace is a partner of the throne:
　　Thy grace and justice, mighty Lord,
　　Shall well divide our last reward.

PSALM LXIII. 1, 2, 5, 3, 4. *First Part.*
Common Metre.
The Morning of a Lord's Day.

1　EARLY, my God, without delay,
　　　　I haste to seek thy face;
　　My thirsty spirit faints away
　　　　Without thy cheering grace.

2　So pilgrims on the scorching sand
　　　　Beneath a burning sky,
　　Long for a cooling stream at hand,
　　　　And they must drink or die.

3　I've seen thy glory and thy power
　　　　Through all thy temple shine;
　　My God, repeat that heavenly hour,
　　　　That vision so divine.

4　Not all the blessings of a feast
　　　　Can please my soul so well,
　　As when thy richer grace I taste,
　　　　And in thy presence dwell.

5 Not life itself, with all its joys,
 Can my best passions move,
 Or raise so high my cheerful voice,
 As thy forgiving love.

6 Thus till my last expiring day
 I'll bless my God and king;
 Thus will I lift my hands to pray,
 And tune my lips to sing.

PSALM LXIII. 6—10. Second Part
Common Metre.

Midnight Thoughts recollected.

1 'TWAS in the watches of the night
 I thought upon thy power,
 I kept thy lovely face in sight
 Amidst the darkest hour.

2 My flesh lay resting on my bed,
 My soul arose on high;
 My God, my Life, my Hope, I said,
 Bring thy salvation nigh.

3 My spirit labours up thine hill,
 And climbs the heavenly road:
 But thy right hand upholds me still,
 While I pursue my God.

4 Thy mercy stretches o'er my head
 The shadow of thy wings,
 My heart rejoices in thine aid,
 My tongue awakes and sings.

5 But the destroyers of my peace
 Shall fret and rage in vain;
 The tempter shall forever cease,
 And all my sins be slain.

6 Thy sword shall give my foes to death,
 And send them down to dwell
 In the dark caverns of the earth,
 Or in the deeps of hell.

PSALM LXIII. Long Metre.

nging after God; or, The Love of God better than Life.

GREAT God, indulge my humble claim,
 Thou art my hope, my joy, my rest;

The glories that compose thy name
Stand all engag'd to make me blest.

2 Thou great and good, thou just and wise,
Thou art my father and my God;
And I am thine by sacred ties;
Thy son, thy servant bought with blood.

3 With heart and eyes and lifted hands
For thee I long, to thee I look,
As travellers in thirsty lands
Pant for the cooling water brook.

4 With early feet I love t' appear
Among thy saints and seek thy face,
Oft have I seen thy glory there,
And felt the power of sovereign grace.

5 Not fruits nor vines that tempt our taste,
No pleasures that to sense belong,
Could make me so divinely blest,
Or raise so high my cheerful song.

6 My life itself without thy love
No taste or pleasure could afford,
'Twould but a tiresome burden prove,
If I were banish'd from the Lord.

7 Amidst the wakeful hours of night,
When busy cares afflict my head,
One thought of thee gives new delight,
And adds refreshment to my bed.

8 I'll lift my hands, I'll raise my voice,
While I have breath to pray or praise;
This work shall make my heart rejoice,
And bless the remnant of my days.

PSALM LXIII. Short Metre.
Seeking God.

1 MY God, permit my tongue
This joy, to call thee mine;
And let thy early cries prevail
To taste thy love divine.

2 My thirsty fainting soul
Thy mercy does implore:

Not travellers in desert lands
  Can pant for water more.

3 Within thy churches, Lord,
    I long to find my place,
  Thy power and glory to behold,
    And feel thy quickening grace.

4 For life without thy love
    No relish can afford ;
  No joy can be compar'd with this,
    To serve and please the Lord.

5 To thee I'll lift my hands,
    And praise thee while I live ;
  Not the rich dainties of a feast
    Such food or pleasure give.

6 In wakeful hours of night,
    I call my God to mind :
  I think how wise thy counsels are,
    And all thy dealings kind.

7 Since thou hast been my help,
    To thee my spirit flies,
  And on thy watchful providence,
    My cheerful hope relies.

8 The shadow of thy wings,
    My soul in safety keeps ;
  I follow where my father leads,
    And he supports my steps.

PSALM LXIV. Long Metre.

1 GREAT God attend to my complaint,
    Nor let my drooping spirit faint ;
  When foes in secret spread the snare,
  Let my salvation be thy care.

2 Shield me without and guard within,
  From treacherous foes and deadly sin ;
  May envy, lust and pride depart,
  And heavenly grace expand my heart.

3 Thy justice and thy power display,
  And scatter far thy foes away ;

While listening nations learn thy word,
And saints triumphant bless the Lord.

4 Then shall thy church exalt her voice,
And all that love thy name rejoice;
By faith approach thine awful throne,
And plead the merits of thy Son.

PSALM LXV. 1—5 *First Part.* Long Metre.

Public Prayer and Praise.

1 THE praise of Sion waits for thee,
My God; and praise becomes thy house;
There shall thy saints thy glory see
And there perform their public vows.

2 O thou whose mercy bends the skies
To save when humble sinners pray;
All lands to thee shall lift their eyes,
And every yielding heart obey.

3 Against my will my sins prevail,
But grace shall purge away the stain:
The blood of Christ will never fail
To wash my garments white again.

4 Blest is the man whom thou shalt chuse,
And give him kind access to thee;
Give him a place within thy house,
To taste thy love divinely free.

PAUSE.

5 Let Babel fear when Sion prays;
Babel, prepare for long distress,
When Sion's God himself arrays
In terror and in righteousness.

6 With dreadful glory God fulfils
What his afflicted saints request;
And with Almighty wrath reveals
His love to give his churches rest.

7 Then shall the flocking nation run
To Sion's hill and own their Lord;
The rising and the setting sun,
Shall see the Saviour's name adored.

PSALM LXV. 6—13. Second Part. Long Metre.
Divine Providence in Air, Earth, and Sea ; or, the God of Nature and Grace.

1 THE God of our Salvation hears
   The groans of Sion mix'd with tears ;
Yet when he comes with kind designs,
Through all the way his terror shines.

2 On him the race of man depends,
Far as the earth's remotest ends,
Where the Creator's name is known,
By nature's feeble light alone.

3 Sailors that travel o'er the flood,
Address their frighted souls to God,
When tempests rage and billows roar
At dreadful distance from the shore.

4 He bids the noisy tempest cease ;
He calms the raging crowd to peace,
When a tumultuous nation raves,
Wide as the winds, and loud as waves.

5 Whole kingdoms shaken by the storm,
He settles in a peaceful form,
Mountains establish'd by his hand
Firm on their old foundation stand.

6 Behold his ensigns sweep the sky,
New comets blaze, and lightnings fly ;
The Heathen lands with swift surprise,
From the bright horrors turn their eyes.

7 At his command the morning ray
Smiles in the East, and leads the day,
He guides the sun's declining wheels
Over the tops of western hills.

8 Seasons and times obey his voice ;
The evening and the morn rejoice
To see the earth made soft with showers,
Laden with fruit and drest with flowers.

9 'Tis from his watry stores on high,
He gives the thirsty ground supply ;
He walks upon the clouds, and thence
Doth his enriching drops dispense.

10 The desert grows a fruitful field,
   Abundant fruit the vallies yield;
   The vallies shout with cheerful voice,
   And neighbouring hills repeat their joys.

11 The pasture smile in green array,
   There lambs and larger cattle play;
   The larger cattle and the lamb,
   Each in his language speaks thy name.

12 Thy works pronounce thy power divine;
   O'er every field thy glories shine;
   Through every month thy gifts appear;
   Great God, thy goodness crowns the year.

PSALM LXV. *First Part.* Common Metre.
A Prayer-hearing God, and the Gentiles called.

1 PRAISE waits in Sion, Lord, for thee;
   There shall our vows be paid;
  Thou hast an ear when sinners pray,
   All flesh shall seek thine aid.

2 Lord, our iniquities prevail,
   But pardoning grace is thine,
  And thou wilt grant us power and skill
   To conquer every sin.

3 Blest are the men whom thou wilt chuse
   To bring them near thy face,
  Give them a dwelling in thine house,
   To feast upon thy grace.

4 In answering what thy church requests,
   Thy truth and terror shine,
  And works of dreadful righteousness,
   Fulfil thy kind design.

5 Thus shall the wondering nations see
   The Lord is good and just;
  And distant islands fly to thee,
   And make thy name their trust.

6 They dread thy glittering tokens, Lord,
   When signs in heaven appear;
  But they shall learn thy holy word,
   And love as well as fear.

PSALM LXV. Second Part. Common Metre.

The Providence of God in Air, Earth, and Sea; or, the Blessings of Rain.

1 'TIS by thy strength the mountains stand,
   God of eternal power;
The sea grows calm at thy command,
   And tempests cease to roar.

2 Thy morning light and evening shade,
   Successive comforts bring:
Thy plenteous fruits make harvest glad,
   Thy flowers adorn the spring.

3 Seasons and times, and moons and hours,
   Heaven, earth and air are thine:
When clouds, distil in fruitful showers,
   The Author is divine:

4 Those wondering cisterns in the sky
   Borne by the winds around,
Whose watery treasures well supply
   The furrows of the ground.

5 The thirsty ridges drink their fill,
   And ranks of corn appear;
Thy ways abound with blessings still,
   Thy goodness crowns the year.

PSALM LXV. Third Part. Common Metre.

The Blessings of the Spring; or God gives Rain.

A Psalm for the Husbandman.

1 GOOD is the Lord, the heavenly King,
   Who makes the earth his care;
Visits the pastures every spring,
   And bids the grass appear.

2 The clouds like rivers rais'd on high,
   Pour out at his command
Their watry blessings from the sky,
   To cheer the thirsty land.

3 The soften'd ridges of the field
   Permit the corn to spring:

PSALM LXVI.

 The vallies rich provision yield,
  And the poor laborers sing.

4 The little hills on every side
  Rejoice at falling showers,
 The meadows dress'd in buteous pride
  Perfume the air with flowers.

5 The barren clouds refresh'd with rain
  Promise a joyful crop;
 The parched grounds look green again,
  And raise the reper's hope.

6 The various months thy goodness crowns
  How bounteous are thy ways!
 The bleating flocks spread o'er the downs,
  And shepherds shout thy praise.

PSALM LXVI. *First Part.* Common Metre.

Governing Power and Goodness; or, Our Grace tried by Afflictions.

1 SING, all the nations to the Lord,
  Sing with a joyful noise;
 With melody of sound record
  His honours and your joys.

2 Say to the Power that form'd the sky,
  " How terrible art thou!
 " Sinners before thy presence fly,
  " Or at thy feet they bow."

3 [Come see the wonders of our God,
  How glorious are his ways?
 In Moses hand he put the rod,
  And clave the frighted seas.

4 He made the ebbing channel dry,
  While Israel pass'd the flood;
 There did the church begin their joy,
  And triumph in their God.]

5 He rules by his resistless might:
  Will rebel mortals dare
 Provoke th' Eternal to the fight,
  And tempt that dreadful war.

PSALM LXVI. LXVII.

6 Oh bless our God, and never cease;
　Ye saints, fulfil his praise;
He keeps our life, maintains our peace,
　And guides our doubtful ways.

7 Lord, thou hast prov'd our suffering souls,
　To make our graces shine;
So silver bears the burning coals,
　The metal to refine.

8 Through watery deeps and firey ways
　We march at thy command,
Led to possess the promis'd place
　By thine unerring hand.

PSALM LXVI. 13—20. Second Part.
Praise to God for hearing Prayer.

1 NOW shall my solemn vows be paid
　　To that Almighty power
That heard the long requests I made
　In my distressful hour.

2 My lips and cheerful heart prepare
　To make his mercies known:
Come ye that fear my God, and hear
　The wonders he has done.

3 When on my head huge sorrows fell,
　I sought the heavenly aid;
He sav'd my sinking soul from hell,
　And death's eternal shade.

4 If sin lay cover'd in my heart
　While prayer employ'd my tongue;
The Lord had shewn me no regard,
　Nor I his praises sung.

5 But God (his name be ever blest)
　Has set my spirit free;
Nor turn'd from him my poor request,
　Nor turn'd his heart from me.

PSALM LXVII.
The Nation's Prosperity, and the Church's Increase.

1 SHINE, mighty God, on Sion, shine,
　With beams of heavenly grace;

Reveal thy power through all our coasts,
   And shew thy smiling face.

2 [Amidst our realm exalted high
   Do thou our glory stand,
And like a wall of guardian fire
   Surround the favourite land.]

3 When shall thy name from shore to shore
   Sound all the earth abroad ;
And distant nations know and love
   Their Saviour and their God.

4. Sing to the Lord, ye distant lands,
   Sing loud with solemn voice ;
Let every tongue exalt his praise,
   And every heart rejoice.

5 He, the great Lord, the sovereign Judge,
   That sits enthron'd above,
In wisdom rules the worlds he made
   And bids them taste his love.

6 Earth shall obey his high command,
   And yield a full increase ;
Our God will crown his chosen land
   With fruitfulness and peace.

7 God the Redeemer scatters round
   His choicest favours here,
While the creation's utmost bound
   Shall see, adore, and fear.

PSALM LXVIII. *First Part. ver. 1—6, 32, 35.*
The Vengeance and Compassion of God.

1 LET God arise in all his might,
   And put the troops of hell to flight ;
As smoak that sought to cloud the skies
Before the rising tempest flies.

2 [He comes array'd in burning flames ;
Justice and judgment are his names :
Behold his fainting foes expire
Like melting wax before the fire.]

3 He rides and thunders through the sky ;
   His name *Jehovah* sounds on high :

PSALM LXVIII.

Sing to his name, ye sons of grace;
Ye saints rejoice before his face.

4 The widow and the fatherless
Fly to his aid in sharp distress;
In him the poor and helpless find
A judge that's just, a father kind.

5 He breaks the captive's heavy chain,
And prisoners see the light again;
But rebels that dispute his will,
Shall dwell in chains and darkness still.

PAUSE.

6 Kingdoms and thrones to God belong;
Crown him, ye nations, in your song;
His wondrous names and powers rehearse,
His honours shall enrich your verse.

7 He shakes the heavens with loud alarms;
How terrible is God in arms!
In Israel are his mercies known,
Israel is his peculiar throne.

8 Proclaim him king, pronounce him blest;
He's your defence, your joy, your rest:
When terrors rise, and nations faint,
God is the strength of every saint.

PSALM LXVIII. *Second Part. ver.* 17, 18.
Christ's Ascension, and the Gift of the Spirit.

1 LORD, when thou didst ascend on high,
Ten thousand angels fill'd the sky;
Those heavenly guards around thee wait,
Like chariots that attend thy state.

2 Not Sinai's mountain could appear
More glorious when the Lord was there;
While he pronounc'd his dreadful law,
And struck the chosen tribes with awe.

3 How bright the triumph none can tell,
When the rebellious powers of hell,
That thousand souls had captives made,
Were all in chains like captives led.

4 Rais'd by his father to the throne,
He sent his promis'd spirit down,

With gifts and grace for rebel-men
That God might dwell on earth again.

PSALM LXVIII. 3d Part. ver. 19, 9, 20, 21, 22.
Praise for Temporal Blessings; or, common and special Mercies.

1 WE bless the Lord, the just, the good,
  Who fills our hearts with heavenly food;
  Who pours his blessings from the skies,
  And loads our days with rich supplies.

2 He sends his sun his circuit round,
  To cheer the fruits, to warm the ground;
  He bids the clouds with plenteous rain
  Refresh the thirsty earth again.

3 'Tis to his care we owe our breath,
  And all our near escape from death:
  Safety and health to God belong;
  He heals the weak, and guards the strong.

4 He makes the saint and sinner prove
  The common blessings of his love;
  But the wide difference that remains
  Is endless joy or endless pains.

5 The Lord that bruis'd the serpent's head,
  On all the serpent's seed shall tread,
  The stubborn sinner's hope confound,
  And smite him with a lasting wound.

6 But his right hand his saints shall raise,
  From the deep earth, or deeper seas,
  And bring them to his court above;
  There shall they taste his special love.

PSALM LXIX. 1,—14. *First Part.* Com. Metre.
The Sufferings of CHRIST *for our Salvation.*

1 "SAVE me, O God, the swelling floods
  "Break in upon my soul;
  "I sink and sorrows o'er my head
  "Like mighty waters roll.

2 "I cry till all my voice be gone,
  "In tears I waste the day;
  "My God, behold my longing eyes,
  "And shorten thy delay.

PSALM LXIX.

3 " They hate my soul without a cause,
   " And still their number grows
   " More than the hairs around my head,
   " And mighty are my foes.

4 " 'Twas then I paid that dreadful debt
   " That men could never pay,
   " And gave those honours to thy law
   " Which sinners took away.

5 " Thus in the great Messiah's name,
   " The royal prophet mourns ;
   " Thus he awakes our hearts to grief,
   " And gives us joy by turns.

6 " Now shall the saints rejoice and find
   " Salvation in thy name,
   " For I have borne their heavy load
   " Of sorrow, pain, and shame.

7 " Grief like a garment cloth'd me round,
   " And sackcloth was my dress,
   " While I procured for naked souls
   " A robe of righteousness.

8 " Among my brethren and the Jews
   " I like a stranger stood,
   " And bore their vile reproach to bring
   " The Gentiles near to God.

9 " I came in sinful mortals stead
   " To do my father's will ;
   " Yet when I cleans'd my father's house,
   " They scandaliz'd my zeal.

10 " My fastings and my holy groans
   " Were made the drunkard's song ;
   " But God from his celestial throne
   " Heard my complaining tongue.

11 " He sav'd me from the dreadful deep,
   " Where fears beset me round ;
   " He rais'd and fix'd my sinking feet
   " On well-establish'd ground.

12 " 'Twas in a most accepted hour,
   " My prayer arose on high,

"And for my sake my God shall hear
"The dying sinner's cry."

PSALM LXIX. 14, 21, 26, 29, 32. *Second Part.*
Common Metre.
The Passion and Exaltation of Christ.

1 NOW let our lips with holy fear
And mournful pleasure sing
The sufferings of our great High-Priest,
The sorrows of our King.

2 He sinks in floods of deep distress;
How high the waters rise!
While to his heavenly Father's ear
He sends perpetual cries.

3 "Hear me, O Lord, and save thy Son,
"Nor hide thy shining face;
"Why should thy favourite look like one
"Forsaken of thy grace?

4 "With rage they persecute the man
"That groans beneath thy wound,
"While for a sacrifice I pour
"My life upon the ground.

5 "They tread my honour to the dust,
"And laugh when I complain;
"Their sharp insulting slanders add
"Fresh anguish to my pain.

6 "All my reproach is known to thee,
"The scandal and the shame;
"Reproach has broke my bleeding heart,
"And lies defil'd my name.

7 "I look'd for pity, but in vain;
"My kindred are my grief;
"I ask my friends for comfort round,
"But meet with no relief.

8 "With vinegar they mock my thirst,
"They give me gall for food;
"And sporting with my dying groans,
"They triumph in my blood.

9 "Shine into my distressed soul,
"Let thy compassion save;

" And though my flesh sink down to death,
" Redeem it from the grave.
10 " I shall arise to praise thy name,
" Shall reign in worlds unknown;
" And thy salvation, O my God,
" Shall seat me on thy throne.

PSALM LXIX. *Third Part.* Common Metre.
Christ's Obedience and Death; or, God glorified and Sinners saved.

1 FATHER, I sing thy wondrous grace,
I bless my Saviour's name,
He brought salvation for the poor,
And bore the sinner's shame.

2 His deep distress has rais'd us high,
His duty and his zeal
Fulfill'd the law which mortals broke,
And finish'd all thy will.

3 His dying groans, his living songs
Shall better please my God,
Than harp or trumpet's solemn sound,
Than goat's or bullock's blood.

4 This shall his humble followers see,
And set their hearts at rest;
They by his death draw near to thee,
And live forever blest.

5 Let heaven and all that dwell on high
To God their voices raise,
While lands and seas assist the sky,
And join t' advance his praise.

6 *Zion* is thine, most holy God,
Thy Son shall bless her gates;
And glory purchas'd by his blood
For thine own *Israel* waits.

PSALM LXIX. *First Part.* Long Metre.
Christ's Passion and Sinner's Salvation.

1 DEEP in our hearts let us record
The deeper sorrows of the Lord;

Behold the rising billows roll
To overwhelm his holy soul.

2 In long complaints he spends his breath,
While hosts of hell and powers of death,
And all the sons of malice join
To execute their curst design.

3 Yet gracious God, thy power and love
Have made the curse a blessing prove;
Those dreadful sufferings of thy Son
Aton'd for crimes which we had done.

4 The pangs of our expiring Lord
The honours of thy law restor'd:
His sorrows made thy justice known
And paid for follies not his own.

5 Oh for his sake our guilt forgive,
And let the mourning sinner live:
The Lord will hear us in his name,
Nor shall our hope be turn'd to shame.

PSALM LXIX. ver. 7, &c. Second Part.
Long Metre.
Christ's Sufferings and Zeal.

1 'TWAS for our sake eternal God,
Thy Son sustain'd, that heavy load
Of base reproach and sore disgrace,
While shame defil'd his sacred face.

2 The *Jews* his brethren and his kin,
Abus'd the man that check'd their sin;
While he fulfill'd thy holy laws,
They hate him, but without a cause.

3 [My *Father's house*, said he, *was made
A place for worship, not for trade.*
Then scattering all their gold and brass,
He scourg'd the merchants from the place.]

4 [Zeal for the temple of his God
Consum'd his life, expos'd his blood:
Reproaches at thy glory thrown
He felt and mourn'd them as his own.]

5 [His friends forsook, his followers fled,
While foes and arms surround his head;

They curse him with a slandering tongue,
And the false judge maintains the wrong.]

6 His life they load with hateful lies,
And charge his lips with blasphemies:
They nail him to the shameful tree;
There hung the man that dy'd for me.

7 But God beheld, and from his throne
Marks out the men that hate his son;
The hand that rais'd him from the dead,
Shall pour the vengeance on their head.

PSALM LXX. Common Metre.
Protection against Personal Enemies.

1 IN haste, O God, attend my call,
  Nor hear my cries in vain;
Oh let thy speed prevent may fall,
  And still my hope sustain.

2 When foes insidious wound my name,
  And tempt my soul astray,
Then let them fall with lasting shame,
  To their own plots a prey.

3 While all that love thy name rejoice,
  And glory in thy word,
In thy salvation raise their voice,
  And magnify the Lord.

4 O thou my help in time of need,
  Behold my sore dismay;
In pity hasten to my aid,
  Nor let thy grace delay.

PSALM LXXI. 5—9. First Part.
The aged Saint's Reflection and Hope.

1 MY God, my everlasting hope,
   I live upon thy truth;
Thine hands have held my childhood up,
  And strengthen'd all my youth.

2 My flesh was fashion'd by thy power
  With all these limbs of mine:
And from my mother's painful hour
  I've been entirely thine.

3 Still has my life new wonders seen
    Repeated every year;
Behold my days that yet remain,
    I trust them to thy care.

4 Cast me not off when strength declines,
    When hoary hairs arise;
And round me let thy glory shine,
    When e'er thy servant dies.

5 Then in the history of my age,
    When men review my days,
They'll read thy love in every page.
    In every line thy praise.

PSALM LXXI. 15, 14, 16, 23, 22, 24. Sec. Part.

Christ our Strength and Righteousness.

1 MY Saviour, my almighty Friend,
    When I begin thy praise,
Where will the growing numbers end,
    The numbers of thy grace?

2 Thou art my everlasting trust,
    Thy goodness I adore
And since I know thy graces first
    I speak thy glories more.

3 My feet shall travel all the length
    Of the celestial road,
And march with courage in thy strength
    To see my father God.

4 When I am fill'd with sore distress
    For some surprising sin,
I'll plead thy perfect righteousness,
    And mention none but thine.

5 How will my lips rejoice to tell
    The victories of my king!
My soul, redeem'd from sin and hell,
    Shall thy salvation sing.

6 [My tongue shall all the day proclaim
    My Saviour and my God,
His death has brought my foes to shame,
    And sav'd me by his blood.

7 Awake, awake, my tuneful powers ;
  With this delightful song
I'll entertain the darkest hours
  Nor think the season long.]

PSALM LXXI. 17—21. Third Part.
The aged Christian's Prayer and Song ; or, old Age, Death and the Resurrection.

1 GOD of my childhood, and my youth,
    The guide of all my days,
  I have declar'd thy heavenly truth,
    And told thy wondrous ways.

2 Wilt thou forsake my hoary hairs,
    And leave my fainting heart ;
  Who shall sustain my sinking years
    If God my strength depart ?

3 Let me thy power and truth proclaim
    Before the rising age,
  And leave a savour of thy name
    When I shall quit the stage.

4 The land of silence and of death
    Attends my next remove ;
  Oh may these poor remains of breath
    Teach the wide world thy love !

PAUSE.

5 Thy righteousness is deep and high,
    Unsearchable thy deeds ;
  Thy glory spreads beyond the sky,
    And all my praise exceeds.

6 Oft have I heard thy threatenings roar,
    And oft endur'd the grief :
  But when thy hand has prest me sore,
    Thy grace was my relief.

7 By long experience have I known
    Thy sovereign power to save ;
  At thy command I venture down
    Securely to the grave.

8 When I lie buried deep in dust,
    My flesh shall be thy care ;

These wither'd limbs with thee I trust
To raise them strong and fair.

Psalm LXXII. First Part.
The Kingdom of Christ.

1 GREAT God, whose universal sway
The known and unknown worlds obey,
Now give the kingdom to thy Son,
Extend his power, exalt his throne.

2 Thy sceptre well becomes his hands,
All heaven submits to his commands;
His justice shall avenge the poor,
And pride and rage prevail no more.

3. With power he vindicates the just,
And treads th' oppressor in the dust;
His worship and his fear shall last,
Till hours, and years, and time be past.

4 As rain on meadows newly mown,
So shall he send his influence down:
His grace on fainting souls distils,
Like heavenly dew on thirsty hills.

5 The *heathen* lands that lie beneath
The shades of overspreading death,
Revive at his first dawning light,
And deserts blossom at the sight.

6. The saints shall flourish in his days,
Drest in the robes of joy and praise;
Peace, like a river from his throne
Shall flow to nations yet unknown.

Psalm LXXII. Second Part.
Christ's Kingdom among the Gentiles.

1 JESUS shall reign where e'er the sun
Does his successive journies run:
His kingdom stretch from shore to shore,
Till moons shall wax and wane no more.

2 [Behold the nations with their kings;
There *Europe* her best tribute brings;
From north to south the princes meet,
To pay their homage at his feet.

3 There *Persia*, glorious to behold,
And *India* shines in eastern gold;
While western empires own their Lord,
And savage tribes attend his word.]

4 For him shall endless prayer be made,
And endless praises crown his head;
His name like sweet perfume shall rise
With every morning sacrifice.

5 People and realms of every tongue
Dwell on his love with sweetest song,
And infant voices shall proclaim
Their early blessings on his name.

6 Blessings abound where e'er he reigns,
The joyful prisoner bursts his chains;
The weary find eternal rest,
And all the sons of want are blest.

7 [Where he displays his healing power,
Death and the curse are known no more;
In him the tribes of Adam boast
More blessings than their father lost.

8 Let every creature rise and bring,
Peculiar honors to our king:
Angels descend with songs again,
And earth repeat the loud amen.]

PSALM LXXIII. *First Part.* Com. Metre.
Afflicted Saints happy, and prosperous Sinners cursed.

1 NOW I'm convinc'd the Lord is kind
To men of heart sincere,
Yet once my foolish thoughts repin'd,
And border'd on despair.

2 I griev'd to see the wicked thrive,
And spoke with angry breath,
" How pleasant and profane they live!
" How peaceful is their death!

3 " With well fed flesh and haughty eyes
" They lay their fears to sleep;
" Against the heavens their slanders rise,
" While saints in silence weep.

4 " In vain I lift my hands to pray,
   " And cleanse my heart in vain ;
   " For I am chastened all the day,
   " The night renews my pain."

5 Yet while my tongue indulg'd complaints,
   I felt my heart reprove ;
   " Sure I shall thus offend thy saints,
   " And grieve the men I love."

6 But still I found my doubts too hard,
   The conflict too severe,
   'Till I retir'd to search thy word,
   And learn thy secrets there.

7 There, as in some prophetic glass,
   I saw the sinner's feet
   High mounted on a slippery place
   Beside a fiery pit.

8 I heard the wretch profanely boast,
   'Till at thy frown he fell ;
   His honors in a dream were lost,
   And he awakes in hell.

9 Lord, what an envious fool I was !
   How like a thoughtless beast ;
   Thus to suspect thy promis'd grace,
   And think the wicked blest.

10 Yet I was kept from full dispair,
   Upheld by power unknown :
   That blessed hand that broke the snare
   Shall guide me to thy throne.

PSALM LXXIII. 23—28. *Second Part.*
Common Metre.
God our Portion here and hereafter.

1 GOD, my supporter and my hope
   My help forever near,
   Thine arm of mercy held me up
   When sinking in dispair.

2 Thy counsels, Lord, shall guide my feet
   Through life's bewildered race ;
   Thine hand conduct me near thy seat,
   To dwell before thy face.

3 Were I in heaven without my God,
   'Twould be no joy to me ;
And whilst this earth is my abode,
   I long for none but thee.

4 What if the springs of life were broke,
   And flesh and heart should faint,
God is my soul's eternal rock,
   The strength of every saint.

5 Behold the sinners that remove
   Far from thy presence die ;
Not all the idol gods they love
   Can save them when they cry.

6 But to draw near to thee, my God,
   Shall be my sweet employ ;
My tongue shall sound thy works abroad,
   And tell the world my joy.

PSALM LXXIII. 22, 3, 6, 17—20. Long Metre.
The Prosperity of Sinners cursed.

1 LORD, what a thoughtless wretch was I,
   To mourn, and murmur and repine
To see the wicked plac'd on high,
In pride and robes of honour shine.

2 But, oh their end, their dreadful end !
Thy sanctuary taught me so :
On slippery rocks I see them stand,
And fiery billows roll bellow.

3 Now let them boast how tall they rise,
I'll never envy them again,
There they may stand with haughty eyes,
Till they plunge deep in endless pain.

4 Their fancy'd joys how fast they flee !
Like dreams, as fleeting and as vain ;
Their songs of softest harmony,
Are but a preface to their pain.

5 Now I esteem their mirth and wine,
Too dear to purchase with my blood ;
Lord, 'tis enough that thou art mine,
My life, my portion and my God.

PSALM LXXIII. Short Metre.

The Mystery of Providence unfolded.

1 SURE there's a righteous God,
    Nor is religion vain;
Though men of vice may boast aloud,
    And men of grace complain.

2 I saw the wicked rise,
    And felt my heart repine,
While haughty fools with scornful eyes,
    In robes of honour shine.

3 [Pamper'd with wonton ease,
    Their flesh looks full and fair,
Their wealth rolls in like flowing seas,
    And grows without their care.

4 Free from the plagues and pains
    That pious souls endure,
Through all their life oppression reigns,
    And racks the humble poor.

5 Their impious tongues blaspheme
    The everlasting God;
Their malice blasts the good man's name,
    And spreads their lies abroad.

6 But I with flowing tears
    Indulg'd my doubts to rise;
" Is there a God that sees or hears
" The things below the skies?

7 The tumult of my thought
    Held me in hard suspense,
Till to thy house my feet were brought
    To learn thy justice thence.

8 Thy word with light and power,
    Did my mistake amend:
I view'd the sinners's life before,
    But here I learnt their end.

9 On what a slippery steep
    The thoughtless wretches go;
And oh that dreadful firey deep
    That waits their fall below!

10 Lord, at thy feet I bow,
  My thoughts no more repine:
I call my God my portion now,
  And all my powers are thine.

PSALM LXXIV.
The Church pleading with God under sore Persecution.

1 WILL God forever cast us off!
  His wrath forever smoke
Against the people of his love,
  His little chosen flock?

2 Think of the tribes so dearly bought
  With their Redeemer's blood;
Nor let thy Sion be forgot,
  Where once thy glory stood.

3 Lift up thy feet, and march in haste,
  Aloud our ruin calls;
See what a wide and fearful waste
  Is made within thy walls.

4 Where once thy churches pray'd and sang
  Thy foes profanely rage;
Amid thy gates their ensigns hang,
  And there their hosts engage.

5 How are the seats of worship broke?
  They tear the buildings down,
And he that deals the heaviest stroke,
  Procures the chief renown.

6 With flames they threaten to destroy
  Thy children in their rest;
Come let us burn at once, they cry,
  The temple and the priest.

7 And still to heighten our distress,
  Thy presence is withdrawn;
Thy wanted signs of power and grace,
  Thy power and grace are gone.

8 No prophet speaks to calm our grief,
  But all in silence mourn;
Nor know the times of our relief
  The hour of thy return.

PAUSE.

9 How long, eternal God, how long,
   Shall men of pride blaspheme;
Shall saints be made their endless song,
   And bear immortal shame?

10 Canst thou forever sit and hear
   Thine holy name profan'd?
And still thy jealousy forbear,
   And still with-hold thine hand?

11 What strange deliverance hast thou shown
   In ages long before!
And now no other God we own,
   No other God adore.

12 Thou didst divide the raging sea
   By thy resistless might,
To make thy tribes a wondrous way,
   And then secure their flight.

13 Is not the world of nature thine,
   The darkness and the day?
Didst thou not bid the morning shine,
   And mark the sun his way?

14 Hath not thy power formed every coast,
   And set the earth its bounds,
With summer's heat, and winter's frost,
   In their perpetual rounds?

15 And shall the sons of earth and dust
   That sacred power blaspheme?
Will not thy hand that form'd them first
   Avenge thine injur'd name?

16 Think on the covenant thou hast made,
   And all thy words of love;
Nor let the birds of prey invade
   And vex thy trembling dove.

17 Our foes would triumph in our blood,
   And make our hope their jest;
Plead thine own cause, almighty God,
   And give thy children rest.

Psalm LXXV. Long Metre.

Praise to God for the return of Peace.

1 TO thee, most high and holy God,
   To thee our thankful hearts we raise;
Thy works declare thy name abroad,
   Thy wondrous works demand our praise.

2 To slavery doom'd, thy chosen sons
   Behold their foes triumphant rise:
And sore opprest by earthly thrones,
   They sought the sovereign of the skies.

3 'Twas then, great God, with equal power,
   Arose thy vengeance and thy grace,
To scourge their legions from the shore,
   And save the remnant of thy race.

4 Thy hand, that form'd the restless main,
   And rear'd the mountain's awful head,
Bade raging seas their course restrain,
   And desert wilds receive their dead.

5 Such wonders never come by chance,
   Nor can the winds such blessings blow;
'Tis God the Judge doth one advance,
   'Tis God that lays another low.

6 Let haughty tyrants sink their pride,
   Nor lift so high their scornful head;
But lay their impious thoughts aside,
   And own the empire God hath made.

Psalm LXXVI.

Israel saved, and the Assyrians destroyed; or, God's Vengeance against his Enemies proceeds from his Church.

1 IN Judah God of old was known;
   His name in Israel great;
In Salem stood his holy throne,
   And Zion was his seat.

2 Among the praises of his saints,
   His dwelling there he chose;
There he receiv'd their just complaints,
   Against their haughty foes.

3 From Zion went his dreadful word,
    And broke that threatening spear;
The bow, the arrows, and the sword,
    And crush'd the Assyrian war.

4 What are the earth's wide kingdoms else
    But mighty hills of prey?
The hill on which Jehovah dwells
    Is glorious more than they.

5 'Twas Zion's king that stop'd the breath
    Of captains and their bands:
The men of might sleep fast in death,
    That quells their warlike hands.

6 At thy rebuke, O Jacob's God,
    Both horse and chariot fell:
Who knows the terrors of thy rod?
    Thy vengeance who can tell?

7 What power can stand before thy sight
    When once thy wrath appears?
When heaven shines round with dreadful light,
    The earth adores and fears.

8 When God in his own sovereign ways
    Comes down to save th' opprest,
The wrath of man shall work his praise,
    And he'll restrain the rest.

9 [Vows to the Lord, and tribute bring,
    Ye princes, fear his frown:
His terrors shake the proudest king,
    And smite his armies down.

10 The thunder of his sharp rebuke
    Our haughty foes shall feel;
For Jacob's God hath not forsook,
    But dwells in Zion still.]

PSALM LXXVII. *First Part.*

Melancholy assaulting, and Hope prevailing.

1 TO God I cry'd with mournful voice,
    I sought his gracious ear,
In the sad hour, when troubles rose,
    And fill'd my heart with fear.

2 Sad were my days, and dark my nights,
    My soul refus'd relief;
I thought on God, the just and wise,
    But thoughts increas'd my grief.

3 Still I complain'd and still opprest,
    My heart began to break;
My God, thy wrath forbade my rest,
    And kept my eyes awake.

4 My overwhelming sorrows grew,
    'Till I could speak no more;
Then I within myself withdrew,
    And call'd thy judgments o'er.

5 I call'd back years and ancient times
    When I beheld thy face;
My spirit search'd for secret crimes
    That might with-hold thy grace.

6 I call'd thy mercies to my mind,
    Which I enjoy'd before;
And will the Lord no more be kind;
    His face appear no more?

7 Will he forever cast me off?
    His promise ever fail?
Has he forgot his tender love?
    Shall anger still prevail?

8 But I forbid this hopeless thought,
    This dark despairing frame:
Rememb'ring what thy hand hath wrought;
    Thy hand is still the same.

9 I'll think again of all thy ways,
    And talk thy wonders o'er,
Thy wonders of recovering grace,
    When flesh could hope no more.

10 Grace dwelt with justice on the throne;
    And men that love thy word,
Have in thy sanctuary known
    The counsels of the Lord.

PSALM LXXVII. Second Part.
Comfort derived from ancient Providence; or Israel derived from Egypt, and brought to Canaan.

1 " How awful is thy chastening rod!
   " (May thy own children say)
   " The great, the wise, the dreadful God!
   " How holy is his way!

2 I'll meditate his works of old,
   Who reigns in heaven above,
   I'll hear his ancient wonders told,
   And learn to trust his love.

3 He saw the house of Joseph lie
   With Egypt's yoke opprest;
   Long he delay'd to hear their cry,
   Nor gave his people rest.

4 The sons of pious Jacob seem'd
   Abandon'd to their foes;
   But his Almighty arm redeem'd
   The nation whom he chose.

5 From slavish chains he set them free,
   They follow where he calls;
   He bade them venture through the sea,
   And made the waves their walls.

6 The waters saw thee, mighty God,
   The waters saw thee come;
   Backward they fled, and frighted stood,
   To make thine armies room.

7 Strange was thy journey through the sea,
   Thy footsteps, Lord, unknown;
   Terrors attend the wondrous way
   That brings thy mercies down.

8 [Thy voice with terror in the sound
   Through clouds and darkness broke;
   All heaven in lightening shone around,
   And earth with thunder shook.

9 Thine arrows through the skies were hurl'd,
   How glorious is the Lord!
   Surprise and trembling seiz'd the word,
   And all his saints ador'd.

10 He gave them water from the rock;
   And safe by Moses' hand,
Through a dry desert led his flock
   To Canaan's promis'd land.

PSALM LXXVIII. First Part.

Providence of God recorded; or, pious Education and Instruction of Children.

1 LET children hear the mighty deeds
   Which God perform'd of old;
Which in your younger years we saw,
   And which our fathers told.

2 He bids us make his glories known;
   His works of power and grace;
And we'll convey his wonders down
   Through every rising race.

3 Our lips shall tell them to our sons,
   And they again to theirs,
That generations yet unborn
   May teach them to their heirs.

4 Thus shall they learn, in God alone
   Their hope securely stands,
That they may ne'er forget his works,
   But practise his commands.

PSALM LXXVIII. Second Part.

Israel's Rebellion and Punishment; or, the Sins and Chastisements of God's People.

1 OH what a stiff rebellious house
   Was Jacob's ancient race!
False to their own most solemn vows,
   And to their Maker's grace.

2 They broke the covenant of his love,
   And did his laws despise,
Forgot the works he wrought to prove
   His power before their eyes.

3 They saw the plagues on Egypt light
   From his avenging hand;
What dreadful tokens of his might
   Spread o'er the stubborn land.

4 They saw him cleave the mighty sea,
    And march'd with safety through,
With watery walls to guard their way,
    'Till they had 'scap'd the foe.

5 A wondrous pillar mark'd the road,
    Compos'd of shade and light;
By day it prov'd a sheltering cloud,
    A leading fire by night.

6 He from the rock their thirst supply'd;
    The gushing waters flow'd,
And ran in rivers by their side,
    Along the desert road.

7 Yet they provok'd the Lord most high,
    And dar'd distrust his hand;
" *Can he with bread our host supply*
" *Amidst this barren land?*"

8 The Lord with indignation heard,
    And caus'd his wrath to flame:
His terrors ever stand prepar'd
    To vindicate his name.

PSALM LXXVIII. *Third Part.*

The Punishment of Luxury and Intemperance; or, Chastisement and Salvation.

1 WHEN Israel sinn'd the Lord reprov'd,
    And fill'd their heart with dread;
Yet he forgave the men he lov'd,
    And sent them heavenly bread.

2 He fed them with a liberal hand,
    And made his treasures known;
He gave the midnight clouds command
    To pour provision down.

3 The manna like a morning shower
    Lay thick around their feet;
The food of heaven, so light so pure;
    As though 'twere angels meat.

4 But they in murmuring language said,
    " Is manna all our feast?
" We loath this light, this airy bread;
    " We must have flesh to taste."

PSALM LXXVIII.

5 " *Ye shall have flesh to please your lust,*"
   The Lord in wrath reply'd,
And sent them quails like sand or dust,
   Heap'd up on every side.

6 He gave them all their own desire;
   And greedy as they fed,
His vengeance burnt with secret fire,
   And smote the rebels dead.

7 When some were slain the rest return'd,
   And sought the Lord with tears;
Under the rod they fear'd and mourn'd,
   But soon forgot their fears.

8 Oft he chastis'd, and still forgave,
   'Till by his gracious hand
The nations he resolv'd to save
   Possess'd the promis'd land.

PSALM LXXVIII. ver. 32, &c. Fourth Part.
Backsliding and Forgiveness; or, Sin punished and Saints saved.

1 GREAT God, how oft did Israel prove
By turns thine anger, and thy love;
There is a glass our hearts may see
How fickle and how false they be

2 How soon the faithless Jews forgot
The dreadful wonders God had wrought!
Then they provoke him to his face,
Nor fear his power, nor trust his grace.

3 Then Lord confum'd their years in pain,
And made their travels long and vain;
A tedious march through unknown ways
Wore out their strength, and spent their days.

4 Oft when they saw their brethren slain,
They mourn'd, and sought the Lord again;
Call'd him the rock of their abode,
Their high Redeemer, and their God.

5 Their prayers and vows before him rise
As flattering words or solemn lies,
While their rebellious tempers prove
False to his covenant and his love.

6 Yet could his sovereign grace forgive
   The men who ne'er deserv'd to live;
   His anger oft away he turn'd,
   Or else with gentle flame it burn'd.

7 He saw their flesh was weak and frail,
   He saw temptations still prevail;
   The God of Abraham lov'd them still,
   And led them to his holy hill.

PSALM LXXIX. Long Metre.
For the Distress of War.

1 BEHOLD, O God, what cruel foes,
   Thy peaceful heritage invade;
   Thy holy temple stands defil'd,
   In dust thy sacred walls are laid.

2 Wide o'er the vallies drench'd in blood,
   Thy people fall'n in death remain;
   The fowls of heaven their flesh devour,
   And savage beasts divide the slain.

3 Th' insulting foes, with impious rage,
   Reproach thy children to their face;
   " Where is your God of boasted power,
   " And where the promise of his grace?"

4 Deep from the prison's horrid glooms,
   Oh hear the mournful captives sigh,
   And let thy sovereign power reprieve,
   The trembling souls condem'd to die.

5 Let those, who dar'd insult thy reign,
   Return dismay'd with endless shame,
   While heathens, who thy grace despise,
   Shall from thy vengeance learn thy name.

6 So shall thy children, freed from death,
   Eternal songs of honour raise,
   And every future age shall tell,
   Thy sovereign power and pardoning grace.

PSALM LXXX.
The Church's Prayer under Affliction; or, the Vineyard of God wasted.

1 GREAT Shepherd of thine Israel,
   Who didst between the cherubs dwell,

And lead the tribes, thy chosen sheep;
Safe through the desert and the deep.

2 Thy church is in the desert now,
Shine from on high, and guide us through;
Turn us to thee, thy love restore,
We shall be sav'd and sigh no more.

3 Great God, whom heavenly hosts obey,
How long shall we lament and pray,
And wait in vain thy kind return?
How long shall thy fierce anger burn?

4 Instead of wine and cheerful bread,
Thy saints with their own tears are fed;
Turn us to thee, thy love restore,
We shall be sav'd and sigh no more.

PAUSE I.

5 Hast thou not planted with thy hands
A lovely vine in heathen lands?
Did not thy power defend it round,
And heavenly dews enrich the ground?

6 How did the spreading branches shoot,
And bless the nations with the fruit;
But now, dear Lord, look down and see
Thy mourning vine, that lovely tree.

7 Why is her beauty thus defac'd?
Why hast thou laid her fences waste?
Strangers and foes against her join,
And every beast devours the vine.

8 Return, almighty God, return;
Nor let thy bleeding vineyard mourn;
Turn us to thee, thy love restore,
We shall be sav'd and sigh no more.

PAUSE II.

9 Lord, when this vine in Canaan grew,
Thou wast its strength and glory too;
Attack'd in vain by all its foes,
Till the fair branch of promise rose.

10 Fair branch, ordain'd of old to shoot
From David's stock, from Jacob's root;
Himself a noble vine, and we
The lesser branches of the tree;

11 'Tis thy own Son; and he shall stand
Girt with thy strength at thy right hand;
Thy first-born Son, adorn'd and blest
With power and grace above the rest.

12 Oh! for his sake attend our cry,
Shine on thy churches lest they die;
Turn us to thee, thy love restore,
We shall be sav'd and sigh no more.

PSALM LXXXI. 1, 8—16.
The Warning of God to his People; or, Spiritual Blessings and Punishments.

1 SING to the Lord aloud,
  And make a joyful noise;
God is our strength, our Saviour God;
  Let Israel hear his voice.

2 " From idols false and vain,
  " Preserve my rites divine;
  " I am the Lord who broke thy chain
  " Of slavery and of sin.

3 " Stretch thy desires abroad,
  " And I'll supply them well;
  " But if ye will refuge your God,
  " If Israel will rebel:

4 I'll leave them, saith the Lord,
  " To their own lusts a prey,
  " And let them run the dangerous road,
  " 'Tis their own chosen way.

5 " Yet oh! that all my saints,
  " Would hearken to my voice!
  " Soon I would ease their sore complaints,
  " And bid their hearts rejoice.

6 " While I destroy their foes,
  " I'll richly feed my flock,
  " And they shall taste the stream that flows
  " From their eternal rock."

PSALM LXXXII.
God the supreme Governor; or, Magistrates warned.

1 AMONG th' assemblies of the great
  A greater ruler takes his seat;

The God of heaven as judge surveys
Those gods on earth and all their ways.

2 Why will ye frame oppressive laws ?
Or why support th' unrighteous cause ?
When will ye once defend the poor,
That foes may vex the saints no more ?

3 They know not, Lord, nor will they know ;
Dark are the ways in which they go ;
Their name of earthly gods is vain,
For they shall fall and die like men.

4 Arise, O Lord, and let thy Son
Possess his universal throne,
And rule the nations with his rod ;
He is our Judge, and he our God.

PSALM LXXXIII.
A Complaint against Persecutors.

1 AND will the God of grace
    Perpetual silence keep ;
The God of justice hold his peace,
    And let his vengeance sleep ?

2 Behold what cursed snares
    The men of mischief spread ;
The men that hate thy saints and thee,
    Lift up their threatening head.

3 Against thy hidden ones,
    Their counsels they employ,
And malice with her watchful eye
    Pursues them to destroy.

4 " Come, let us join, they cry,
    " To root them from the ground,
" Till not the name of saints remain,
    " Nor memory shall be found,"

5 Awake, almighty God,
    And call thy wrath to mind :
Give them like forests to the fire,
    Or stuble to the wind

6 Convince their madness, Lord,
    And make them seek thy name ;

PSALM LXXXIV.

  Or else their stubborn rage confound,
   That they may die in shame.

7 Then shall the nations know
 Thy glorious, dreadful word,
Jehovah is thy name alone,
 And thou the sovereign Lord.

PSALM LXXXIV. *First Part.* Long Metre.
The Pleasure of Public Worship.

1 HOW pleasant, how divinely fair,
 O Lord of hosts, thy dwellings are!
With long desire my spirit faints
To meet th' assemblies of thy saints.

2 My flesh would rest in thine abode,
My panting heart cries out for God;
My God! my King! why should I be
So far from all my joys and thee.

3 The sparrow chuses where to rest,
And for her young provides a nest;
But will my God to sparrows grant
That pleasure which his children want?

4 Blest are the saints who sit on high,
Around thy throne above the sky;
Thy brightest glories shine above,
And all their work is praise and love.

5 Blest are the souls who find a place
Within the temple of thy grace;
There they behold thy gentler rays,
And seek thy face and learn thy praise.

6 Blest are the men whose hearts are set
To find the way to *Zion*'s gate;
God is their strength, and through the road
They lean upon their helper God.

7 Cheerful they walk with growing strength,
Till all shall meet in heaven at length,
Till all before thy face appear,
And join in nobler worship there.

PSALM LXXXIV. *Second Part.* Long Metre.
God and his Church; or, Grace and Glory.

1 GREAT God attend, while *Zion* sings
　　The joy that from thy presence springs;
To spend one day with thee on earth
Exceeds a thousand days of mirth.

2 Might I enjoy the meanest place
Within thy house, O God of grace,
Not tents of ease, nor thrones of power
Should tempt my feet to leave thy door.

3 God is our sun, he makes our day;
God is our shield, he guards our way
From all th' assaults of hell and sin,
From foes without and foes within.

4 All needful grace will God bestow,
And crown that grace with glory too:
He gives us all things, and with-holds
No real good from upright souls.

5 Oh God, our King, whose sovereign sway
The glorious hosts of heaven obey,
And devils at thy presence flee,
Blest is the man that trusts in thee.

PSALM LXXXIV. *ver.* 1, 2, 3, 10.
Paraphrased in Common Metre.
Delight on Ordinances of Worship; or, God present in his Churches.

1 MY soul, how lovely is the place
　　To which thy God resorts!
'Tis heaven to see his smiling face,
　　Though in his earthly courts.

2 There the great Monarch of the skies
　　His saving power displays,
And light breaks in upon our eyes,
　　With kind and quickening rays.

3 With his rich gifts the heavenly *Dove*
　　Descends, and fills the place,
While *Christ* reveals his wondrous love,
　　And sheds abroad his grace.

4 There, mighty God, thy words declare
    The secrets of thy will:
And still we seek thy mercies there,
    And sing thy praises still.

PAUSE.

5 My heart and flesh cry out for thee,
    While far from thine abode;
When shall I tread thy courts and see
    My Saviour and my God!

6 The sparrow builds her self a nest,
    And suffers no remove;
Oh make me like the sparrows, blest,
    To dwell but where I love.

7 To set one day beneath thine eye,
    And hear thy gracious voice,
Exceeds a whole eternity
    Employ'd in carnal joys.

8 Lord, at thy threshold I would wait,
    While Jesus is within.
Rather than fill a throne of state,
    Among the tents of sin.

9 Could I command the spacious land,
    And the more boundless sea,
For one blest hour at thy right hand
    I'd give them both away.

PSALM LXXXIV. As the 148th Psalm.
Longing for the house of God.

1 LORD of the worlds above,
        How pleasant and how fair
    The dwellings of thy love,
    Thy earthly temples are;
        To thine abode
        My heart aspires
        With warm desires
        To see my God.

2 The sparrow for her young
    With pleasure seeks a nest,
And wandering swallows long
    And find their wonted rest;

My spirit faints
With equal zeal
To rise and dwell
Among thy saints.

3 O happy souls that pray,
Where God appoints to hear;
O happy men that pay
Their constant service there!
   They praise thee still;
   And happy they
   That love the way
   To *Zion's* hill.

4 They go from strength to strength,
Thro' this dark vale of tears,
Till each arrives at length,
Till each in heaven appears;
   O glorious seat
   When God our King
   Shall thither bring
   Our willing feet!

P A U S E.

5 To spend one sacred day,
Where God and saints abide,
Affords diviner joy
Than thousand days beside:
   Where God resorts,
   I love it more
   To keep the door
   Than shine in courts.

6 God is our sun and shield,
Our light and our defence;
With gifts our hands are fill'd
We draw our blessings thence;
   He shall bestow
   On *Jacob's* race
   Peculiar grace
   And glory too.

7 The Lord his people loves;
His hand no good with-holds
From those his heart approves,
From pure and pious souls:

Thrice happy he,
O God of hosts,
Whose spirit trusts
Alone in thee.

PSALM LXXXV. Ver. 1—3. First Part.
Waiting for an Answer to Prayer; or, Deliverance begun and compleated.

1 LORD, thou hast call'd thy grace to mind;
    Thou hast revers'd our heavy doom:
So God forgave when *Israel* sinn'd,
And brought his wandering captives home.

2. Thou hast begun to set us free,
And made thy fiercest wrath abate:
Now let our hearts be turn'd to thee,
And thy salvation be complete.

3 Revive our dying graces, Lord,
And let thy saints in thee rejoice;
Make known thy truth, fulfil thy word:
We wait for praise to tune our voice.

4 We wait to hear what God will say:
He'll speak, and give his people peace:
But let them run no more astray,
Lest his returning wrath increase.

PSALM LXXXV. Ver. 9. &c. Second Part.
Salvation by Christ.

1 SALVATION is forever nigh
    The souls that fear and trust the Lord;
And grace descending from on high
Fresh hopes of glory shall afford.

2 Mercy and truth on earth are met,
Since Christ the Lord came down from heaven;
By his obedience so complete
Justice is pleas'd, and peace is given.

3 Now truth and honour shall abound,
Religion dwell on earth again,
And heavenly influence bless the ground
In our Redeemer's gentler reign.

4 His righteousness is gone before,
To give us free access to God;

Our wandering feet shall stray no more,
But mark his steps, and keep the road.

PSALM LXXXVI. Ver. 8—13.
A General Song of Praise to GOD.

1 AMONG the princes, earthly gods,
   There's none hath power divine;
Nor is their nature, mighty Lord,
   Nor are their works like thine.

2 The nations, thou hast made shall bring
   Their offerings round thy throne;
For thou alone dost wondrous things,
   For thou art God alone.

3 Lord, I would walk with holy feet,
   Teach me thine heavenly ways,
And all my wandering thoughts unite
   In God my father's praise.

4 Great is thy mercy, and my tongue
   Shall those sweet wonders tell,
How by thy grace my sinking soul
   Rose from the deeps of hell.

PSALM LXXXVII.
The Church the Birth Place of the Saints; or Jews and Gentiles united in the Christian Church.

1 GOD in his earthly temple lays
   Foundation for his heavenly praise;
He lik'd the tents of *Jacob* well,
But still in *Sion* loves to dwell.

2 His mercy visits every house,
   That pay their night and morning vows;
But makes a more delightful stay,
Where churches meet to praise and pray.

3 What glories were describ'd of old!
What wonders are in *Sion* told!
Thou city of our God below,
Thy fame shall *Tyre* and *Egypt* know.

4 *Egypt* and *Tyre*, and *Greek* and *Jew*,
Shall there begin their lives anew;

Angels and men shall join to sing.
The hill where living waters spring.

5 When God makes up his last account
Or natives in his holy mount,
Twill be an honour to appear
As one new-born and nourish'd there.

PSALM LXXXVIII. As the 113th.
Loss of Friends, and absence of Divine Grace,

1 O GOD of my salvation, hear
   My nightly groan, my daily prayer,
That still employ my waiting breath;
My soul, declining to the grave,
Implores thy sovereign power to save
   From dark despair and lasting death.

2 Thy wrath lies heavy on my soul,
And waves of sorrows o'er me roll,
   While dust and silence spread the gloom;
My friends, belov'd in happier days,
The dear companions of my ways,
   Descend around me to the tomb.

3 As, lost in lonely grief, I tread
The mournful mansions of the dead,
   Or to some throng'd assembly go;
Through all alike I rove alone,
While, here forgot and there unknown,
   The change renews my piercing woe.

4 And why will God neglect my call?
Or who shall profit by my fall,
   When life departs and love expires!
Can dust and darkness praise the Lord?
Or wake, or brighten at his word,
   And tune the harp with heavenly quires?

5 Yet through each melancholy day,
I've pray'd to thee, and still will pray,
   Imploring still thy kind return—
But oh! my friends, my comforts, fled,
And all my kindred of the dead
   Recal my wandering thoughts to mourn.

PSALM LXXXIX. First Part. Long Metre.

The Covenant made with Christ; or, the true David.

1 FOREVER shall my song record
  The truth and mercy of the Lord;
Mercy and truth forever stand
Like heaven establish'd by his hand.

2 Thus to his Son he sware and said,
  " With thee my covenant first is made;
  " In thee shall dying sinners live;
  " Glory and grace are thine to give.

3 " Be thou my prophet; thou my priest,
  " Thy children shall be ever blest;
  " Thou art my chosen king, thy throne
  " Shall stand eternal like my own.

4 " There's none of all my sons above
  " So much my image or my love;
  " Celestial powers thy subjects are,
  " Then what can earth to thee compare?

5 " *David*, my servant, whom I chose
  " To guard my flock, to crush my foes;
  " And rais'd him to the *Jewish* throne,
  " Was but a shadow of my Son."

6 Now let the church rejoice and sing,
Jesus her saviour and her king:
Angels his heavenly wonders show,
And saints declare his works below.

PSALM LXXXIX. First Part. Com. Metre.
The Faithfulness of God.

1 MY never-ceasing song shall show
  The mercies of the Lord;
And make succeeding ages know
  How faithful is his word.

2 The sacred truths his lips pronounce
  Shall firm as heaven endure;
And if he speak a promise once,
  Th' eternal grace is sure.

3 How long the race of *David* held!
  The promis'd *Jewish* throne

But there's a nobler covenant seal'd
  To *David*'s greater son.

4 His seed forever shall possess
  A throne above the skies;
The meanest subjects of his grace
  Shall to that glory rise.

5 Lord God of hosts, thy wondrous ways
  Are sung by saints above;
And saints on earth their honours raise
  To thy unchanging love.

PSALM LXXXIX. 7, &c. Second Part.
The Power and Majesty of God; or Reverential Worship.

1 WITH reverence let the saints appear,
  And bow before the Lord;
His high commands with reverence hear,
  And tremble at his word.

2 How terrible thy glories rise!
  Aow bright thine armies shine!
Where is the power with thee that vies,
  Or truth compar'd with thine?

3 The *Northern* pole and *Southern* rest
  On thy supporting hand;
Darkness and day from *East* to *West*
  Move round at thy command.

4 Thy word the raging winds controul,
  And rule the boisterous deep;
Thou mak'st the sleeping billows roll,
  The rolling billows sleep.

5 Heaven, earth, and air, and sea are thine,
  And the dark world of hell;
They saw thine arm in vengeance shine
  When *Egypt* durst rebel.

6 Justice and judgment are thy throne,
  Yet wondrous is thy grace!
While truth and mercy join'd in one,
  Invite us near thy face.

PSALM LXXXIX. 15, &c. Third Part.
A blessed Gospel.

1 BLEST are the souls who hear and know
   The gospel's joyful sound !
Peace shall attend the path the go,
   And light their steps surround.

2 Their joy shall bear their spirits up,
   Through their Redeemer's name ;
His righteousness exalts their hope,
   And fills their foes with shame.

3 The Lord our glory and defence
   Strength and salvation gives ;
Israel, thy king forever reigns.
   Thy God forever lives.

PSALM LXXXIX. 19, &c. Fourth Part.
Christ's meditorial Kingdom ; or, *his divine and humane Nature.*

1 HEAR what the Lord in vision said,
   And made his mercy known :
" Sinners, behold, your help is laid
   " On my almighty Son.

2. Behold the man my wisdom chose
   Among your mortal race :
His head my holy oil o'erflows,
   With full supplies of grace.

3 High shall he reign on *David*'s throne,
   My people's better king ;
My arm shall beat his rivals down,
   And still new subjects bring.

4 My truth shall guard him in his way
   With mercy by his side ;
While in my name o'er earth and sea
   He shall in triumph ride.

5 Me for his father and his God,
   He shall forever own,
Call me his rock, his high abode,
   And I'll support my son.

6 My first-born son array'd in grace,
  At my right hand shall sit,
Beneath him angels know their place,
  And monarchs at his feet.
7 My covenant stands forever fast,
  My promises are strong:
Firm as the heavens his throne shall last,
  His seed endure as long.

PSALM LXXXIX. 30, &c. Fifth Part.
The Covenant of Grace unchangeable; or, Affliction without Rejection.

1 YET (saith the Lord) if *David*'s race,
    The children of my son,
  Should break my laws, abuse my grace
    And tempt mine anger down.
2 Their sins I'll visit with the rod,
    And make their folly smart;
  But I'll not cease to be their God,
    Nor from my truth depart.
3 My covenant I will ne'er revoke,
    But keep my grace in mind;
  And what eternal love hath spoke,
    Eternal truth shall bind.
4 Once have I sworn, (I need no more)
    And pledg'd my holiness,
  To seal the sacred promise sure
    To *David* and his race.
5 The sun shall see his offspring rise,
    And spread from sea to sea,
  Long as he travels round the skies
    To give the nations day.
6 Sure as the moon that rules the night
    His kingdom shall endure,
  Till the fix'd laws of shade and light
    Shall be observ'd no more.

PSALM LXXXIX. 47, &c. Sixth Part.
Long Metre
Mortality and Hope.
A Funeral Psalm.

1 REMEMBER Lord, our mortal state;
  How frail our life, how short our date!

PSALM LXXXIX.

Where is the man that draws his breath
Safe from disease, secure from death.

2 Lord, while we see whole nations die,
Our flesh and strength repine and cry;
" Must death forever rage and reign,
" Or hast thou made mankind in vain."

3 Where is thy promise to the just?
Are not thy servants turn'd to dust?
But faith forbids these mournful sighs,
And sees the sleeping dust arise.

4 That glorious hour, that dreadful day
Wipes the reproach of saints away,
And clears the honour of thy word:
Awake, our souls, and bless the Lord.

PSALM LXXXIX. 47, &c. *Last Part.*
As the 113th Psalm.
Life, Death, and the Resurrection.

1 THINK, mighty God, on feeble man,
 How few his hours, how short his span!
Short from the cradle to the grave:
Who can secure his vital breath
Against the bold demands of death
 With skill to fly, or power to save?

2 Lord, shall it be forever said,
" The race of man was only made
" For sickness, sorrow and the dust?"
Are not thy servants day by day
Sent to their graves, and turn'd to clay?
 Lord, where's thy kindness to the just?

3 Hast thou not promis'd to thy son,
And all his seed a heavenly crown?
 But flesh and sense indulge dispair;
Forever blessed be the Lord,
That faith can read his holy word,
 And find a resurrection there.

4 Forever blessed be the Lord,
Who gives his saints a long reward,
 For all their toil, reproach and pain;
Let all below, and all above,

Join to proclaim thy wondrous love,
And each repeat their loud *Amen.*

PSALM XC. 1—5 *First Part.*
Man Mortal, and GOD Eternal.

A mournful Song at a Funeral.

1 THRO' every age, eternal God,
Thou art our rest, our safe abode :
High was thy throne ere heaven was made,
Or earth thy humble foot-stool laid.

2 Long had'st thou reign'd ere time began,
Or dust was fashion'd to a man ;
And long thy kingdom shall endure
When earth and time shall be no more.

3 But man, weak man, is born to die,
Made up of guilt and vanity :
Thy dreadful sentence, Lord, was just,
" *Return ye sinners, to your dust.*

4 [A thousand of our years amount
Scarce to a day in thine account,
Like yesterday's departed light ;
Or the last watch of ending night.

PAUSE.

5 Death, like an overflowing stream,
Sweeps us away ; our life's a dream ;
An empty tale ; a morning flower,
Cut down and wither'd in an hour.]

6 [Our age to seventy years is set ;
How short the time ! how frail the state !
And if to eighty we arrive,
We rather sigh, and groan than live.

7 But oh how oft thy wrath appears,
And cuts off our expected years !
Thy wrath awakes our humble dread !
We fear the power that strikes us dead.]

8 Teach us O Lord, how frail is man ;
And kindly lengthen out the span,
'Till a wise care of piety
Fit us to die, and dwell with thee.

PSALM XC.

PSALM XC, 1—5 First Part.
Common Metre.
Man Frail and God Eternal.

1 OUR God, our help in ages past,
  Our hope for years to come,
Our shelter from the stormy blast,
  And our eternal home.

2 Beneath the shadow of thy throne
  Thy saints have dwelt secure;
Sufficient is thine arm alone,
  And my defence is sure.

3 Before the hills in order stood,
  Or earth receiv'd her frame,
From everlasting thou art God,
  To endless years the same.

4 Thy word commands our flesh to dust,
  Return ye sons of men;
All nations rose from earth at first,
  And turn to earth again.

5 A thousand ages in thy sight.
  Are like an evening gone;
Short as the watch that ends the night
  Before the rising dawn.

6 [The busy tribes of flesh and blood,
  With all their lives and cares,
Are carried downwards by the flood,
  And lost in following years.

7 Time, like an ever-rolling stream,
  Bears all its sons away;
They fly, forgotten, as a dream
  Dies at the opening day.

8 Like flowery fields the nations stand
  Pleas'd with the morning light;
The flowers beneath the mower's hand
  Lie withering ere 'tis night.

9 Our God, our help in ages past,
  Our hope for years to come,

Be thou our guard while troubles last,
And our eternal home.

PSALM XC. 8, 11, 2, 10, 12. Second Part.
Common Metre.

Infirmities and Mortality the effect of sin; or, Life, old Age, and Preparation for Death.

1 LORD, if thine eyes survey our faults,
   And justice grow severe,
Thy dreadful wrath exceeds our thoughts,
   And burns beyond our fear.

2 Thine angers turns our frame to dust;
   By one offence to thee,
Adam, with all his sons, have lost
   Their immortality.

3 Life, like a vain amusement flies,
   A fable or a song;
By swift degrees our nature dies,
   Nor can our joys be long.

4 'Tis but a few whose days amount
   To three score years and ten;
And all beyond that short account
   Is sorrow, toil, and pain.

5 [Our vitals with laborious strife
   Bear up the crazy load,
And drag these poor remains of life
   Along the tiresome road.

6 Almighty God, reveal thy love,
   And not thy wrath alone;
Oh let our sweet experince prove
   The mercies of thy throne.

7 Our souls would learn the heavenly art
   T' improve the hours we have,
That we may act the wiser part,
   And live beyond the grave.

PSALM XC. Ver. 13, &c. Third Part.
Common Metre.

Breathing after Heaven.

1 RETURN, O God of love, return;
   Earth is a tiresome place:

PSALM XC. XCI.

How long shall we thy children mourn
   Our absence from thy face?

2 Let heaven succeed our painful years,
   Let sin and sorrow cease,
And in proportion to our tears
   So make our joys increase.

3 Thy wonders to thy servants show,
   Make thy own work complete;
Then shall our souls thy glory know,
   And own thy love was great.

4 Then shall we shine before thy throne
   In all thy beauty, Lord;
And the poor service we had done
   Meet a divine reward.

PSALM XC. Ver. 5, 10, 12, Short Metre.
The Frailty and Shortness of Life.

1 LORD, what a feeble piece
      Is this our mortal frame!
   Our life how poor a trifle 'tis,
      That scarce deserves the name!

2 Alas, the brittle clay
      That built our body first!
   And every month and every day,
      'Tis mouldering back to dust.

3 Our moments fly apace.
      Our feeble powers decay,
   Swift as a flood our hasty days
      Are sweeping us away.

4 Yet, if our days must fly,
      We'll keep their end in sight,
   We'll spend them all in wisdom's way,
      And let them speed their flight.

5 They'll waft us sooner o'er
      This life's tempestuous sea;
   Soon we shall reach the peaceful shore
      Of blest eternity.

PSALM XCI. 1—7 *First Part.*
Safety and public Diseases and Dangers.

1 HE that hath made his refuge God,
      Shall find a most secure abode;

Shall walk all day beneath his shade,
And there at night shall rest his head.

2 Then will I say, " my God, thy power
" Shall be my fortress and my tower:
" I that am form'd of feeble dust
" Make thine Almighty arm my trust."

3 Thrice happy man ! thy Maker's care
Shall keep thee from the fowler's snare;
From Satan's wiles, who still betrays
Unguarded souls a thousand ways.

4 Just as a hen protects her brood,
From birds of prey that seek their blood,
The Lord his faithful sains shall guard,
And endless life be their reward.

5 If burning beams of noon conspire
To dart a pestilential fire;
God is their life, his wings are spread
To shield them with a healthful shade.

6 If vapours with malignant breath
Rise thick, and scatter midnight death,
Israel is safe: the poisoned air
Grows pure, if *Israel's* God be there.

P A U S E.

7 What though a thousand at thy side,
Around thy path ten thousand dy'd,
Thy God his chosen people saves
Amongst the dead, amidst the graves.

8 So when he sent his angel down
To make his wrath in *Egypt* known,
And slew their sons, his careful eye
Past all the doors of *Jacob* by.

9 But if the fire, or plague, or sword,
Receive commission from the Lord,
To strike his saints among the rest,
Their very pains and deaths are blest.

10 The sword, the pestilence, or fire
Shall but fulfil their best desire;
From sins and sorrows set them free,
And bring thy children, Lord, to thee.

PSALM XCI. 9—16. Second Part.

Protection from Death, Guard of Angels, Victory and Deliverance.

1 YE sons of men, a feeble race,
  Expos'd to every snare,
Come make the Lord your dwelling place,
  And try, and trust his care.

2 No ill shall enter where you dwell;
  Or if the plague come nigh,
And sweep the wicked down to hell,
  'Twill raise the saints on high.

3 He'll give his angels charge to keep
  Your feet in all their ways;
To watch your pillow while you sleep,
  And guard your happy days.

4 Their hands shall bear you, lest you fall
  And dash against the stones;
Are they not servants at his call,
  And sent t' attend his sons?

5 Adders and lions ye shall tread;
  The tempter's wiles defeat:
He that hath broke the serpent's head
  Puts him beneath your feet.

6 " Because on me they set their love,
  " I'll save them (saith the Lord;)
  " I'll bear their joyful souls above
  " Destruction and the sword.

7 " My grace shall answer when they call,
  " In trouble I'll be nigh:
  " My power shall help them when they fall,
  " And raise them when they die.

8 " Those that on earth my name have known,
  " I'll honour them in heaven;
  " There my salvation shall be shown,
  " And endless life be given."

PSALM XCII. First Part.
A Psalm for the Lord's Day

1 SWEET is the work, my God, my King,
To praise thy name, give thanks and sing,
To shew thy love by morning light,
And talk of all thy truth at night.

2 Sweet is the day of sacred rest,
No mortal care shall seize my breast,
Oh may my heart in tune be found,
Like David's harp of solemn sound.

3 My heart shall triumph in my Lord,
And bless his works, and bless his word;
Thy works of grace how bright they shine!
How deep thy counsels! how divine!

4 Fools never raise their thoughts so high;
Like brutes they live, like brutes they die;
Like grass they flourish, 'till thy breath
Blast them in everlasting death.

5 But I shall share a glorious part
When grace hath well refin'd my heart,
And fresh supplies of joy are shed
Like holy oil to cheer my head.

6 Sin (my worst enemy before)
Shall vex my eyes and ears no more:
My inward foes shall all be slain,
Nor satan break my peace again.

7 Then shall I see and hear and know
All I desir'd, or wish'd below;
And every power find sweet employ
In that eternal world of joy.

PSALM XCII. ver. 12, &c. Second Part.
The Church is the Garden of God.

1 LORD, 'tis a pleasant thing to stand
In gardens planted by thine hand;
Let me within thy courts be seen
Like a young cedar, fresh and green.

2 There grow thy saints in faith and love,
Blest with thine influence from above;

Not *Lebanon* with all its trees
Yields such a comely sight as these.

3 The plants of grace shall ever live;
(Nature decays, but grace must thrive)
Time, that doth all things else impair,
Still makes them flourish strong and fair.

4 Laden with fruits of age they shew,
The Lord is holy just and true;
None that attend his gates shall find
A God unfaithful or unkind.

PSALM XCIII. 1st Metre. As the 100th Psalm.
The Eternal and the Sovereign God.

1 JEHOVAH reigns: he dwells in light,
Girded with majesty and might:
The world created by his hands
Still on its first foundation stands.

2 But ere this spacious world was made
Or had its first foundation laid,
Thy throne eternal ages stood,
Thyself the ever-living God.

3 Like floods the angry nations rise,
And aim their rage against the skies,
Vain floods, that aim their rage so high!
At thy rebuke the billows die.

4 Forever shall thy throne endure;
Thy promise stand forever sure;
And everlasting holiness
Becomes the dwellings of thy grace.

PSALM XCIII. 2d Metre. As the old 50th Psalm.

1 THE God of glory reigns, he reigns on high;
His robes of state are strength and majesty:
This wide creation rose at his command,
Built by his word and 'stablish'd by his hand.
Long stood his throne ere he began creation,
And his own godhead is the firm foundation.

2 God is th' eternal King: Thy foes in vain
Raise their rebellions to oppose thy reign;

In vain the storms, in vain the floods arise,
And roar, and toss their waves against the skies;
Foaming at heaven they rage with wild commotion,
But heaven's high arches scorn the swelling ocean.

3 Ye tempests rage no more ; ye floods be still,
And the mad world submissive to his will :
Built on his truth his church must ever stand ;
Firm are his promises, and strong his hand ;
See his own sons, when they appear before him,
Bow at his foot-stool, and with fear adore him.

PSALM XCIII. 3d Metre.
As the old 122d Psalm.

1 THE Lord *Jehovah* reigns,
    And royal state maintains,
His head with awful glories crown'd ;
    Array'd in robes of light,
    Begirt with sovereign might,
And rays of majesty around.

2 Upheld by thy commands
    The world securely stands,
And skies and stars obey thy word ;
    Thy throne was fixt on high
    Ere stars adorn'd the sky :
Eternal is thy kingdom, Lord.

3 In vain the noisy croud,
    Like billows fierce and loud,
Against thine empire rage and roar ;
    In vain with angry spite
    The surly nations fight,
And dash like waves against the shore.

4 Let floods and nations rage,
    And all their power engage,
Let swelling tides assault the sky ;
    The terrors of thy frown
    Shall bear their madness down ;
Thy throne forever stands on high.

5 Thy promises are true, .
    Thy grace is ever new,

There fix'd thy church shall ne'er remove;
  Thy saints with holy fear
  Shall in thy courts appear,
And sing thine everlasting love.

Repeat the fourth Stanza to complete the Tune.

PSALM XCIV. 1, 2, 7—14. First Part.

Saints chastised, and Sinners destroyed; or, Instructive Afflictions.

1 O God! to whom revenge belongs,
    Proclaim thy wrath aloud;
  Let sovereign power redress our wrongs,
    Let justice smite the proud.

2 They say, "*The Lord nor sees nor hears;*"
    When will the vain be wise?
  Can he be deaf, who form'd their ears?
    Or blind, who made their eyes?

3 He knows their impious thoughts are vain,
    And they shall feel his power;
  His wrath shall pierce their souls with pain
    In some surprising hour.

4 But if thy saints deserve rebuke,
    Thou hast a gentler road;
  Thy providence, thy sacred book
    Shall make them know their God.

5 Blest is the man thy hands chastise,
    And to his duty draw;
  Thy scourges make thy children wise
    When they forget thy law.

6 But God will ne'er cast off his saints,
    Nor his own promise break;
  He pardons his inheritance
    For their Redeemer's sake.

PSALM XCIV. ver. 16—23. Second Part.

God our Support and Comfort; or Deliverance from Temptation and Persecution.

1 WHO will arise and plead my right
    Against my numerous foes?

While earth and hell their force unite,
And all my hopes oppose.

2 Had not the Lord, my rock, my help,
Sustain'd my fainting head;
My life had now in silence dwelt,
My soul amongst the dead.

3 *Alas my sliding feet!* I cry'd,
Thy promise bore me up,
Thy grace stood constant by my side,
And rais'd my sinking hope.

4 While multitudes of mournful thoughts,
Within my bosom roll,
Thy boundless love forgives my faults,
Thy comforts cheer my soul.

5 Powers of iniquity may rise,
And frame pernicious laws;
But God my refuge rules the skies,
He will defend my cause.

6 Let malice vent her rage aloud,
Let bold blasphemers scoff;
The Lord our God shall judge the proud,
And cut the sinners off.

PSALM XCV. Common Metre.
A Psalm before Prayer.

1 SING to the Lord, *Jehovah*'s name,
And in his strength rejoice;
When his salvation is our theme,
Exalted be our voice.

2 With thanks approach his awful sight,
And psalms of honour sing;
The Lord's a God of boundless might,
The whole creation's King.

3 Let princes hear, let angels know,
How mean their natures seem,
Those gods on high, and gods below,
When once compar'd with him.

4 Earth, with its caverns dark and deep,
Lies in his spacious hand;

He fix'd the seas what bounds to keep,
  And where the hills must stand.

5 Come, and with humble souls adore,
  Come, kneel before his face;
Oh may the creatures of his power
  Be children of his grace!

6 Now is the time, he bends his ear,
  And waits for your request;
Come, lest he rouze his wrath, and swear.
  " *Ye shall not see my rest.*"

PSALM XCV. Short Metre.

A Psalm before Sermon.

1 COME, sound his praise abroad,
    And hymns of glory sing:
  Jehovah is the sovereign God,
    The universal King.

2 He form'd the deeps unknown;
    He gave the seas their bound;
  The watery worlds are all his own,
    And all the solid ground.

3 Come, worship, at his throne,
    Come, bow before the Lord:
  We are his works, and not our own;
    He form'd us by his word.

4 To day attend his voice,
    Nor dare provoke his rod;
  Come, like the people of his choice,
    And own your gracious God.

5 But if your ears refuse
    The language of his grace,
  And hearts grow hard like stubborn *Jews*
    That unbelieving race.

6 The Lord, in vengeance drest
    Will lift his hand and swear,
  " *You that despise my promis'd rest,*
    Shall have no portion there."

PSALM XCV. 1, 2, 3, 6—11. Long Metre.
Canaan lost through Unbelief; or, a Warning to delaying Sinners.

1 COME let our voices join to raise
A sacred song of solemn praise;
God is a sovereign King; rehearse
His honour in exalted verse.

2 Come, let our souls address the Lord,
Who fram'd our natures with his word,
He is our shepherd; we the sheep
His mercy chose, his pastures keep.

3 Come, let us hear his voice to-day,
The counsels of his love obey,
Nor let our harden'd hearts renew
The sins and plagues that *Israel* knew.

4 *Israel*, that saw his works of grace
Yet tempt their Maker to his face;
A faithless unbelieving brood,
That tir'd the patience of their God.

5 Thus saith the Lord, " How false they prove!
" Forget my power, abuse my love;
" Since they despise my rest, I swear,
" Their feet shall never enter there."

6 [Look back, my soul, with holy dread,
And view those ancient rebels dead;
Attend the offer'd grace to day,
Nor lose the blessings by delay.

7 Seize the kind promise while it waits,
And march to *Zion*'s heavenly gates;
Believe, and take the promis'd rest,
Obey, and be forever blest.]

PSALM XCVI. 2, 10, &c. Common Metre.
Christ's first and second Coming.

1 SING to the Lord, ye distant lands,
Ye tribes of every tongue;
His new discover'd grace demands
A new and nobler song.

2 Say to the nations, *Jesus* reigns,
God's own almighty Son;

PSALM XCVII.

His power the sinking world sustains,
  And grace surrounds his throne.

3 Let heaven proclaim the joyful day,
  Joy through the earth be seen;
Let cities shine in bright array,
  And fields in cheerful green.

4 The joyous earth, the bending skies
  His glorious train display;
Ye mountains sink, ye vallies rise,
  Prepare the Lord his way.

5 Behold he comes; he come to bless
  The nations as their God;
To shew the world his righteousness
  And send his truth abroad.

6 His voice shall raise the slumbering dead,
  And bid the world draw near;
But how will guilty nations dread,
  To see their Judge appear!

PSALM XCVII. As the 113th Psalm.
The God of the Gentiles.

1 LET all the earth their voices raise,
    To sing the choicest psalm of praise,
  To sing and bless *Jehovah*'s name:
  His glory let the heathens know,
  His wonders to the nations show,
    And all his saving works proclaim.

2 The heathens know thy glory, Lord,
  The wondering nations read thy word,
    But here *Jehovah*'s name is known;
  Nor shall our worship e'er be paid
  To gods which mortal hands have made;
    Our maker is our God alone.

3 He fram'd the globe, he built the sky,
  He made the shining worlds on high,
    And reigns complete in glory there;
  His beams are majesty and light;
  His beauties how divinely bright!
    His temple how divinely fair!

4 Come the great day, the glorious hour,
   When earth shall feel his saving power,
     And barbarous nations fear his name ;
   Then shall the race of men confess
   The beauty of his holiness,
     And in his courts his grace proclaim.

PSALM XCVII. 1—5. *First Part.*
Christ reigning in Heaven, and coming to Judgment.

1 HE reigns ; the Lord, the Saviour reigns !
     Praise him in evangelic strains :
   Let the whole earth in songs rejoice,
   And distant islands join their voice.

2 Deep are his counsels and unknown ;
   But grace and truth support his throne ;
   Though gloomy clouds his ways surround :
   Justice is their eternal ground.

3 In robes of judgment, lo, he comes,
   Shakes the wide earth and cleaves the tombs,
   Before him burns devouring fire,
   The mountains melt, the seas retire.

4 His enemies with sore dismay,
   Fly from the sight, and shun the day ;
   Then lift your heads, ye saints, on high,
   And sing, for your redemption's nigh.

PSALM XCVII. 6—9. *Second Part.*
Christ's Incarnation.

1 THE Lord is come ; the heavens proclaim
     His birth ; the nations learn his name ;
   An unknown star directs the road
   Of *Eastern* sages to their God.

2 All ye bright armies of the skies,
   Go, worship where the Saviour lies :
   Angels and kings before him bow,
   Those gods on high, and gods below.

3 Let idols totter to the ground,
   And their own worshippers confound :
   But Zion shall his glories sing,
   And earth confess her sovereign King.

PSALM XCVII. Third Part.
Grace and Glory.

1 TH' Almighty reigns exalted high
　　O'er all the earth, o'er all the sky;
Though clouds and darkness veil his feet,
His dwelling is the mercy seat.

2 O ye that love his holy name,
Hate every work of sin and shame:
He guards the souls of all his friends,
And from the snares of hell defends.

3 Immortal light, and joys unknown,
Are for the saints in darkness sown:
Those glorious seeds shall spring and rise,
And the bright harvest bless our eyes.

4 Rejoice, ye righteous, and record
The sacred honours of the Lord;
None but the soul that feels his grace
Can triumph in his holiness.

PSALM XCVII. 3, 5—7, 11. Com. Metre.
Christ's Incarnation and the last Judgment.

1 LET earth, with every isle and sea
　　Rejoice, the Saviour reigns:
His word like fire prepares his way,
　　And mountains melt to plains.

2 His presence sinks the proudest hills,
　　And makes the vallies rise;
The humble soul enjoys his smiles,
　　The haughty sinner dies.

3 The heavens his rightful power proclaim;
　　The idol gods around
Fill their own worshippers with shame,
　　And totter to the ground.

4 Adoring angels at his birth
　　Make the Redeemer known;
Thus shall he come to judge the earth,
　　And angels guard his throne.

5 His foes shall tremble at his sight,
　　And hills and seas retire:

His children take their unknown flight,
    And leave the world in fire.

6 The seeds of joy and glory sown
    For saints in darkness here,
Shall rise and spring in worlds unknown,
    And a rich harvest bear.

PSALM CXVIII. First Part.
Praise for the Gospel.

1 TO our almighty Maker, God,
    New honours be address'd;
His great salvation shines abroad,
    And makes the nations blest.

2 To Abraham first he spoke the word,
    And taught his numerous race;
The Gentiles own him sovereign Lord,
    And learn to trust his grace.

3 Let the whole earth his love proclaim
    With all their different tongues;
And spread the honour of his name
    In melody and songs.

PSALM XCVIII. Second Part.
The Messiah's Coming and Kingdom.

1 JOY to the world; the Lord is come;
    Let earth receive her King:
Let every heart prepare him room,
    And heaven and nature sing.

2 Joy to the earth, the Saviour reigns;
    Let men their songs employ;
While fields and floods, rocks, hills and plains,
    Repeat the sounding joy.

3 No more let sins and sorrows grow,
    Nor thorns infest the ground;
He comes to make his blessings flow,
    Far as the curse is found.

4 He rules the world with truth and grace,
    And makes the nations prove
The glories of his righteousness,
    And wonders of his love.

Psalm XCIX. First Part.
Christ's Kingdom and Majesty.

1 THE God *Jehovah* reigns,
   Let all the nations fear;
Let sinners tremble at his throne,
   And saints be humble there.

2 *Jesus* the Saviour reigns,
   Let earth adore its Lord;
Bright cherubs his attendants stand,
   Swift to fulfil his word.

3 In *Zion* stands his throne,
   His honours are divine,
His church shall make his wonders known,
   For there his glories shine.

4 How holy is his name?
   How terrible his praise!
Justice and truth, and judgment join
   In all his works of grace.

Psalm XCIX. Second Part.
A holy God worshipped with Reverence.

1 EXALT the Lord our God,
   And worship at his feet;
His nature is all holiness,
   And mercy is his seat.

2 When *Israel* was his church,
   When *Aaron* was his priest,
When *Moses* cry'd, when *Samuel* pray'd,
   He gave his people rest.

3 Oft he forgave their sins;
   Nor would destroy their race;
And oft he made his vengeance known,
   When they abus'd his grace.

4 Exalt the Lord our God,
   Whose grace is still the same;
Still he's a God of holiness,
   And jealous for his name.

PSALM C. First Metre. *A plain Translation.*
Praise to our Creator.

1 YE nations round the earth rejoice,
 Before the Lord, your sovereign King;
Serve him with cheerful heart and voice,
With all your tongues his glory sing.

2 The Lord is God; 'tis he alone
Doth life and breath, and being give:
We are his work, and not our own;
The sheep that in his pastures live.

3 Enter his gates with songs of joy,
With praises to his courts repair;
And make it your divine employ
To pay your thanks and honours there.

4 The Lord is good, the Lord is kind,
Great is his grace, his mercy sure:
And the whole race of man shall find
His truth from age to age endure.

PSALM C. Second Metre. A Paraphrase.

1 BEFORE Jehovah's awful throne,
 Ye nations, bow with sacred joy:
Know that the Lord is God alone;
He can create, and he destroy.

2 His sovereign power without our aid
Made us of clay, and form'd us men:
And when like wandering sheep we stray'd,
He brought us to his fold again.

3 We are his people, we his care,
Our souls, and all our mortal frame:
What lasting honours shall we rear,
Almighty Maker, to thy name?

4 We'll croud thy gates with thankful songs,
High as the heaven, our voices raise
And earth with her ten thousand tongues,
Shall fill thy courts with sounding praise.

5 Wide as the world is thy command
Vast as eternity thy love!
Firm as a rock thy truth must stand,
When rolling years shall cease to move.

PSALM CI. Long Metre.
The Magistrate's Psalm.

1 MERCY and judgment are my song,
   And since they both to thee belong,
My gracious God, my righteous King,
To thee my songs and vows I bring.

2 If I am rais'd to bear the sword,
   I'll take my counsel from thy word;
Thy justice and thy heavenly grace,
Shall be the pattern of my ways.

3 Let wisdom all my actions guide,
   And let my God with me reside;
No wicked thing shall dwell with me,
Which may provoke thy jealousy.

4 No sons of slander, rage and strife
   Shall be companions of my life;
The haughty look, the heart of pride
Within my doors shall ne'er abide.

5 [I'll search the land and raise the just
   To posts of honour, wealth and trust;
The men that work thy holy will
Shall be my friends and favourite still.]

6 In vain shall sinners hope to rise
   By flattering or malicious lies:
Nor, while the innocent I guard,
Shall bold offenders e'er be spar'd.

7 The impious crew (that factious band)
   Shall hide their heads, or quit the land;
And all that break the public rest,
Where I have power shall be supprest.

PSALM CI. Common Metre.
A Psalm for a Master of a Family.

1 OF justice and of grace I sing,
     And pay my God my vows,
   Thy grace and justice, heavenly King,
     Teach me to rule my house.

2 Now to my tent, O God, repair,
     And make thy servant wise:

> I'll suffer nothing near me there
> That shall offend thine eyes.

3 The man that doth his neighbour wrong
> By falsehood or by force,
> The scornful eye, the slanderous tongue,
> I'll thrust him from my doors.

4 I'll seek the faithful and the just,
> And will their help enjoy;
> These are the friends that I shall trust,
> The servants I'll employ.

5 The wretch that deals in sly deceit
> I'll not endure a night;
> The liar's tongue I ever hate,
> And banish from my sight.

6 I'll purge my family around,
> And make the wicked flee;
> So shall my house be ever found
> A dwelling fit for thee.

PSALM CII. 1—13, 20, 21. *First Part.*
A Prayer of the afflicted.

1 HEAR me, O God, nor hide thy face,
> But answer, lest I die:
> Hast thou not built a throne of grace,
> To hear when sinners cry?

2 My days are wasted like the smoke
> Dissolving in the air;
> My strength is dry'd, my heart is broke,
> And sinking in despair.

3 My spirits flag like withering grass
> Burnt with excessive heat:
> In secret groans my minutes pass,
> And I forgot to eat.

4 As on some lonely building's top,
> The sparrow tells her moan,
> Far from the tents of joy and hope
> I sit and grieve alone.

5 My soul is like a wilderness,
> Where beasts of midnight howl;

Where the sad raven finds her place,
  And where the screaming owl.

6 Dark dismal thoughts and boding fears
  Dwell in my troubled breast;
While sharp reproaches wound my ears,
  Nor give my spirit rest.

7 My cup is mingled with my woes,
  And tears are my repast:
My daily bread like ashes grows
  Unpleasant to my taste.

8 Sense can afford no real joy
  To souls that feel thy frown;
Lord 'twas thy hand advanc'd me high,
  Thy hand hath cast me down.

9 My looks like wither'd leaves appear;
  And life's declining light
Grows faint as evening-shadows are,
  That vanish into night.

10 But thou forever art the same,
  O my eternal God;
Ages to come shall know thy name,
  And spread thy works abroad.

11 Thou wilt arise, and show thy face,
  Nor will my Lord delay,
Beyond th' appointed hour of grace,
  That long expected day.

12 He hears his saints, he knows their cry,
  And by mysterious ways,
Redeems the prisoners, doom'd to die,
  And fills their tongues with praise.

PSALM CII. 13—21. *Second Part.*

Prayer heard, and Zion restored

1 LET Zion, and her sons rejoice,
  Behold the promis'd hour:
Her God hath heard her mourning voice,
  And comes t' exalt his power.

2 Her dust and ruins that remain,
  Are precious in our eyes;

Those ruins shall be built again,
  And all that dust shall rise.

3 The Lord will raise Jerusalem,
  And stand in glory there;
Nations shall bow before his name,
  And kings attend with fear.

4 He sits a sovereign on his throne,
  With pity in his eyes:
He hears the dying prisoners groan,
  And sees their sighs arise.

5 He frees the souls condemn'd to death,
  And when his saints complain,
It shan't be said, " That praying breath
  " Was ever spent in vain."

6 This shall be known when we are dead,
  And left on long record;
That ages yet unborn may read,
  And trust, and praise the Lord.

PSALM CII. 23.—28. Third Part.
Man's mortality, and Christ's eternity; or, Saints die,
but Christ and the Church live.

1 IT is the Lord our Saviour's hand,
   Weakens our strength amidst the race;
Disease and death at his command
   Arrest us, and cut short our days.

2 Spare us, O Lord, aloud we pray,
   Nor let our sun go down at noon;
Thy years are one eternal day,
   And must thy children die so soon?

3 Yet in the midst of death and grief
   This thought our sorrow shall assuage;
" Our Father and our Saviour live;
   " Christ is the same through every age."

4 'Twas he this earth's foundation laid;
   Heaven is the building of his hand;
This earth grows old, these heavens shall fade:
   And all be chang'd at his command.

5 The starry curtains of the sky
   Like garments shall be laid aside:

But still thy throne stands firm and high,
　Thy church forever must abide.

6 Before thy face thy church shall live;
　And on thy throne thy children reign;
This dying world shall they survive,
　And the dead saints be rais'd again.

PSALM CIII. 1—7. *First* Part. Long Metre.
Blessing God for his Goodness to Soul and Body.

1 BLESS, O my soul, the living God,
　Call home thy thoughts that rove abroad,
Let all the powers within me join
In work and worship so divine.

2 Bless, O my soul, the God of grace;
His favours claim thy highest praise:
Why should the wonders he hath wrought
Be lost in silence, and forgot?

3 'Tis he, my soul, that sent his Son
To die for crimes which thou hast done:
He owns the ransom, and forgives
The hourly follies of our lives.

4 The vices of the mind he heals,
And cures the pains that nature feels,
Redeems the soul from hell, and saves
Our wasting life from threatening graves.

5 Our youth decay'd his power repairs,
His mercy crowns our growing years:
He fills our store with every good,
And feeds our souls with heavenly food.

6 He sees th' oppressor and th' opprest,
And often gives the sufferers rest:
But will his justice more display
In the last great rewarding day.

7 [His power he shew'd by Moses' hands,
And gave to Israel his commands;
But sent his truth and mercy down
To all the nations by his Son.]

8 Let the whole earth his power confess,
Let the whole earth adore his grace;

The Gentile with the Jew shall join
In work and worship so divine.

PSALM CIII. Second Part. Long Metre.

God's gentle Chastisement; or his tender Mercy to his People.

1 THE Lord, how wondrous are his ways!
  How firm his truth! how large his grace
He takes his mercy for his throne,
And thence he makes his glories known.

2 Not half so high his power hath spread
The starry heavens above our head,
As his rich love exceeds our praise,
Exceeds the highest hopes we raise.

3 Not half so far hath nature plac'd
The rising morning from the west
As his forgiving grace removes:
The daily guilt of those he loves.

4 How slow his awful wrath to rise!
On swifter wings salvation flies;
And if he lets his anger burn,
How soon his frowns to pity turn!

5 Amidst his wrath compassion shines;
His strokes are lighter than our sins:
And while his rod corrects his saints,
His ear indulges their complaints.

6 So fathers their young sons chastise,
With gentle hands and melting eyes:
The children weep beneath the smart,
And move the pity of their heart.

PAUSE.

7 The mighty God, the wise and just,
Knows that our frame is feeble dust;
And will no heavy loads impose
Beyond the strength that he bestows.

8 He knows how soon our nature dies,
Blasted by every wind that flies;
Like grass we spring, and die as soon,
Or morning flowers that fade at noon.

9 But his eternal love is sure
   To all the saints, and shall endure:
   From age to age his truth shall reign,
   Nor children's children hope in vain.

PSALM CIII. *First Part.* Short Metre.
Praise for Spiritual and Temporal Mercies.

1 OH bless the Lord, my soul!
   Let all within me join,
   And aid my tongue to bless his name,
   Whose favours are divine.

2 Oh bless the Lord, my soul;
   Nor let his mercies lie,
   Forgotten in unthankfulness;
   And without praises die.

3 'Tis he forgives thy sins,
   'Tis he relieves thy pain,
   'Tis he that heals thy sicknesses,
   And makes the young again.

4 He crowns thy life with love,
   When ransom'd from the grave;
   He that redeem'd my soul from hell
   Hath sovereign power to save.

5 He fills the poor with good;
   He gives the sufferers rest;
   The Lord hath judgments for the proud,
   And justice for th' opprest.

6 His wondrous works and ways
   He made by Moses known;
   But sent the world his truth and grace
   By his beloved Son.

PSALM CIII. 1—18. *Second Part.* Short Metre.

Abounding Compassion of God; or, Mercy in the midst of Judgment.

1 MY soul, repeat his praise,
   Whose mercies are so great;
   Whose anger is so slow to rise,
   So ready to abate.

2 God will not always chide;
    And when his strokes are felt,
His strokes are fewer than our crimes,
    And lighter than our guilt.

3 High as the heavens are rais'd
    Above the ground we tread,
So far the riches of his grace
    Our highest thoughts exceed.

4 His power subdues our sins,]
    And his forgiving love
Far as the east is from the west,
    Doth all our guilt remove.

5 The pity of the Lord
    To those that fear his name,
Is such as tender parents feel;
    He knows our feeble frame.

6 He knows we are but dust,
    Scatter'd with every breath:
His anger like a rising wind
    Can send us swift to death.

7 Our days are as the grass,
    Or like the morning flower!
If one sharp blast sweep o'er the field,
    It withers in an hour,

8 But thy compassions, Lord,
    To endless years endure;
And children's children ever find
    Thy words of promise sure.

PSALM CIII. 15—22. *Third Part.* Short Metre.

God's universal Dominion; or, Angels praise the Lord.

1 THE Lord, the sovereign King,
    Hath fix'd his throne on high,
O'er all the heavenly world he rules,
    And all beneath the sky.

2 Ye angels great in might,
    And swift to do his will,
Bless ye the Lord, whose voice ye hear,
    Whose pleasure ye fulfil.

3 Let the bright hosts, who wait
   The orders of their King,
And guard his churches when they pray,
   Join in the praise they sing,
4 While all his wondrous works,
   Through his vast kingdom, shew,
Their maker's glory, thou my soul,
   Shall sing his graces too.

PSALM CIV.
The Glory of God in Creation and Providence

1 MY soul, thy great Creator praise;
   When cloth'd in his celestial rays,
He in full majesty appears,
And like a robe his glory wears.

Note, *This Psalm may be sung to the Tune of the Old 112th or 127th Psalm, by adding these two Lines to every Stanzas viz.*
   Great is the Lord; what tongue can frame
   An equal honour to his name?

[*Otherwise it must be sung as the* 100*th Psalm.*]

2 The heavens are for his curtains spread;
Th' unfathom'd deep he makes his bed;
Clouds are his chariot when he flies
On winged storms a-cross the skies.

3 Angels, whom his own breath inspires,
His ministers, are flaming fires;
And swift as thought their armies move
To bear his vengeance or his love.

4 The world's foundations by his hand
Are pois'd and shall forever stand:
He binds the ocean in his chain,
Lest it should drown the earth again.

5 When earth was cover'd with the flood
Which high above the mountains stood,
He thunder'd and the ocean fled,
Confin'd to its appointed bed.

6 The swelling billows know their bound,
And in their channels walk their round;
Yet thence convey'd by secret veins,
They spring on hills and drench the plains.

7 He bids the chryftal fountains flow,
  And cheer the vallies as they go;
  There gentle herds their thirft allay,
  And for the ftream wild affes bray.

8 From pleafant trees which fhades the brink,
  The lark and linnet light to drink;
  Their fongs the lark and linnet raife,
  And chide our filence in his praife.

PAUSE I.

9 God from his cloudy ciftern pours
  On the parch'd earth enriching fhowers;
  The grove, the garden, and the field,
  A thoufand joyful bleffings yield.

10 He makes the graffy food arife,
  And gives the cattle large fupplies;
  With herbs for man of various power,
  To nourifh nature, or to cure.

11 What noble fruits the vines produce!
  The olive yields a pleafing juice;
  Our hearts are cheer'd with generous wine,
  His gifts proclaim his love divine.

12 His bounteous hands our table fpread,
  He fills our cheerful ftores with bread;
  While food our vital ftrength imparts,
  Let daily praife infpire our hearts.

PAUSE II.

13 Behold the ftately cedar ftands
  Rais'd in the foreft by his hands;
  Birds to the boughs for fhelter fly,
  And build their nefts fecure on high.

14 To craggy hills afcends the goat;
  And at the airy mountain's foot;
  The feebler creatures make their cell;
  He gives them wifdom where to dwell.

15 He fets the fun his circling race,
  Appoints the moon to change her face;
  And when thick darknefs veils the day,
  Calls out wild beafts to hunt their prey.

16 Fierce lions lead their young abroad,
  And roaring afk their meat from God;

PSALM CIV.

But when the morning beams arise,
The savage beast to covert flies.

1 Then man to daily labour goes;
The night was made for his repose:
Sleep is thy gift, that sweet relief
From tiresome toil, and wasting grief.

18 How strange thy works! how great thy skill!
While every land thy riches fill:
Thy wisdom round the world we see,
This spacious earth is full of thee.

19 Nor less thy glories in the deep,
Where fish in millions swim and creep,
With wondrous motions, swift or slow,
Still wandering in the paths below.

20 There ships divide their watery way,
And flocks of scaly monsters play;
The huge Leviathan resides,
And fearless sports amid the tides.

PAUSE III.

21 Vast are thy works, almighty Lord,
All nature rests upon thy word,
And the whole race of creatures stands,
Waiting their portion from thy hands.

22 While each receives his different food,
Their cheerful looks pronounce it good:
Eagles and bears, and whales and worms
Rejoice and praise in different forms.

23 But when thy face is hid they mourn.
And dying to their dust return;
Both man and beast their souls resign:
Life, breath and spirit, all are thine.

24 Yet thou canst breathe on dust again,
And fill the world with beasts and men;
A word of thy creating breath
Repairs the wastes of time and death.

25 His works the wonders of his might,
Are honour'd with his own delight:
How awful are his glorious ways!
The Lord is dreadful in his praise.

26 The earth stands trembling at thy stroke,
And at thy touch the mountains smoke;
Yet humble souls may see thy face,
And tell their wants to sovereign grace.

27 In thee my hopes and wishes meet,
And make my meditations sweet;
Thy praises shall my breath employ
Till it expire in endless joy.

28 While haughty sinners die accurst,
Their glory bury'd with their dust,
I to my God, my heavenly King
Immortal Hallelujahs sing.

PSALM CV. Abridged.
God's conduct of Israel, and the Plagues of Egypt.

1 GIVE thanks to God, invoke his name,
And tell the world his grace;
Sound through the earth his deeds of fame,
That all may seek his face.

2 His covenant which he kept in mind
For numerous ages past,
To numerous ages yet behind
In equal force shall last.

3 He sware to Abraham and his seed,
And made the blessing sure:
Gentiles the ancient promise read,
And find his truth endure.

4 " Thy seed shall make all nations blest,
(Said the Almighty voice)
" And Canaan's land shall be their rest,
" The type of heavenly joys.

5 (How large the grant! how rich the grace!
To give them Canaan's land,
When they were strangers in the place,
A small and feeble band!

6 Like pilgrims through the countries round
Securely they remov'd:
And haughty kings that on them frown'd
Severely he reprov'd.

PSALM CV.

7 " Touch mine anointed, and mine arm
  " Shall soon avenge the wrong:
  " The man that does my prophets harm
  " Shall know their God is strong."

8 *Then let the world forbear its rage,*
  Nor put the church in fear:
  Israel must live through every age,
  And be th' Almighty's care.

PAUSE I.

9 When Pharaoh dar'd to vex the saints,
   And thus provok'd their God,
  Moses was sent at their complaints,
   Arm'd with his dreadful rod.

10 He call'd for darkness: darkness came
   Like an o'erwhelming flood;
   He turn'd each lake and every stream
   To lakes and streams of blood.

11 He gave the sign, and noisome flies
   Through the whole country spread;
   And frogs in baleful armies rise
   About the monarch's bed.

12 Through fields and towns and palaces
   The tenfold vengeance flew;
   Locusts in swarms devour'd their trees,
   And hail their cattle slew.

13 Then by an Angel's midnight stroke
   The flower of *Egypt* dy'd;
   The strength of every house was broke,
   Their glory and their pride.

14 *Now let the world forbear its rage,*
   Nor put the church in fear;
   Israel must live through every age,
   And be th' Almighty's care.

PAUSE II.

15 Thus were the tribes from bondage freed,
   And left the hated ground;
   Rich with *Egyptian* spoils they fled,
   Nor was one feeble found.

16 The Lord himself chose out their way,
   And mark'd their journies right;
   Give them a leading cloud by day,
   A firey guide by night.

17 They thirst; and waters from the rock
  In rich abundance flow,
 And following still the course they took
  Ran all the desert through.

18 O wondrous stream! O blessed type
  Of ever-flowing grace!
 So Christ our rock maintains our life
  And aids our wandering race.

19 Thus guarded by th' Almighty hand,
  The chosen tribes possest
 Canaan the rich, the promis'd land,
  And there enjoy'd their rest.

20 *Then let the world forbear its rage,*
 The church renounce her fear;
 Israel must live through every age,
  And be th' Almighty's care.

PSALM CVI. 1—5. *First Part.*
Praise to God; or, Communion with Saints.

1 TO God, the great, the ever blest,
   Let songs of honour be addrest;
 His mercy firm forever stands;
 Give him the thanks his love demands.

2 Who knows the wonders of thy ways?
 Who shall fulfil thy boundless praise?
 Blest are the souls that fear thee still,
 And pay their duty to thy will.

3 Remember what thy mercy did
 For *Jacob*'s race, thy chosen seed;
 And with the same salvation bless
 The meanest suppliant of thy grace.

4 Oh may I see thy tribes rejoice.
 And aid their triumphs with my voice!
 This is my glory, Lord, to be
 Join'd to thy saints, and near to thee.

PSALM CVI. *Second Part. ver.* 7, 8, 12, 14, 43, 48.

Israel punished and pardoned; or, God's unchangeable Love.

1 GOD of eternal love,
   How fickle are our ways!

And yet how oft did *Israel* prove
  Thy constancy of grace!

2 They saw thy wonders wrought,
  And then thy praise they sung;
 But soon thy works of power forgot,
  And murmur'd with their tongue.

3 Now they believe his word,
  While rocks with rivers flow;
 Now with their lusts provoke the Lord,
  And he reduc'd them low.

4 Yet when they mourn'd their faults,
  He hearken'd to their groans;
 Brought his own covenant to his thoughts,
  And call'd them still his sons.

5 There names were in his book,
  He sav'd them from their foes;
 Oft he chastis'd, but ne'er forsook
  The people that he chose.

6 Let Israel bless the Lord,
  Who lov'd their ancient race;
 And christians join the solemn word,
  Amen to all the praise.

PSALM CVII. *First Part.*
Israel led to Canaan, and Christians to Heaven.

1 GIVE thanks to God, he reigns above,
  Kind are his thoughts, his name is love,
 His mercy ages past have know,
 And ages long to come shall own.

2 Let the redeemed of the Lord
 The wonders of his grace record;
 Israel, the nation whom he chose,
 And rescued from their mighty foes.

3 [When God's almighty arm had broke
 Their fetters and th' Egyptian yoke,
 They trac'd the desert, wandering round
 A wild and solitary ground.

4 There they could find no leading road,
  Nor city for their fix'd abode;

Nor food, nor fountain to asswage
Their burning thirst, or hunger's rage.]

5 In their distress to God they cry'd,
God was their saviour and their guide;
He led their wandering march around,
And brought their tribes to Canaan's ground.

6 Thus when our first release we gain
From sin's old yoke, and satan's chain,
We have this desert world to pass,
A dangerous and a tiresome place.

7 He feeds and clothes us all the way,
He guides our footsteps lest we stray,
He guards us with a powerful hand,
And brings us to the heavenly land.

8 Oh let the saints with joy record
The truth and goodness of the Lord!
How great his works! how kind his ways!
Let every tongue pronounce his praise.

PSALM CVII. *Second Part.*
Corrections for Sin, and release by Prayer.

1 FROM age to age exalt his name,
God and his grace are still the same;
He fills the hungry soul with food,
And feeds the poor with every good.

2 But if their hearts rebel and rise
Against the God that rules the skies;
If they reject his heavenly word,
And slight the counsels of the Lord:

3 He'll bring their spirits to the ground,
And no deliverance shall be found;
Laden with grief they waste their breath
In darkness and the shades of death.

4 Then to the Lord they raise their cries,
He makes the dawning light arise,
And scatters all that dismal shade
That hung so heavy round their head.

5 He cuts the bars of brass in two,
And lets the smiling prisoners through,
Takes off the load of guilt and grief,
And gives the labouring soul relief.

6 Oh may the sons of men record
　The wondrous goodness of the Lord!
　How great his works! how kind his ways!
　Let every tongue pronounce his praise.

PSALM CVII. Third Part.
Intemperance punished and pardoned; or, a Psalm for the Glutton and the Drunkard.

1 VAIN man on foolish pleasures bent,
　　Prepares for his own punishment;
　What pains, what loathsome maladies
　From luxury and lust arise!

2 The drunkard feels his vitals waste;
　Yet drowns his health to please his taste;
　'Till all his active powers are lost,
　And fainting life draws near the dust.

3 The glutton groans, and loaths to eat,
　His soul abhors delicious meet;
　Nature with heavy loads opprest
　Would yield to death to be releas'd.

4 Then how the frighten'd sinners fly
　To God for help with earnest cry!
　He hears their groans, prolongs their breath,
　And saves them from approaching death.

5 No med'cines could effect the cure
　So quick, so easy, or so secure:
　The deadly sentence God repeals,
　He sends his sovereign word, and heals.

6 Oh may the sons of men record
　The wondrous goodness of the Lord!
　And let their thankful offering prove
　How they adore their Maker's love.

PSALM CVII. Fourth Part. Long Metre.
Deliverance from Storms and Shipwreck; or, the Seamen's Song.

1 WOULD you behold the works of God,
　　His wonders in the world abroad,
　With the bold mariner, survey
　The unknown regions of the sea.

2 They leave their native shores behind,
  And seize the favour of the wind!
  'Till God commands, and tempests rise
  That heave the ocean to the skies.

3 Now to the heavens they mount amain,
  Now sink to dreadful deeps again;
  What strange affrights young sailors feel,
  And like a staggering drunkard reel.

4 When land is far, and death is nigh,
  Lost to all hope, to God they cry:
  His mercy hears the loud address,
  And sends salvation in distress.

5 He bids the winds their wrath assuage,
  And stormy tempests cease to rage;
  The gladsome train their fears give o'er,
  And hail with joy their native shore.

6 Oh may the sons of men record
  The wondrous goodness of the Lord!
  Let them their private offerings bring,
  And in the church his glory sing.

PSALM CVII. *Fourth Part.* Common Metr

The Mariner's Psalm.

1 THY works of glory, mighty Lord,
    That rule the boisterous sea,
  The sons of courage shall record,
    Who tempt that dangerous way.

2 At thy commands the winds arise,
    And swell the towering waves!
  The men astonish'd mount the skies,
    And sink in gaping graves.

3 [Again they climb the watery hills,
    And plunge in deeps again;
  Each like a tottering drunkard reels,
    And finds his courage vain.

4 Frighted to hear the tempest roar,
    They pant with fluttering breath;
  And hopeless of the distant shore
    Expect immediate death.]

PSALM CVII.

5 Then to the Lord they raise their cries,
   He hears the loud request,
And orders silence through the skies,
   And lays the floods to rest.

6 Sailors rejoice to lose their fears,
   And see the storms allay'd ;
Now to their eyes the port appears ;
   There let their vows be paid.

7 'Tis God that brings them safe to land ;
   Let stupid mortals know,
That waves are under his command,
   And all the winds that blow.

8 Oh that the sons of men would praise
   The goodness of the Lord !
And those that see thy wondrous ways
   Thy wondrous love record.

PSALM CVII. *Last Part.*
Colinies planted ; or, Nations blest and punished.

1 WHEN God, provok'd with daring crimes,
   Scourges the madness of the times,
He turns their fields to barren sand,
And dries the rivers from the land.

2 His word can raise the springs again,
And make the wither'd mountains green,
Send showery blessings from the skies ;
And harvests in the desert rise.

3 [Where nothing dwelt but beasts of prey,
Or men as fierce and wild as they,
He bids th' opprest and poor repair,
And builds them towns and cities there.

4 They sow the fields, and trees they plant,
Whose yearly fruit supplies their want ;
Their race grows up from fruitful stocks,
Their wealth increases with their flocks.

5 Thus they are blest ; but if they sin,
He lets the heathen nations in,
A savage crew invades their lands,
Their princes die by barbarous hands.

R

6 Their captive sons, expos'd to scorn,
  Wander unpity'd and forlorn;
  The country lies unfenc'd, untill'd,
  And desolation spreads the field.

7 Yet if the humbled nations mourns,
  Again his dreadful hand he turns:
  Again he makes their cities thrive,
  And bids the dying churches live.

8 The righteous with a joyful sense
  Admire the works of providence;
  And tongues of atheists shall no more,
  Blaspheme the God that saints adore.

9 How few with pious care record
  These wondrous dealings of the Lord!
  But wise observers still shall find
  The Lord is holy, just and kind.

PSALM CVIII. Common Metre.
A Song of Praise.

1 AWAKE, my soul, to sound his praise,
    Awake my harp to sing;
  Join all my powers the song to raise,
    And morning incense bring.

2 Among the people of his care,
    And through the nations round;
  Glad songs of praise will I prepare,
    And there his name resound.

3 Be thou exalted, O my God,
    Above the starry train;
  Diffuse thy heavenly grace abroad,
    And teach the world thy reign.

4 So shall thy chosen sons rejoice,
    And throng thy courts above;
  While sinners hear thy pardoning voice,
    And taste redeeming love.

PSALM CIX. ver. 1—5, 31.
Love to Enemies from the Example of Christ.

1 GOD of my mercy and my praise,
    Thy glory is my song;
  Though sinners speak against thy grace
    With a blaspheming tongue.

2 When in the form of mortal man
   Thy Son on earth was found;
   With cruel slanders false and vain
   They compass'd him round.

3 Their mis'ries his compassion move,
   Their peace he still pursu'd;
   They render hatred for his love,
   And evil for his good.

4 Their malice rag'd without a cause,
   Yet with his dying breath
   He pray'd for murderers on his cross,
   And bless'd his foes in death.

5 Lord, shall thy bright example shine
   In vain before my eyes;
   Give me a soul a-kin to thine,
   To love mine enemies.

6 The Lord shall on my side engage,
   And in my Saviour's name
   I shall defeat their pride and rage,
   Who slander and condemn.

PSALM CX. *First Part.* Long Metre.

Christ exalted, and Multitudes converted; or the Success of the Gospel.

1 THUS God th' eternal Father spake
   To Christ the Son; "Ascend and sit
   "At my right hand, 'till I shall make
   "Thy foes submissive at thy feet.

2 "From Zion shall thy word proceed,
   "Thy word, the sceptre in thy hand,
   "Shall make the hearts of rebels bleed,
   "And bow their wills to thy command.

3 "That day shall shew thy power is great,
   "When saints shall flock with willing minds,
   And sinners croud thy temple-gate,
   "Where holiness in beauty shines."

4 O blessed power! O glorious day!
   What a large vict'ry shall ensue!
   And converts, who thy grace obey,
   Exceed the drops of morning dew.

PSALM CX. Second Part. Long Metre.
The Kingdom and Priesthood of Christ.

1 THUS the great Lord of earth and sea
　　Spake to his Son, and thus he swore;
" Eternal shall thy priesthood be,
" And change from hand to hand no more.

2 " Aaron, and all his sons must die:
" But everlasting life is thine,
" To save forever those that fly
" For refuge from the wrath divine.

3 " By me Melchisedec was made
" On earth a king and priest at once;
" And thou, my heavenly priest shalt plead,
" And thou my king shalt rule my sons."

4 Jesus the priest ascends his throne,
While counsels of eternal peace,
Between the father and the son,
Proceed with honour and success.

5 Through the whole earth his reign shall spread,
And crush the powers that dare rebel:
Then shall he judge the rising dead,
And send the guilty world to hell.

6 Though while he treads his glorious way,
He drinks the cup of threats and blood,
The sufferings of that dreadful day
Shall but advance him near to God.

PSALM CX. Common Metre.
Christ's Kingdom and Priesthood.

1 JESUS, our Lord, ascend thy throne,
　　And near thy Father sit;
In Zion shall thy power be known,
　　And make thy foes submit.

2 What wonders shall thy gospel do?
　　Thy converts shall surpass
The numerous drops of morning dew,
　　And own thy sovereign grace.

3 God hath pronounc'd a firm decree,
　　Nor changes what he swore;

"Eternal shall thy priesthood be,
 "When Aaron is no more,
4 "Melchisedec, that wondrous priest,
 "That king of high degree,
 "That holy man who Abraham blest
 "Was but a type of thee."

5 Jesus our priest forever lives
 To plead for us above;
Jesus our King forever gives
 The blessings of his love.

6 God shall exalt his glorious head,
 And his high throne maintain,
Shall strike the powers and princes dead,
 Who dare oppose his reign.

PSALM CXI. *First Part.*
The Wisdom of God in his Works.

1 SONGS of immortal praise belong
 To my almighty God;
He has my heart and he my tongue
 To spread his name abroad.

2 How great the works his hand has wrought!
 How glorious in our sight!
And men in every age have sought
 His wonders with delight.

3 How fair and beauteous nature's frame!
 How wise th' eternal mind!
His counsels never change the scheme
 That his first thoughts design'd.

4 When he redeem'd his chosen sons,
 He fix'd his covenant sure:
The orders that his lips pronounce
 To endless years endure.

5 Nature and time, and earth and skies,
 Thy heavenly skill proclaim;
What shall we do to make us wise,
 But learn to read thy name?

6 To fear thy power, to trust thy grace,
 Is our divinest skill!

And he's the wisest of our race
That best obeys thy will.

PSALM CXI. Second Part.
The Perfections of God.

1 GREAT is the Lord; his works of might
    Demand our noblest songs;
Let his assembled saints unite
    Their harmony of tongues.

2 Great is the mercy of the Lord,
    He gives his children food;
And ever mindful of his word,
    He makes his promise good.

3 His Son, the great Redeemer, came
    To seal his covenant sure:
Holy and reverend is his name,
    His ways are just and pure.

4 They that would grow divinely wise,
    Must with his fear begin;
Our fairest proof of knowledge lies
    In hating every sin.

PSALM CXII. As the 113th Psalm.
The Blessings of the liberal Man.

1 THAT man is blest who stands in awe
    Of God, and loves his sacred law:
  His seed on earth shall be renown'd;
  His house the seat of wealth shall be,
  An unexhausted treasury,
    And with successive honours crown'd.

2 His liberal favours he extends,
  To some he gives, to others lends:
    A generous pity fills his mind:
  Yet what his charity impairs,
  He saves by prudence in affairs,
    And thus he's just to all mankind.

3 His hands, while they his alms bestow'd,
  His glory's future harvest sow'd,
    The sweet remembrance of the just,
  Like a green root revives and bears,

PSALM CXII.

A train of blessings for his heirs,
When dying nature sleep in dust.

4 Beset with threatening dangers round,
Unmov'd shall he maintain his ground ;
His conscience holds his courage up ;
The soul that's fill'd with virtue's light,
Shines brightest in affliction's night :
And sees in darkness beams of grace.

PAUSE.

5 [Ill tidings never can surprise
His heart that fix'd on God relies,
Though waves and tempests roar around ;
Safe on a rock he sits, and sees
The shipwreck of his enemies,
And all their hope and glory drown'd.

6 The wicked shall his triumph see,
And gnash their teeth in agony,
To find their expectations crost :
They and their envy, pride and spite,
Sink down to everlasting night,
And all their names in darkness lost.

PSALM CXII. Long Metre.

The Blessings of the Pious and Charitable.

1 THRICE happy man who fears the Lord,
Loves his command, and trusts his word ;
Honour and peace his days attend,
And blessings to his seed descend.

2 Compassion dwells upon his mind,
To works of mercy still inclin'd :
He lends the poor some present aid,
Or gives them, not to be repaid.

3 When times grow dark, and tiding spread
That fill his neighbours round with dread,
His heart is armed against the fear,
For God with all his power is there.

4 His spirit fix'd upon the Lord
Draws heavenly courage from his word ;
Amidst the darkness light shall rise,
To cheer his heart and bless his eyes.

5 He hath dispers'd his alms abroad,
　His works are still before his God;
　His name on earth shall long remain,
　While envious sinners rage in vain.

PSALM CXII. Common Metre.
Liberality rewarded.

1 HAPPY is he that fears the Lord,
　　And follows his commands,
Who lends the poor without reward,
　Or gives with liberal hands

2 As pitty dwells within his breast
　　To all the sons of need;
So God shall answer his request
　With blessings on his seed.

3 No evil tidings shall surprise
　　His well-establish'd mind!
His soul to God, his refuge flies,
　And leaves his fears behind.

4 In times of danger and distress
　　Some beams of light shall shine,
To shew the world his righteousness,
　And give him peace divine.

5 His works of piety and love
　　Remain before the Lord;
Honour on earth and joys above,
　Shall be his sure reward.

PSALM CXIII. Proper Tune.
The Majesty and Condescention of God.

1 YE that delight to serve the Lord,
　　The honours of his name record;
　His sacred name forever bless:
Where'er the circling sun displays
His rising beams or setting rays,
　Let lands and seas his power confess.

2 Not time, nor nature's narrow rounds,
Can give his vast dominion bounds;
　The heavens are far below his height;
Let no created greatness dare
With our eternal God compare,
　Arm'd with his uncreated might.

3 He bows his glorious head to view
What the bright hosts of angels do,
   And bends his care to mortal things;
His sovereign hand exalts the poor,
He takes the needy from the door,
   And seats them on the throne of kings.

4 When childless families despair,
He sends the blessings of an heir,
   To rescue their expiring name;
The mother with a thankful voice
Proclaims his praises and her joys;
   Let every age advance his praise.

PSALM CXIII. Long Metre.
God sovereign and gracious

1 YE servants of th' almighty King,
   In every age his praises sing;
Where e'er the sun shall rise or set,
The nations shall his praise repeat.

2 Above the earth, beyond the sky
His throne of glory stands on high;
Nor time nor place his power restrains,
Nor bound his universal reign.

3 Which of the sons of Adam dare,
Or angels with their God compare?
His glories how divinely bright!
Who dwells in uncreated light.

4 Behold his love, he stoops to view
What saints above the angels do;
And condescends yet more to know
The mean affairs of men below.

5 From dust and cottages obscure
His grace exalts the humble poor!
Gives them the honour of his sons,
And fits them for their heavenly thrones.

6 [A word of his creating voice
Can make the barren house rejoice;
Tho' Sarah's ninety years were past,
The promis'd seed is born at last.

7 With joy the mother views her son,
And tells the wonders God has done;

Faith may grow strong when sense despaire:
If nature fails the promise bears.

PSALM CXIV.
Miracles attending Israel's Journey.

1 WHEN Israel, freed from Pharaoh's hand,
  Left the proud tyrant and his land,
The tribes with cheerful homage own
Their king, and Judah was his throne.

2 A-cross the deep their journey lay;
The deep divide to make them way;
Jordan beheld their march, and fled
With backward current to his head.

3 The mountains shook like frighted sheep,
Like lambs the little hillocks leap:
Not Sinai on her base could stand,
Conscious of sovereign power at hand.

4 What power could make the deep divide?
Make Jordan backward roll his tide?
Why did ye leap, ye little hills?
And whence the dread that Sinai feels?

5 Let every mountain, every flood
Retire and know th' approaching God,
The King of Israel: see him here;
Tremble thou earth, adore and fear.

6 He thunders, and all nature mourns,
The rock to standing pools he turns;
Flints spring with fountains at his word,
And fires and seas confess the Lord.

PSALM CXV. First Metre.
The true God our Refuge; or, Idolatry reproved.

1 NOT to ourselves, who are but dust,
   Not to ourselves is glory due,
Eternal God, thou only just,
Thou only gracious, wise and true.

2 Display to earth thy dreadful name;
Why should a heathen's haughty tongue
Insult us, and to raise our shame,
Say, *Where's the God you've serv'd so long?*

3 The God we serve maintains his throne,
Above the clouds, beyond the skies;

Through all the earth his will is done,
He knows our groans, he hears our cries.

4 But the vain idols they adore
Are senseless shapes of stone and wood:
At best a mass of glittering ore,
A silver saint, and golden god.

5 [With eyes and ears, they carve the head
Deaf are their ears, their eyes are blind;
In vain are costly offerings made,
And vows are scatter'd in the wind.

6 Their feet were never made to move,
Nor hands to save when mortals pray;
Mortals that pay them fear or love,
Seem to be blind and deaf as they.]

7 Oh Israel, make the Lord thy hope,
Thy help, thy refuge, and thy rest;
The Lord shall build thy ruins up,
And bless the people and the priest.

8 The dead no more can speak thy praise,
They dwell in silence in the grave;
But we shall live to sing thy grace,
And tell the world thy power to save.

PSALM CXV. Second Metre.
As the new Tune of the 50th Psalm.
Idolatry reproved.

1 NOT to our names, thou only just and true
Not to our worthly names is glory due:
Thy power and grace, thy truth and justice claim
Immortal honours to thy sovereign name;
Shine thro' the earth from heaven thy blest abode,
Nor let the heathen say, *And where's your God.*

2 Heaven is thine higher court there stands thy throne
And through the lower worlds thy will is done:
God fram'd this earth, the starry heavens he spread,
But fools adore the gods their hands have made;
The kneeling croud, with looks devout behold
Their silver saviours, and their saints of gold.

3 [Vain are those artful shapes of eyes and ears!
The molten image neither sees nor hears;

Their hands are helpless, nor their feet can move,
They have no speech, nor thought, nor power, nor love
Yet sottish mortals make their long complaints
To their deaf idols, and their moveless saints.

4 The rich have statutes well adorn'd with gold;
The poor content with gods of coarser mould,
With tools of iron carve the senseless stock
Lopt from a tree, or broken from a rock:
People and priests drive on the solemn trade,
And trust the gods that saws and hammers made.

5 Be heaven and earth amaz'd! 'Tis hard to say
Which are more stupid, or their gods, or they:
O Israel trust the Lord: He hears and sees,
He knows thy sorrows and restores thy peace:
His worship does a thousand comforts yield,
He is thy help, and he thine heavenly shield.

6 In God we trust; our impious foes in vain
Attempt our ruin and oppose his reign;
Had they prevail'd darkness had clos'd our days
And death and silence had forbid his praise:
But we are sav'd, and live: Let songs arise,
And Zion bless the God that built the skies.

PSALM CXVI. *First Part.*
Recovery from Sickness.

1 I Love the Lord: He heard my cries,
    And pity'd every groan,
Long as I live, when troubles rise,
    I'll hasten to his throne.

2 I love the Lord: He bow'd his ear,
    And chas'd my griefs away:
Oh let my heart no more despair,
    When I have breath to pray!

3 My flesh declin'd my spirits fell,
    And I drew near the dead,
While inward pangs and fears of hell
    Perplex'd my wakeful head.

4 " My God, I cry'd, thy servant save,
    " Thou ever good and just:
    " Thy power can rescue from the grave,
    " Thy power is all my trust."

5 The Lord beheld me fore diſtreſt,
  He bade my pains remove :
Return, my ſoul, to God my reſt,
  For thou haſt known his love.

6 My God hath ſav'd my ſoul from death,
  And dry'd my falling tears :
Now to his praiſe I'll ſpend my breath,
  And my remaining years.

PSALM CXVI. 12. &c. Second Part.
Thanks for private Deliverance.

1 WHAT ſhall I render to my God
    For all his kindneſs ſhown?
  My feet ſhall viſit thine abode,
    My ſongs addreſs thy throne.

2 Among the ſaints that fill thine houſe
    My offerings ſhall be paid;
  There ſhall my zeal perform my vows,
    My ſoul in anguiſh made.

3 How much is mercy thy delight,
    Thou ever-bleſſed God!
  How dear thy ſervants in thy ſight?
    How precious is their blood?

4 How happy all thy ſervants are!
    How great thy grace to me!
  My life which thou haſt made thy care,
    Lord, I devote to thee.

5 Now I am thine, forever thine,
    Nor ſhall my purpoſe move;
  Thy hand has looſ'd my bonds of pain,
    And bound me with thy love.

6 Here in thy courts I leave my vow,
    And thy rich grace record :
  Witneſs, ye ſaints, who hear me now,
    If I forſake the Lord.

PSALM CXVII. Common Metre.
Praiſe to God from all Nations.

1 O All ye nations, praiſe the Lord,
    Each with a different tongue;

In every language learn his word,
  And let his name be sung,
2 His mercy reigns thro' every land:
  Proclaim his grace abroad;
  Forever firm his truth shall stand;
  Praise ye the faithful God.

PSALM CXVII. Long Metre.

1 FROM all that dwell below the skies
    Let the Creator's praise arise:
  Let the Redeemer's name be sung
  Thro' every land, by every tongue.

2 Eternal are thy mercies, Lord;
  Eternal, truth attends thy word;
  Thy praise shall sound from shore to shore,
  Till suns shall rise and set no more.

PSALM CXVII. Short Metre.

1 THY name, almighty Lord,
    Shall sound through distant lands:
  Great is thy grace, and sure thy word:
    Thy truth forever stands.

2 Far be thine honor spread,
    And long thy praise endure,
  Till morning light and evening shade
    Shall be exchang'd no more.

PSALM CXVIII. First Part. Ver. 6—15.

Deliverance from a Tumult.

1 THE Lord appears my helper now,
    Nor is my faith afraid
  What all the sons of earth can do,
    Since heaven affords its aid.

2 'Tis safer, Lord, to hope in thee,
    And have my God my friend,
  Than trust in men of high degree,
    And on their truth depend.

3 'Tis thro' the Lord my heart is strong,
    In him my lips rejoice;
  While his salvation is my song,
    How cheerful is my voice!

4 Like angry bees they girt me round;
  When God appears they fly;
So burning thorns with crackling sound
  Make a fierce blaze, and die.

5 Joy to the saints and peace belongs;
  The Lord protects their days:
Let Israel tune immortal songs
  To his Almighty grace.

PSALM CXVIII. *Second Part.* Ver. 17—21.
  Public Praise for Deliverance from Death.

1 LORD, thou hast heard thy servant cry.
    And rescu'd from the grave;
  Now shall he live: (and none can die,
    If God resolve to save.)

2 Thy praise more constant than before,
    Shall fill his daily breath;
  Thy hand that hath chastis'd him sore
    Defends him still from death.

3 Open the gate of Zion now,
    For we shall worship there,
  The house where all the righteous go
    Thy mercy to declare.

4 Among th' assemblies of thy saints
    Our thankful voice we raise;
  There we have told thee our complaints,
    And there we speak thy praise.

PSALM CXVIII. *Third Part.* Ver. 21, 23.
  Christ the foundation of the Church.

1 BEHOLD the sure foundation stone
    Which God in Zion lays,
  To build our heavenly hopes upon,
    And his eternal praise.

2 Chosen of God, to sinners dear,
    And saints adore the name,
  They trust their whole salvation here,
    Nor shall they suffer shame.

3 The foolish builders scribe and priest,
    Reject it with disdain;

Firm on this rock the church shall rest,
 And envy rage in vain.

4 What tho' the gates of hell withstood?
 Yet must this building rise:
'Tis thy own work, Almighty God,
 And wondrous in our eyes.

PSALM CXVIII. *Fourth Part.* Ver. 24, 25, 26.

*Hosannah; the Lord's day; or, Christ's Resurrection,
and our Salvation.*

1 THIS is the day the Lord hath made,
 He calls the hours his own;
Let heaven rejoice, let earth be glad,
 And praise surround the throne.

2 To day he rose and left the dead;
 And Satan's empire fell;
To day the saints his triumph spread,
 And all his wonders tell.

3 *Hosannah* to th' anointed king,
 To David's holy son,
Help us, O Lord; descend and bring
 Salvation from thy throne.

4 Blest is the Lord, who comes to men
 With messages of grace:
Who comes in God his father's name,
 To save our sinful race.

5 *Hosannah* in the highest strains
 The church on earth can raise;
The highest heavens, in which he reigns,
 Shall give him nobler praise.

PSALM CXVIII Ver. 12—27. Short Metre.

*An Hosannah for the Lord's-Day; or, a new song of
Salvation by Christ.*

1 SEE what a living stone
 The builders did refuse;
Yet God hath built his church thereon
 In spite of envious Jews.

2 The scribe and angry priest
 Reject thine only Son;

Yet on this rock shall Zion rest,
 As the chief corner-stone.

3 The work, O Lord, is thine,
 And wondrous in our eyes:
This day declares it all divine,
 This day did Jesus rise.

4 This is the glorious day
 That our Redeemer made;
Let us rejoice and sing, and pray,
 Let all the church be glad.

5 *Hosannah* to the king
 Of David's royal blood:
Bless him, ye saints, he comes to bring
 Salvation from your God.

6 We bless thine holy word
 Which all this grace displays;
And offer on thine altar, Lord,
 Our sacrifice of praise.

PSALM CXVIII. 22—27. Long Metre.
An Hosannah for the Lord's-Day; or, a new song of Salvation by Christ.

1 LO! what a glorious corner-stone
 The Jewish builders did refuse:
But God hath built his church thereon,
In spite of envy and the Jews.

2 Great God, the work is all divine,
The joy and wonder of our eyes;
This is the day that proves it thine,
The day that saw our Saviour rise.

3 Sinners rejoice, and saints be glad;
Hosannah, let his name be blest;
A thousand honours on his head,
With peace and light and glory rest!

4 In God's own name he comes to bring
Salvation to our dying race;
Let the whole church address their king
With hearts of joy, and songs of praise.

PSALM CXIX.
[*I have collected and disposed the most useful Verses of this Psalm under eighteen different Heads, and formed a*

Divine Song upon each of them. But the Verses are much transposed to attain some Degree of Connection.

In some places, among the words Law, Commands, Judgments, Testimonies, I have used Gospel, Word, Grace, Truth, Promise, &c. as more agreeable to the New Testament, and the common Language of Christians, and it equally answers the Design of the Psalmist, which was to recommend the holy Scriptures.

PSALM CXIX. First Part.
The blessedness of Saints, and misery of Sinners.

V. 1, 2, 3.

1 BLEST are the undefil'd in heart,
    Whose ways are right and clean;
Who never from thy law depart,
    But fly from every sin.

2 Blest are the men that keep thy word,
    And practise thy commands;
With their whole heart they seek the Lord
    And serve thee with their hands.

Ver. 165.
3 Great is their peace who love thy law;
    How firm their souls abide;
Nor can a bold temptation draw
    Their steady feet aside.

Ver. 21, 118.
4 Then shall my heart have inward joy,
    And keep my face from shame,
When all thy statutes I obey
    And honour all thy name.

5 But haughty sinners God will hate,
    The proud shall die accurst;
The sons of falshood and deceit
    Are troden to the dust.

Ver 119, 153.
6 Vile as the dross the wicked are;
    And those that leave thy ways
Shall see salvation from afar,
    But never taste thy grace.

PSALM CXIX. Second Part.

Secret Devotion and Spiritual Mindedness; or Constant Converse with God.

Ver. 147, 55.

1 TO thee, before the dawning light,
  My gracious God, I pray;
I meditate thy name by night,
  And keep thy law by day.

Ver. 81.

2 My spirit faints to see thy grace,
  Thy promise bears me up;
And while salvation long delays,
  Thy word supports my hope.

Ver. 164.

3 Seven times a day I lift my hands,
  And pay my thanks to thee,
Thy righteous providence demands
  Repeated praise from me.

Ver. 62.

4 When midnight darkness veils the skies
  I call thy works to mind;
My thoughts in warm devotion rise,
  And sweet acceptance find.

PSALM CXIX. Third Part.

Profession of Sincerity, Repentance, and Obedience.

Ver. 57, 50.

1 THOU art my portion, O my God:
  Soon as I know thy way.
My heart makes haste t' obey thy word,
  And suffers no delay.

Ver. 27, 90.

2 I chose the path of heavenly truth,
  And glory in my choice:
Not all the riches of the earth
  Could make me so rejoice.

3 The testimonies of thy grace
  I set before my eyes:
Thence I derive my daily strength,
  And there my comfort lies.

Ver. 59.

4 If once I wander from the path,
  I think upon my ways,

Then turn my feet to thy commands,
And trust thy pardoning grace.

Ver. 94, 112.

5 Now I am thine, forever thine,
Oh save thy servant Lord,
Thou art my shield, my hiding-place,
My hope is in thy word.

Ver. 112.

6 Thou hast inclin'd this heart of mine
Thy statutes to fulfil;
And thus till mortal life shall end
Would I perform thy will.

PSALM CXIX. *Fourth Part.*
Instruction from Scripture.

1 HOW shall the young secure their hearts,
And guard their lives from sin?
Thy word the choicest rules imparts
To keep the conscience clean.

Ver. 130.

2 When once it enters to the mind,
It spreads such light abroad,
The meanest souls instruction find,
And raise their thoughts to God.

Ver. 105.

3 'Tis like the sun, a heavenly light,
That guides us all the day;
And through the dangers of the night,
A lamp to lead our way.

Ver. 99, 100.

4 The men that keep thy law with care,
And meditate thy word,
Grow wiser than their teachers are,
And better know the Lord.

Ver. 104. 113.

5 Thy precepts make me truly wise;
I hate the sinner's road:
I hate my own vain thoughts that rise,
But love thy law, my God.

Ver. 19, 90, 91.

6 [The starry heavens thy rule obey,
The earth maintains her place;

And these thy servants night and day
  Thy skill and power express.
7 But still thy law, and gospel, Lord,
  Have lessons more divine:
Not earth stands firmer than thy word,
  Nor stars so nobly shine.]

> Ver. 190, 140, 9, 119.

8 Thy word is everlasting truth,
  How pure is every page!
That holy book shall guide our youth,
  And well support our age.

PSALM CXIX. *Fifth Part.*
Delight in Scripture; or, the Word of God dwelling in us.

> Ver. 97.

1 OH how I love thy holy law
    'Tis daily my delight;
  And thence my meditations draw
    Divine advice by night.

> Ver. 148.

2 My waking eyes prevent the day
    To meditate thy word:
  My soul with longing melts away
    To hear thy gospel, Lord.

> Ver. 3, 13, 44.

3 Thy heavenly words my heart engage,
    And well employ my tongue,
  And in my tiresome pilgrimage
    Yield me a heavenly song.

> Ver. 19, 103.

4 Am I a stranger, or at home,
    'Tis my perpetual feast;
  Not honey dropping from the comb
    So much allures the taste.

> Ver. 72, 127.

5 No treasures so enrich the mind;
    Nor shall thy word be sold
  For loads of silver well refin'd,
    Nor heaps of choicest gold.

> Ver. 28, 49, 175.

6 When nature sinks, and spirits droop,
    Thy promises of grace

Are pillars to support my hope,
And there I write thy praise.

PSALM CXIX. Sixth Part.
Holiness and Comfort from the Word.

Ver. 128.
1 LORD, I esteem thy judgments right
And all thy statutes just;
Thence I maintain a constant fight
With every flattering lust.

Ver. 97, 9.
2 Thy precepts often I survey;
I keep thy law in sight
Through all the business of the day,
To form my actions right.

Ver. 62.
3 My heart in midnight silence cries,
" How sweet thy comforts be;"
My thoughts in holy wonder rise,
And bring their thanks to thee.

Ver. 162.
4 And when my spirit drinks her fill,
At some good word of thine,
Not mighty men that share the spoil,
Have joys compar'd to mine.

PSALM CXIX. Seventh Part.
Imperfection of Nature, and Perfection of Scripture.

Ver. 96. Paraphrased.
1 LET all the heathen writers join
To form one perfect book,
Great God, if once compar'd with thine,
How mean their writings look.

2 Not the most perfect rules they gave
Could shew one sin forgiven;
Nor lead a step beyond the grave,
But thine conduct to heaven.

3 I've seen an end to what we call
Perfection here below;
How short the powers of nature fall,
And can no father go.

4 Yet man would fain be just with God,
By works their hands have wrought:

PSALM CXIX.

But thy commands, exceeding broad,
   Extend to every thought.

5 In vain we boast perfection here,
   While sin defiles our frame;
And sinks our virtues down so far,
   They scarce deserve the name.

6 Our faith, and love, and every grace
   Fall far below thy word;
But perfect truth and righteousness
   Dwell only with the Lord.

PSALM CXIX. *Eighth Part.*
Excellency and Variety of Scripture,
Ver. 111 Paraphrased.

1 LORD I have made thy word my choice,
   My lasting heritage;
There shall my noblest powers rejoice,
   My warmest thoughts engage.

2 I'll read the histories of thy love,
   And keep thy laws in sight,
While through the promises I rove,
   With ever-fresh delight.

3 'Tis a broad land of wealth unknown,
   Where springs of life arise;
Seeds of immortal bliss are sown,
   And hidden glory lies.

4 The best relief that mourners have,
   It makes our sorrows blest;
Our fairest hope beyond the grave,
   And our eternal rest.

PSALM CXIX. *Ninth Part.*
Desire of Knowledge.
Ver. 64, 68, 18.

1 THY mercies fill the earth, O Lord,
   How good thy works appear!
Open my eyes to read thy word,
   And see thy wonders there.

Ver. 73, 125.
2 My heart was fashion'd by thy hand,
   My service is thy due,

Oh make thy servant understand
 The duties I must do.
3 Since I'm a stranger here below,
 Let not thy path be hid,
But mark the road my feet should go,
 And be my constant guide.

Ver. 26.
4 When I confess'd my wandering ways,
 Thou heardst my soul complain;
Grant me the teachings of thy grace,
 Or I shall stray again.

Ver. 33, 34.
5 If God to me his statutes shew,
 And heavenly truth impart,
His work forever I'll pursue,
 His law shall rule my heart.

Ver. 50, 71.
6 This was my comfort when I bore
 Variety of grief;
It made me learn thy word the more,
 And fly to that relief.

Ver. 51.
7 [In vain the proud deride me now;
 I'll ne'er forget thy law,
Nor let that blessed gospel go
 Whence all my hopes I draw.

Ver. 27, 171.
8 When I have learn'd my Father's will,
 I'll teach the world his ways;
My thankful lips inspir'd with zeal,
 Shall sing aloud his praise.]

PSALM CXIX. *Tenth Part.*
Pleading the Promises.
Ver. 38, 49.

1 BEHOLD thy waiting servant, Lord,
  Devoted to thy fear;
Remember and confirm thy word,
 For all my hopes are there.

Ver. 41, 58, 107.
2 Hast thou not sent salvation down,
 And promis'd quickening grace?
Doth not my heart address thy throne?
 And yet thy love delays.

Ver. 123, 42.
3 Mine eyes for thy salvation fail;
   Oh bear thy servant up;
Nor let the scoffing lips prevail,
   Who dare reproach my hope.

Ver. 49, 74.
4 Didst thou not raise my faith, O Lord?
   Then let thy truth appear:
Saints shall rejoice in my reward,
   And trust as well as fear.

PSALM CXIX. *Eleventh Part.*
Breathing after Holiness.

1 OH that the Lord would guide my ways
      To keep his statutes still!
   Oh that my God would grant me grace
      To know and do his will!

Ver. 29.
2 Oh send thy Spirit down to write
   Thy law upon my heart,
Nor let my tongue indulge deceit,
   Nor act the liar's part.

Ver. 37, 36.
3 From vanity turn off my eyes;
   Let no corrupt design
Nor covetous desires arise
   Within this soul of mine.

Ver. 233.
4 Order my footsteps by thy word,
   And make my heart sincere;
Let sin have no dominion, Lord,
   But keep my conscience clear.

Ver. 176.
5 My soul hath gone too far astray,
   My feet too often slip;
Yet since I've not forgot thy way,
   Restore thy wandering sheep.

6 Make me to walk in thy commands,
   'Tis a delightful road;
Nor let my head, or heart, or hands,
   Offend against my God.

T

PSALM CXIX. *Twelfth Part.*
Breathing after Comfort and Deliverance.
Ver. 153.
1 MY God, consider my distress,
    Let mercy plead my cause;
Though I have sinn'd against thy grace,
    I ne'er forget thy laws.
Ver. 89, 116.
2 Forbid, forbid the sharp reproach,
    Which I so justly fear;
Uphold my life, uphold my hopes,
    Nor let my shame appear.
Ver. 122, 135.
3 Be thou a surety, Lord, for me,
    Nor let the proud oppress;
But make thy waiting servant see
    The shinings of thy face.
Ver. 81.
4 My eyes with expectation fail;
    My heart within me cries,
" When will the Lord his truth fulfil,
" And bid my comforts rise?"
Ver. 132.
5 Look down upon my sorrows, Lord,
    And shew thy grace the same;
Thy tender mercies still afford
    To those that love thy name.

PSALM CXIX. *Thirteenth Part.*
Holy Fear and Tenderness of Conscience.
Ver. 10.
1 WITH my whole heart I've sought thy face;
    Oh let me never stray
From thy commands O God of grace,
    Nor tread the sinner's way.
Ver. 11.
2 Thy word I've hid within my heart,
    To keep my conscience clean,
And be an everlasting guard
    From every rising sin.
Ver. 63, 53, 158.
3 I'm a companion of the saints,
    Who fear and love the Lord;

PSALM CXIX.

My sorrows rise, my nature faints,
 When men transgress thy word.

Ver. 161, 163.

4 While sinners do thy gospel wrong,
 My spirit stands in awe;
My soul abhors a lying tongue,
 But loves thy righteous law.

Ver. 161, 120.

5 My heart with sacred reverence hears
 The threatenings of thy word;
My flesh with holy trembling fears
 The Judgments of the Lord.

Ver. 166, 174.

6 My God, I long, I hope, I wait
 For thy salvation still;
While thy whole law is my delight,
 And I obey thy will.

PSALM CXIX. *Fourteenth Part.*
Benefit of Afflictions, and Support under them.

Ver. 253, 81, 82.

1 CONSIDER all my sorrows, Lord,
 And thy deliverance send;
My soul for thy salvation faints,
 When will my troubles end!

Ver. 71.

2 Yet I have found 'tis good for me
 To bear my Father's rod;
Afflictions make me learn the law,
 And live upon my God.

Ver. 50.

3 This is the comfort I enjoy
 When new distress begins:
I read thy word, I run thy way,
 And hate my former sins.

Ver. 92.

4 Had not thy word been my delight
 When earthly joys were fled,
My soul, opprest with sorrows weight,
 Had sunk amongst the dead.

Ver. 75.

5 I know thy judgments, Lord, are right,
 Though they may seem severe;

The sharpest sufferings I endure,
Flow from thy faithful care.

Ver. 67.

6 Before I knew thy chastening rod,
My feet were apt to stray;
But now I learn to keep thy word,
Nor wander from thy way.

PSALM CXIX. *Fifteenth Part.*
Holy Resolutions.

Ver. 93.

1 OH that thy statutes every hour
Might dwell upon my mind!
Thence I derive a quickening power
And daily peace I find.

Ver. 15, 16.

2 To meditate thy precepts, Lord,
Shall be my sweet employ;
My soul shall ne'er forget thy word,
Thy word is all my joy.

Ver. 32.

3 How would I run in thy commands,
If thou my heart discharge
From sin and satan's hateful chains,
And set my feet at large!

Ver. 13, 46.

4 My lips with courage shall declare
Thy statutes and thy name;
I'll speak thy word tho' kings should hear,
Nor yield to sinful shame.

Ver. 61, 69. 70.

5 Let bands of persecutors rise
To rob me of my right;
Let pride and malice forge their lies,
Thy law is my delight.

Ver. 115.

6 Depart from me, ye wicked race,
Whose hands and hearts are ill:
I love my God, I love his ways,
And must obey his will.

PSALM CXIX.

PSALM CXIX. Sixteenth Part.
Prayer for quickening Grace.

Ver. 25, 37.

1 MY soul lies cleaving to the dust;
  Lord, give me life divine;
From vain desires and every lust
  Turn off these eyes of mine.

2 I need the influence of thy grace
  To speed me in thy way,
Lest I should loiter in my race,
  Or turn my feet astray.

Ver. 107.

3 When sore afflictions press me down,
  I need thy quickening powers;
Thy word that I have rested on
  Shall help my heaviest hours.

Ver. 156, 40.

4 Are not thy mercies sovereign still,
  And thou a faithful God?
Wilt thou not grant me warmer zeal
  To run the heavenly road?

Ver. 159, 40.

5 Does not my heart thy precepts love,
  And long to see thy face?
And yet how slow my spirits move
  Without enlivening grace!

Ver. 93.

6 Then shall I love thy gospel more,
  And ne'er forget thy word,
When I have felt its quickening power
  To draw me near the Lord.

PSALM CXIX Seventeenth Part.
Grace shining in Difficulties and Trials.

Ver. 143, 28.

1 WHEN pain and anguish seize me, Lord,
  All my support is from thy word:
My soul dissolves for heaviness;
Uphold me with thy strengthening grace.

Ver. 51, 69, 110.

2 The proud have fram'd their scoffs and lies,
They watch my feet with envious eyes,

They tempt my soul to snares and sin,
Yet thy commands I ne'er decline.

Ver. 161, 78.

3 They hate me, Lord, without a cause,
They hate to see me love thy laws;
But I will trust and fear thy name,
Till pride and malice die with shame.

PSALM CXIX. Last Part.

Sanctified Afflictions; or, Delight in the Word of God.

Ver. 67, 59.

1 FATHER, I bless thy gentle hand;
How kind was thy chastising rod,
That forc'd my conscience to a stand,
And brought my wandering soul to God!

2 Foolish and vain, I went astray,
Ere I had felt thy scourges, Lord,
I left my guide, and lost my way,
But now I love and keep thy word.

Ver. 71.

3 'Tis good for me to wear the yoke,
For pride is apt to rise and swell;
'Tis good to bear my father's stroke,
That I might learn his statutes well.

Ver. 72.

4 The law that issues from thy mouth
Shall raise my cheerful passions more
Than all the treasures of the south,
Or richest hills of golden ore.

Ver. 73.

5 Thy hands have made my mortal frame,
Thy spirit form'd my soul within:
Teach me to know thy wondrous name,
And guard me safe from death and sin.

Ver. 74.

6 Then all that love and fear the Lord
At my salvation shall rejoice;
For I have trusted in thy word,
And made thy grace my only choice.

PSALM CXX.

Complaint of quarrelsome Neighbours; or, a devote Wish for Peace.

1 THOU God of love, thou ever-blest,
Pity my suffering state;

When wilt thou set my soul at rest,
  From lips that love deceit?

2 Hard lot of mine! My days are cast
    Among the sons of strife,
  Whose never-ceasing quarrels waste
    My golden hours of life.

3 Oh might I fly to change my place,
    How would I choose to dwell
  In some wild lonesome wilderness,
    And leave these gates of hell!

4 Peace is the blessing that I seek,
    How lovely are its charms!
  I am for peace; but when I speak,
    They all declare for arms.

5 New passions still their souls engage,
    And keep their malice strong:
  What shall be done to curb thy rage,
    O though devouring tongue!

6 Should burning arrows smite thee through,
    Strict justice would approve;
  But I would rather spare my foe,
    And melt his heart with love.

PSALM CXXI. Long Metre.
Divine Protection.

1 UP to the hills I lift mine eyes,
    Th' eternal hill beyond the skies;
  Thence all her help my soul derives;
  There my almighty refuge lives.

2 He lives; the everlasting God,
  That built the world, that spread the flood;
  The heavens, with all their host he made,
  And the dark regions of the dead.

3 He guides our feet, he guards our way;
  His morning smiles adorn the day:
  He spreads the evening vail, and keeps
  The silent hours while Israel sleeps.

4 Israel, a name divinely blest,
  May rise secure, securely rest;

Thy holy guardian's wakeful eyes
　　　Admit no slumber, nor surprise.

5 No sun shall smite thy head by day,
　　　Nor the pale moon with sickly ray
　　Shall blast thy couch; nor baleful star
　　　Dart his malignant fire so far.

6 Should earth and hell with malice burn,
　　　Still thou shalt go, and still return
　　Safe in the Lord! his heavenly care
　　　Defends thy life from every snare.

7 On thee foul spirits have no power;
　　　And in thy last departing hour
　　Angels that trace the airy road,
　　　Shall bear thee homeward to thy God.

　　　PSALM CXXI. Common Metre.
　　　　Preservation by Day and Night.

1 TO heaven I lift my waiting eyes,
　　　　There all my hopes are laid:
　　The Lord that built the earth and skies
　　　　Is my perpetual aid.

2 Their stedfast feet shall never fall,
　　　　Whom he designs to keep;
　　His ear attends the softest call;
　　　　His eyes can never sleep.

3 He will sustain our weakest powers
　　　　With his almighty arm,
　　And watch our most unguarded hours
　　　　Against surprising harm.

4 Israel rejoice, and rest secure,
　　　　Thy keeper is the Lord;
　　His watchful eyes employ his power
　　　　For thine eternal guard.

5 Nor scorching sun, nor sickly moon
　　　　Shall have his leave to smite:
　　He shields thy head from burning noon,
　　　　From blasting damps at night.

6 He guards thy soul, he keeps thy breath,
　　　　Where thickest dangers come;
　　Go and return, secure from death,
　　　　Till God commands thee home.

PSALM CXXI. As the 148th Psalm.
God our Preserver.

1 UPWARDS I lift mine eyes,
   From God is all my aid;
The God that built the skies,
And earth and nature made;
   God is the tower
   To which I fly;
   His grace is nigh
   In every hour.

2 My feet shall never slide,
And fall in fatal snares,
Since God my guard and guide,
Defends me from my fears.
   Those wakeful eyes
   That never sleep,
   Shall Israel keep
   When dangers rise.

3 No burning heats by day,
Nor blasts of evening air,
Shall take my health away,
If God be with me there:
   Thou art my sun,
   And thou my shade,
   To guard my head
   By night or noon.

4 Hast thou not given thy word
To save my soul from death?
And I can trust my Lord
To keep my mortal breath;
   I'll go and come,
   Nor fear to die,
   Till from on high
   Thou call me home.

PSALM CXXII. Common Metre.
Going to Church.

1 HOW did my heart rejoice to hear
   My friends devoutly say,
"In Zion let us all appear,
"And keep the solemn day."

2 I love the gates, I love the road;
  The church adorn'd with grace,
Stands like a palace built for God
  To shew his milder face.

3 Up to her courts with joy unknown
  The holy tribes repair;
The son of David holds his throne,
  And sits in judgment there.

4 He hears our praises and complaints;
  And while his awful voice
Divides the sinners from the saints,
  We tremble and rejoice.

5 Peace be within this sacred place,
  And joy a constant guest!
With holy gifts and heavenly grace
  Be her attendants blest!

6 My soul shall pray for Zion still,
  While life or breath remains;
There my best friends, my kindred dwell,
  There God my Saviour reigns.

PSALM CXXII. Proper Tune.
Going to Church.

1 HOW pleas'd and blest was I,
    To hear the people cry,
  Come, let us seek our God to day!
Yes with a cheerful zeal
We haste to Zion's hill,
  And there our vows and honours pay.

2 Zion, thrice happy place,
Adorn'd with wondrous grace,
  And walls of strength embrace thee round;
In thee our tribes appear
To pray, and praise, and hear
  The sacred gospel's joyful sound.

3 There David's greater son
Has fix'd his royal throne.
  He sits for grace and judgment there;
He bids the saints be glad,
He makes the sinner sad;
  And humble souls rejoice with fear.

4 May peace attend thy gate,
  And joy within thee wait
    To bless the soul of every guest;
  The man that seeks thy peace,
  And wishes thine increase,
    A thousand blessings on him rest!

5 My tongue repeats her vows,
  Peace to this sacred house!
    For here my friends and kindred dwell;
  And since my glorious God
  Makes thee his best abode,
    My soul shall ever love thee well.

Repeat the 4th Stanza to complete the Tune.

PSALM CXXIII.
Pleading with Submission.

1 O Thou whose grace and justice reign
    Enthron'd above the skies,
  To thee our hearts would tell their pain,
    To thee we lift our eyes.

2 As servants watch their master's hand,
    And fear the angry stroke!
  Or maids before their mistress stand,
    And wait a peaceful look:

3 So for our sins we justly feel
    Thy discipline, O God;
  Yet wait the gracious moment still,
    Till thou remove the rod.

4 Those that in wealth and pleasure live,
    Our daily groans deride,
  And thy delays of mercy give
    Fresh courage to their pride.

5 Our foes insult us, but our hope
    In thy compassion lies;
  This thought shall bear our spirits up,
    That God will not despise.

PSALM CXXIV. Common Metre.
God gives Victory.

1 HAD not the God of truth and love,
    When hosts against us rose,

Display'd his vengeance from above,
  And crush'd the conquering foes:

2 Their armies like a raging flood
    Had swept the guardless land,
  Destroy'd on earth his blest abode,
    And whelm'd our feeble band.

3 But safe beneath his spreading shield
    His sons securely rest,
  Defy the dangers of the field,
    And bare the fearless breast.

4 And now our souls shall bless the Lord,
    Who broke the deadly snare;
  Who sav'd us from the murdering sword,
    And made our lives his care.

5 Our help is in Jehovah's name,
    Who form'd the heavens above;
  He that supports their wondrous frame
    Can guard his church by love.

PSALM CXXV. Common Metre.
The Saint's Trial and Safety.

1 UNSHAKEN as the sacred hill,
    And firm as mountains stand,
  Firm as a rock the soul shall rest
    That trusts th' almighty hand.

2 Not walls nor hills could guard so well
    Old Salem's happy ground,
  As those eternal arms of love
    That every saint surround.

3 While tyrants are a smarting scourge
    To drive them near to God,
  Divine compassion will assuage
    The fury of the rod.

4 Deal gently, Lord, with souls sincere,
    And lead them safely on
  To the bright gates of paradise,
    Where Christ their Lord is gone.

5 But if we trace those crooked ways
    That the old serpent drew,

The wrath that drove him first to hell,
Shall smite his followers too.

PSALM CXXV. Short Metre.

The Saint's Trial and Safety ; or, moderated Afflictions.

1 FIRM and unmov'd are they
    That rest their souls on God ;
Firm as the mount where David dwelt,
    Or where the ark abode.

2 As mountains stood to guard
    The city's sacred ground,
So God and his almighty love
    Embrace his saints around.

3 What though the Father's rod
    Drop a chastising stroke,
Yet left it wound their souls too deep,
    Its fury shall be broke.

4 Deal gently, Lord, with those
    Whose faith and pious fear,
Whose hope, and love, and every grace,
    Proclaim their hearts sincere.

5 Nor shall the tyrant's rage
    Too long oppress the saints ;
The God of Israel will support
    His children, lest they faint.

6 But if our slavish fear
    Will choose the road to hell,
We must expect our portion there
    Where bolder sinners dwell.

PSALM CXXVI. Long Metre.

Surprising Deliverance.

1 WHEN God restor'd our captive state,
    Joy was our song, and grace our theme
The grace beyond our hopes so great,
That joy appear'd a pleasing dream.

2 The scoffer owns thy hand, and pays
Unwilling honours to thy name ;
While we with pleasure shout thy praise,
Which cheerful notes thy love proclaim.

3 When we review our dismal fears,
   'Twas hard to think they'll vanish so;
   With God we left our flowing tears,
   He makes our joys like rivers flow.

4 The man that in his furrow'd field,
   His scatter'd seed with sadness leaves,
   Will shout to see the harvest yield
   A welcome load of joyful sheaves.

PSALM CXXVI. Common Metre.
The Joy of a remarkable Conversion; or, Melancholy removed.

1 WHEN God reveal'd his gracious name,
      And chang'd my mournful state,
   My rapture seem'd a pleasing dream,
      The grace appear'd so great.

2 The world beheld the glorious change,
      And did thy hand confess;
   My tongue broke out in unknown strains,
      And sung surprising grace.

3 " *Great is the work*, my neighbours cry'd,
      And own'd the power divine:
   " *Great is the work*, my heart reply'd,
   " *And be the glory thine.*"

4 The Lord can clear the darkest skies,
      Can give us day for night;
   Make drops of sacred sorrow rise
      To rivers of delight.

5 Let those that sow in sadness wait
      Till the fair harvest come,
   They shall confess their sheaves are great,
      And shout the blessings home.

6 Though seed lie buried long in dust,
      It shan't deceive their hope;
   The precious grain can ne'er be lost,
      For grace insures the crop.

PSALM CXXVII. Long Metre.
The Blessing of God on the Business and Comfort of Life

1 IF God succeed not, all the cost
      And pains to build the house are lost,

If God the city will not keep,
The watchful guards as well may sleep.

2 What though we rise before the sun,
And work and toil when day is done,
Careful and sparing eat our bread,
To shun that poverty we dread.

3 'Tis all in vain, till God hath blest,
He can make rich, yet give us rest,
On God, our sovereign, still depends
Our joy in children and in friends.

4 Happy the man to whom he sends
Obedient children, faithful friends!
How sweet our daily comforts prove
When they are seafon'd with his love!

PSALM CXXVII. Common Metre.

God all in all.

1 IF God to build the house deny,
  The builders work in vain;
And towns without his wakeful eye
  And useless watch maintain.

2 Before the morning beams arise,
  Your painful work renew,
And till the stars ascend the skies
  Your tiresome toil pursue.

3 Short be your sleep, and coarse your fare;
  In vain till God has blest;
But if his smiles attend your care,
  You shall have food and rest.

4 Nor children, relatives, nor friends,
  Shall real blessings prove,
Nor all the earthly joys he sends,
  If sent without his love.

PSALM CXXVIII.

Family Blessings.

1 O Happy man, whose soul is fill'd
   With zeal and reverent awe!
His lips to God their honours yield,
   His life adorns the law.

2 A careful providence shall stand
  And ever guard thy head,
Shall on the labours of thy hand
  Its kindly blessing shed.

3 Thy wife shall be a fruitful vine;
  Thy children round thy board,
Each like a plant of honour shine,
  And learn to fear the Lord.

4 The Lord shall thy best hopes fulfil
  For months and years to come:
The Lord who dwells on Zion's hill
  Shall send thee blessing home.

5 This is the man whose happy eyes
  Shall see his house increase,
Shall see the sinking church arise,
  Then leave the world in peace.

PSALM CXXIX.

Persecutors punished.

1 UP from my youth, may Israel say,
  Have I been nurs'd in tears;
My griefs were constant as the day,
  And tedious as the years.

2 Up from my youth I bore the rage,
  Of all the sons of strife;
Oft they assail'd my riper age,
  But God preserv'd my life.

3 O'er all my frame their cruel dart
  Its painful wounds impress'd;
Hourly they vex'd my fainting heart,
  Nor let my sorrows rest.

4 The Lord grew angry on his throne,
  And with impartial eye,
Measur'd the mischiefs they had done,
  Then let his arrows fly.

5 How was their insolence surpris'd
  To hear his thunders roll
And all the foes of Zion seiz'd
  With horror to the soul.

PSALM CXXX.

6 Thus shall the men that hate the saints
   Be blasted from the sky;
Their glory fades, their courage faints,
   And all their prospects die.

7 [What though they flourish tall and fair,
   They have no root beneath;
Their growth shall perish in despair,
   And lie despis'd in death.

8 So Scorn that on the house-top stands,
   No hope of harvest gives:
The reaper ne'er shall fill his hands,
   Nor binder fold the sheaves.

PSALM CXXX. Common Metre.

Pardoning Grace.

1 OUT of the deeps of long distress,
   The borders of despair,
I sent my cries to seek thy grace,
   My groans to move thine ear.

2 Great God, should thy severer eye,
   And thine impartial hand,
Mark and revenge iniquity,
   No mortal flesh could stand.

3 But there are pardons with my God,
   For crimes of high degree!
Thy Son has bought them with his blood,
   To draw us near to thee.

4 [I wait for thy salvation, Lord,
   With strong desires I wait;
My soul invited by thy word
   Stands watching at thy gate.]

5 [Just as the guards that keep the night
   Long for the morning skies,
Watch the first beams of breaking light,
   And meet them with their eyes.

6 So waits my soul to see thy grace
   And more intent than they,
Meets the first openings of thy face,
   And finds a brighter day.]

7 Then in the Lord let Israel trust,
  Let Israel seek his face;
The Lord is good as well as just,
  And plenteous in his grace.

8 There's full redemption at his throne,
  For sinners long enslav'd;
The great Redeemer is his son:
  And Israel shall be saved.

PSALM CXXX. Long Metre.
Pardoning Grace.

1 FROM deep distress and troubled thoughts,
  To thee, my God, I rais'd my cries:
If thou severely mark our faults,
No flesh can stand before thine eyes.

2 But thou hast built thy throne of grace
Free to dispense thy pardons there,
That sinners may approach thy face,
And hope, and love, as well as fear.

3 As the benighted pilgrims wait,
And long and wish for breaking day,
So waits my soul before thy gate;
When will my God his face display!

4 My trust is fix'd upon thy word,
Nor shall I trust thy word in vain:
Let mourning souls address the Lord,
And find relief from all their pain.

5 Great is his love, and large his grace,
Through the redemption of his Son:
He turns our feet from sinful ways,
And pardons what our hands have done.

PSALM CXXXI.
Humility and Submission.

1 IS there ambition in my heart?
  Search, gracious God, and see;
Or do I act a haughty part?
  Lord, I appeal to thee.

2 I charge my thoughts, be humble still,
  And all my carriage mild,

Content, My Father, with thy will,
 And peaceful as a child.

3 The patient soul, the lowly mind
 Shall have a large reward :
 Let saints in sorrow lie resign'd,
 And trust a faithful Lord.

PSALM CXXXII. 5, 13—18. Long Metre.

At the Settlement of a Church ; or, the Ordination of a Minister.

1 WHERE shall we go to seek and find
   An habitation for our God,
 A dwelling for th' eternal Mind
 Among the sons of flesh and blood !

2 The God of Jacob chose the hill
 Of Zion for his antient rest ;
 And Zion is his dwelling still,
 His church is with his presence blest.

3 " Here I will fix my gracious throne,
 " And reign forever, saith the Lord ;
 " Here shall my power and love be known,
 " And blessings shall attend my word.

4 " Here will I meet the hungry poor,
 " And fill their souls with living bread ;
 " Sinners that wait before my door
 " With sweet provisions shall be fed.

5 " Girded with truth, and cloth'd with grace
 " My priests, my ministers shall shine ;
 " Not Aaron in his costly dress
 " Appears so glorious and divine.

6 " The saints, unable to contain
 " Their inward joy, shall shout and sing,
 " The son of David here will reign,
 " And Zion triumph in her King.

7 " Jesus shall see a numerous seed
 " Born here t' uphold his glorious name ;
 " His crown shall flourish on his head,
 " While all his foes are cloth'd with shame."

PSALM CXXXIII.

PSALM CXXXII. 4, 5, 7, 8, 15—17.
Common Metre.
A Church Established.

1 [NO sleep nor slumber to his eyes
  Good David would afford,
Till he had found below the skies
  A dwelling for the Lord.

2 The Lord in Zion plac'd his name,
  His ark was settled there:
And there th' assembled nation came
  To worship thrice a year.

3 We trace no more those toilsome ways,
  Nor wander far abroad;
Where e'er thy people meet for praise,
  There is a house for God.]

PAUSE.

4 Arise, O King of grace, arise,
  And enter to thy rest,
Lo! thy church waits with longing eyes
  Thus to be own'd and blest.

5 Enter with all thy glorious train,
  Thy spirit and thy word;
All that the ark did once contain
  Could no such grace afford.

6 Here, mighty God, accept our vows,
  Here let thy praise be spread;
Bless the provision of thy house,
  And fill thy poor with bread.

7 Here let the Son of David reign,
  Let God's anointed shine;
Justice and truth his court maintain,
  With love and power divine.

8 Here let him hold a lasting throne,
  And at his kingdom grows,
Fresh honours shall adorn his crown,
  And shame confound his foes.

PSALM CXXXIII. Common Metre.
Brotherly Love

1 LO, what an entertaining sight
  Those friendly brethren prove,

PSALM CXXXIII.

 Whose cheerful hearts in bands unite
  Of harmony and love.

2 Where streams of bliss from Christ the spring
  Descends to every soul,
 And heavenly peace with balmy wing
  Shades and bedews the whole.

3 'Tis like the oil divinely sweet
  On Aaron's reverend head,
 The trickling drops perfum'd his feet,
  And o'er his garments spread.

4 'Tis pleasant as the morning dews
  That fall on Sion's hill,
 Where God his mildest glory shews,
  And makes his grace distil.

PSALM CXXXIII. Short Metre.
Communion of Saints; or, Love and Worship in a Family.

1 **B**LEST are the sons of peace,
  Whose hearts and hopes are one;
 Whose kind designs to serve and please
  Through all their actions run.

2 Blest is the pious house
  Where zeal and friendship meet,
 Their songs of praise, their mingled vows
  Make their communion sweet.

3 Thus when on Aaron's head
  They pour'd the rich perfume,
 The oil throughout his raiment spread,
  And pleasure fill'd the room.

4 Thus on the heavenly hills
  The saints are blest above,
 Where joy like morning dew distils,
  And all the air is love.

PSALM CXXXIII. As the 122d Psalm.
The Blessings of Friendship.

1 **H**OW pleasant 'tis to see
  Kindred and friends agree,
 Each in his proper station move,
  And each fulfil his part.

With sympathising heart,
In all the cares of life and love.

2 'Tis like an ointment shed
   On Aaron's sacred head,
Divinely rich, divinely sweet;
   The oil thro' all the room
   Diffus'd a choice perfume,
Ran through his robes, and bleft his feet.

3 Like fruitful showers of rain
   That water all the plain,
Defcending from the neighbouring hills;
   Such streams of pleasure roll
   Thro' every friendly foul,
Where love like heavenly dew diftils.

Repeat the first Stanza to complete the Tune.
PSALM CXXXIV.
Daily and Nightly Devotion.

1 YE, that obey th' immortal King,
   Attend his holy place;
Bow to the glories of his power,
   And blefs his wondrous grace.

2 Lift up your hands by morning-light,
   And fend your fouls on high;
Raife your admiring thoughts by night
   Above the starry sky.

3 The God of Zion cheers our hearts
   With rays of quickening grace;
The God that spread the heavens abroad,
   And rules the swelling seas.

PSALM CXXXV. 1—4, 14, 19—21. *First Part.*
Long Metre.
The Church is God's House and Care.

1 PRAISE ye the Lord exalt his name,
   While in his earthly courts ye wait,
Ye faints that to his house belong,
   Or stand attending at his gate.

2 Praife ye the Lord, the Lord is good;
   To praife his name is fweet employ:
Ifrael he chofe of old, and still
   His church is his peculiar joy.

3 The Lord himself will judge his saints;
  He treats his servants as his friends;
  And when he hears their sore complaints,
  Repents the sorrows that he sends.

4 Through every age the Lord declares
  His name, and breaks th' oppressor's rod;
  He gives his suffering servants rest,
  And will be known th' almighty God.

5 Bless ye the Lord, who taste his love,
  People and priests exault his name:
  Amongst his saints he ever dwells;
  His church is his Jerusalem.

PSALM CXXXV. Ver. 5—12. Second Part.
*The Works of Creation, Providence, Redemption of Israel,
and Destruction of Enemies.*

1 GREAT is the Lord, exalted high
  Above all powers and every throne;
  What e'er he please in earth and sea,
  Or heaven, or hell, his hand hath done.

2 At his command the vapours rise,
  The lightnings flash, the thunders roar;
  He pours the rain, he brings the wind
  And tempest from his airy store.

3 'Twas he those dreadful tokens sent,
  O Egypt, through thy stubborn land;
  When all thy first-born, beasts and men,
  Fell dead by his avenging hand.

4 What mighty nations, mighty kings
  He slew, and their whole country gave
  To Israel, whom his hand redeemed,
  No more to be proud Pharaoh's slave.

5 His power the same, the same his grace,
  That saves us from the hosts of hell;
  And heaven he gives us to possess,
  Whence those apostate angels fell.

PSALM CXXXV. Common Metre.

Praise due to God, not to Idols.

1 AWAKE, ye saints: To praise your King
  Your sweetest passions raise.

Your pious pleasure, while you sing,
  Increasing with the praise.

2 Great is the Lord, and works unknown
    Are his divine employ:
  But still his saints are near his throne,
    His treasure and his joy.

3 Heaven, earth, and sea confess his hand;
    He bids the vapours rise;
  Lightning and storm at his command
    Sweep through the sounding skies.

4 All power that gods or kings have claim'd
    Is found with him alone;
  But heathen gods should ne'er be nam'd
    Where our Jehovah's known.

5 Which of the stocks and stones they trust
    Can give them showers of rain?
  In vain they worship glittering dust,
    And pray to gold in vain.

6 [Their gods have tongues that speechless prove,
    Such as their makers gave:
  Their feet were never form'd to move,
    Nor hands have power to save.

7 Blind are their eyes, their ears are deaf,
    Nor hear when mortals pray;
  Mortals that wait for their relief,
    Are blind and deaf as they.]

8 Ye nations, know the living God,
    Serve him with faith and fear;
  He makes the churches his abode,
    And claims your honours there.

PSALM CXXXVI. Common Metre.

God's Wonders of Creation, Providence, Redemption of Israel, and Salvation of his People.

1 GIVE thanks to God, the sovereign Lord;
    His mercies still endure,
  And be the King of kings ador'd,
    His truth is ever sure.

2 What wonders hath his wisdom done!
    How mighty is his hand!

Heaven, earth and sea he fram'd alone :
   How wide is his command!

3 The sun supplies the day with light:
   How bright his counsels shine!
  The moon and stars adorn the night:
   His works are all divine!

4 [He struck the sons of Egypt dead:
   How dreadful is his rod!
  And thence with joy his people led:
   How Gracious is our God.

5 He cleft the swelling sea in two,
   His arm is great in might:
  And gave the tribes a passage through;
   His power and grace unite.

6 But Pharaoh's army there he drown'd:
   How glorious are his ways!
  And brought his saints through desert ground:
   Eternal be his praise.

7 Great monarchs fell beneath his hand;
   Victorious is his sword:
  While Israel took the promis'd land
   And faithful is his word.]

8 He saw the nations dead in sin;
   He felt his pity move:
  How sad the state the world was in!
   How boundless was his love!

9 He sent to save us from our woe;
   His goodness never fails;
  From death and hell, and every foe;
   And still his grace prevails.

10 Give thanks to God the heavenly King;
   His mercies still endure;
  Let the whole earth his praises sing;
   His truth is ever sure.

PSALM CXXXVI. *As the 148th Psalm.*

GIVE thanks to God most high,
   The universal Lord:
The sovereign King of kings:
   And be his grace ador'd.

His power and grace
Are still the same;
And let his name
Have endless praise.

2 How mighty is his hand!
What wonders hath he done!
He form'd the earth and seas,
And spread the heavens alone.
Thy mercy, Lord,
Shall still endure;
And ever sure
Abides thy word.

3 His wisdom fram'd the sun
To crown the day with light;
The moon and twinkling stars
To cheer the darksome night.
His power and grace
Are still the same;
And let his name
Have endless praise.

4 [He smote the first-born sons,
The flower of Egypt, dead:
And thence his chosen tribes
With joy and glory led.
Thy mercy, Lord,
Shall still endure;
And ever sure
Abides thy word.

5 His power and lifted rod
Cleft the red-sea in two;
And for his people made
A wondrous passage through.
His power and grace
Are still the same;
And let his name
Have endless praise.

6 But cruel Pharaoh there
With all his host he drown'd;
And brought his Israel safe
Through a long desert ground
Thy mercy, Lord,
Shall still endure;
And ever sure

PSALM CXXXVI.
PAUSE.

7 The kings of Canaan fell
 Beneath his dreadful hand;
 While his own servants took
 Possession of their land.
   His power and grace
   Are still the same;
   And let his name
   Have endless praise.]

8 He saw the nations lie
 All perishing in sin,
 And pity'd the sad state
 The ruin'd world was in.
   Thy mercy, Lord,
   Shall still endure;
   And ever sure
   Abides thy word.

9 He sent his only Son
 To save us from our woe,
 From satan, sin and death,
 And every hurtful foe.
   His power and grace
   Are still the same;
   And let his name
   Have endless praise.

10 Give thanks aloud to God,
 To God the heavenly king:
 And let the spacious earth
 His works and glories sing,
   Thy mercy, Lord,
   Shall still endure;
   And ever sure
   Abides thy word,

PSALM CXXXVI. *Abridged.* Long Metre.

1 GIVE to our God immortal praise;
 Mercy and truth are all his ways;
 Wonders of grace to God belong
 Repeat his mercies in your song.

2 Give to the Lord of lords renown,
 The King of kings with glory crown;
 His mercies ever shall endure,
 When lords and kings are known no more.

3 He built the earth, he spread the sky,
   And fix'd the starry lights on high:
   Wonders of grace to God belong
   Repeat his mercies in your song.

4 He fills the sun with morning light,
   He bids the moon direct the night:
   His mercies ever shall endure,
   When suns and moons shall shine no more.

5 The Jews he freed from Pharaoh's hand,
   And brought them to the promis'd land:
   Wonders of grace to God belong
   Repeat his mercies in your song.

6 He saw the Gentiles dead in sin,
   And felt his pity move within:
   His mercies ever shall endure
   When death and sin shall reign no more.

7 He sent his Son with power to save
   From guilt, and darkness, and the grave:
   Wonders of grace to God belong
   Repeat his mercies in your song.

8 Thro' this vain world he guides our feet,
   And leads us to his heavenly seat:
   His mercies ever shall endure
   When this vain world shall be no more.

PSALM CXXXVII.
The Babylonian Captivity.

1 ALONG the banks where Babel's current flows,
   Our captive bands in deep despondence stray'd,
While Zion's fall in sad remembrance rose,
   Her friends, her children mingled with the dead.

2 The tuneless harp, that once with joy we strung,
   When praise employ'd and mirth inspir'd the lay,
In mournful silence on the willows hung;
   And growing grief prolong'd the tedious day.

3 The barbarous tyrants, to increase the woe,
   With taunting smiles a song of Zion claim;
Bid sacred praise in strains melodious flow,
   While they blaspheme the great Jehovah's name.

4 But how, in heathen chains and lands unknown,
   Shall Israel's sons, a song of Zion raise?
O hapless Salem, God's terrestial throne,
   Thou land of glory, sacred mount of praise.

5 If e'er my memory lose thy lovely name,
    If my cold heart neglect my kindred race,
Let dire destructions seize this guilty frame;
    My hand shall perish and my voice shall cease.

6 Yet shall the Lord, who hears when Zion calls,
    O'ertake her foes with terror and dismay,
His arm avenge her desolated walls,
    And raise her children to eternal day.

PSALM CXXXVIII.
Restoring and Preserving Grace.

1 WITH all my powers of heart and tongue
    I'll praise my Maker in my song;
Angels shall hear the notes I raise,
Approve the song and join the praise.

2 [Angels that make thy church their care
Shall witness my devotions there,
While holy zeal directs my eyes
To thy fair temple in the skies.]

3 I'll sing thy truth and mercy, Lord,
I'll sing the wonders of thy word;
Not all the works and names below
So much thy power and glory show.

4 To God I cry'd when troubles rose;
He heard me, and subdu'd my foes:
He did my rising fears controul,
And strength diffus'd through all my soul.

5 The God of heaven maintains his state,
Frowns on the proud, and scorns the great;
But from his throne descends to bless
The humble souls that trust his grace.

6 Amidst a thousand snares I stand
Upheld and guarded by thy hand:
Thy words my fainting soul revive,
And keep my dying faith alive.

7 Grace will complete what grace begins,
To save from sorrows or from sins,
The work that wisdom undertakes,
Eternal mercy ne'er forsakes.

PSALM CXXXIX. First Part. Long Metre.
The all-seeing God.

1 LORD, thou hast search'd and seen me thro';
 Thine eye commands with piercing view
My rising and my resting hours,
My heart and flesh with all their powers.

2 My thoughts, before they are my own,
Are to my God distinctly known;
He knows the words I mean to speak
Ere from my opening lips they break.

3 Within thy circling power I stand,
On every side I find thy hand;
Awake, asleep, at home, abroad,
I am surrounded still with God.

4 Amazing knowledge, vast and great!
What large extent! what lofty height!
My soul with all the powers I boast,
Is in the boundless prospect lost.

5 *Oh may these thoughts possess my breast,*
Where-e'er I rove where-e'er I rest;
Nor let my weaker passions dare
Consent to sin, for God is their.

PAUSE I.

6 Could I so false, so faithless prove,
To quit thy service and thy love,
Where, Lord, could I thy presence shun,
Or from thy dreadful glory run?

7 If up to heaven I take my flight,
'Tis there thou dwell'st enthron'd in light;
Or dive to hell, there vengeance reigns,
And Satan groans beneath thy chains.

8 If mounted on a morning ray
I fly beyond the Western sea,
Thy swifter hand would first arrive,
And there arrest thy fugitive.

9 Or should I try to shun thy sight
Beneath the spreading veil of night,
One glance of thine, one piercing ray
Would kindle darkness into day.

10 Oh may these thoughts possess my breast,
　Where-e'er I rove, where-e'er I rest;
　Nor let my weaker passions dare
　Consent to sin, for God is there.

PAUSE II.

11. The veil of night is no disguise,
　No screen from thy All-searching eyes;
　Thy hand can seize thy foes as soon
　Through midnight shades as blazing noon.

12 Midnight and noon in this agree,
　Great God, they'er both alike to thee,
　Not death can hide what God will spy,
　And hell lies naked to his eye.

13 Oh may these thoughts possess my breast,
　Where-e'er I rove, where-e'er I rest!
　Nor let my weaker passions dare
　Consent to sin, for God is there.

PSALM CXXXIX. Second Part. Long Metre.

The wonderful Formation of man.

1 'TWAS from thy hand, my God, I came,
　　A work of such a curious frame;
　In me thy fearful wonders shine.
　And each proclaim thy skill divine.

2 Thine eyes could all my limbs survey,
　Which yet in dark confusion lay:
　Thou saweth the daily growth they took,
　Form'd by the model of thy book.

3 By thee my growing parts were nam'd
　And what thy sovereign counsels fram'd
　The breathing lungs, the beating heart,
　Was copy'd with unerring art.

4 At last to shew my Maker's name,
　God stamp'd his image on my frame,
　And in some unknown moment join'd,
　The finish'd members of the mind.

5 There the young seeds of thought began
　And all the passions of the man,
　Great God, our infant nature pays
　Immortal tribute to thy praise.

PAUSE.

6 Lord, since in my advancing age
I've acted on life's busy stage,
Thy thoughts of love to me surmount
My power of numbers to recount.

7 I could survey the ocean o'er,
And count each sand that makes the shore,
Before my swiftest thoughts could trace
The numerous wonders of thy grace.

8 These on my heart are still imprest,
With these I give my eyes to rest;
And at my waking hour I find
God and his love possess my mind.

PSALM CXXXIX. *Third Part.* Long Metre.
Sincerity profest, and Grace tried; or, the Heartsearching God.

1 MY God, what inward grief I feel,
When impious men transgress thy will!
I mourn to hear their lips profane,
Take thy tremendous name in vain.

2 Does not my soul detest and hate
The sons of malice and deceit?
Those that oppose thy laws and thee,
I count for enemies to me.

3 Lord, search my soul, try every thought,
Though my own heart accuse me not,
Of walking in a false disguise,
I beg the trial of thine eyes.

4 Doth secret mischief lurk within?
Do I indulge some unknown sin?
Oh turn my feet whene'er I stray,
And lead me in thy perfect way.

PSALM CXXXIX. *First Part.* Common Metre.
God is every where.

1 IN all my vast concerns with thee,
In vain my soul would try
To shun thy presence, Lord, or flee
The notice of thine eye.

PSALM CXXXIX.

2 Thy all-surrounding sight surveys
   My rising and my rest,
My public walks, my private ways,
   And secrets of my breast.

3 My thoughts lie open to the Lord
   Before they're form'd within;
And ere my lips pronounce the word,
   He knows the sense I mean.

4 Oh wondrous knowledge, deep and high;
   Where can a creature hide?
Within thy circling arms I lie,
   Enclos'd on every side.

5 So let thy grace surround me still,
   And like a bulwark prove,
To guard my soul from every ill,
   Secur'd by sovereign love.

         PAUSE.
6 Lord, where shall guilty souls retire
   Forgotten and unknown?
In hell they meet thy dreadful fire,
   In heaven thy glorious throne.

7 Should I suppress my vital breath
   To 'scape the wrath divine,
Thy voice would break the bars of death,
   And make the grave resign.

8 If wing'd with beams of morning-light
   I fly beyond the west,
Thy hand, which must support my flight,
   Would soon betray my rest.

9 If o'er my sins I think to draw
   The curtains of the night,
The flaming eyes that guard thy law
   Would turn the shades to light.

10 The beams of noon, the midnight-hour
   Are both alike to thee:
Oh may I ne'er provoke that power
   From which I cannot flee

PSALM CXXXIX *Second Part.* Common Metre.
   The Wisdom of God in the formation of Man.

WHEN I with pleasing wonder stand,
   And all my frame survey,

Lord, tis thy work; I own thy hand
  Thus built my humble clay.

2 Thy hand my heart and reins poffeft
  Where unborn nature grew;
Thy wifdom all my features trac'd,
  And all my members drew.

3 Thine eye with niceft care furvey'd
  The growth of every part;
Till the whole fcheme thy thoughts had laid
  Was copy'd by thy art.

4 Heaven, earth, and fea, and fire and wind
  Shew me thy wondrous fkill;
But I review myfelf, and find
  Diviner wonders ftill.

5 Thy awful glories round me fhine,
  My flefh proclaims thy praife;
Lord, to thy works of nature join
  Thy miracles of grace.

PSALM CXXXIX. 14, 17, 18. *Third Part.*
Common Metre.
The mercies of God innumerable.
An Evening Pfalm.

1 LORD, when I count thy mercies o'er,
    They ftrike me with furprife;
  Not all the fands that fpread the fhore,
    To equal numbers rife.

2 My flefh with fear and wonder ftands,
    The product of thy fkill,
  And hourly bleffings from thy hands
    Thy thoughts of love reveal.

3 Thefe on my heart by night I keep;
    How kind, how dear to me!
  Oh may the hour that ends my fleep
    Still find my thoughts with thee.

PSALM CXL. Common Metre.

1 PROTECT us, Lord, from fatal harm;
    Behold our rifing woes;
  We truft alone thy powerful arm,
    To fcatter all our foes.

2 Their tongue is like a poison'd dart,
  Their thoughts are full of guile,
While rage and carnage swell their heart,
  They wear a peaceful smile.

3 O God of grace, thy guardian care,
  When foes without invade,
Or spread within a deeper snare,
  Supplies our constant aid.

4 Let falsehood flee before thy face,
  Thy heavenly truth extend,
All nations taste thy heavenly grace,
  And all delusion end.

5 With daily bread the poor supply,
  The cause of justice plead,
And be thy church exalted high,
  With Christ the glorious head.

PSALM CXLI. Ver. 2, 3, 4 5.

Watchfulness and Brotherly Love.
A Morning or Evening Psalm.

1 MY God, accept my early vows,
    Like morning incense in thine house,
  And let thy nightly worship rise
  Sweet as the evening sacrifice.

2 Watch o'er my lips, and guard them, Lord,
  From every rash and heedless word;
  Nor let my feet incline to tread
  The guilty path where sinners lead.

3 Oh may the righteous, when I stray,
  Smite and reprove my wandering way!
  Their gentle words, like ointment shed,
  Shall never bruise, but cheer my head.

4 When I behold them prest with grief,
  I'll cry to heaven for their relief;
  And by my warm petitions prove
  How much I prize their faithful love.

PSALM CXLII.
God is the Hope of the Helpless.

1 TO God I made my sorrows known,
    From God I sought relief;

  In long complaints before his throne
   I pour'd out all my grief.

2 My soul was overwhelm'd with woes,
  My heart began to break;
 My God, who all my burdens knows,
  Beholds the way I take.

3 On every side I cast mine eye,
  And found my helper gone,
 While friends and strangers past me by
  Neglected and unknown.

4 Then did I raise a louder cry,
  And call'd thy mercy near,
 " Thou art my portion when I die,
 " Be thou my refuge here."

5 Lord, I am brought exceeding low,
  Now let thine ear attend,
 And make my foes who vex me know
  I'ye an almighty Friend.

6 From my sad prison set me free,
  Then shall I praise thy name,
 And holy men shal join with me,
  Thy kindness to proclaim.

PSALM CXLIII.

Complaint of heavy Afflictions in Mind and Body.

1 MY righteous Judge, my gracious God,
  Hear when I spread my hands abroad,
 And cry for succour from thy throne,
 Oh make thy truth and mercy known.

2 Let judgment not against me pass;
 Behold thy servant pleads thy grace;
 Should justice call us to thy bar,
 No man alive is guiltless there.

3 Look down in pity, Lord, and see
 The mighty woes that burthen me;
 Down to the dust my life is brought,
 Like one long bury'd and forgot.

4 I dwell in darkness and unseen,
  My heart is desolate within,

My thoughts in musing silence trace
The antient wonders of thy grace.

5 Thence I derive a glimpse of hope
To bear my sinking spirits up;
I stretch my hands to God again,
And thirst like parched lands for rain.

6 For thee I thirst, I pray, I mourn;
When will thy smiling face return?
Shall all my joys on earth remove,
And God forever hide his love?

7 My God, thy long delay to save,
Will sink thy prisoner to the grave;
My heart grows faint, and dim mine eye;
Make haste to help before I die.

8 The night is witness to my tears,
Distressing pains, distressing fears;
Oh might I hear thy morning voice,
How would my wearied powers rejoice!

9 In thee I trust, to thee I sigh,
And lift my weary soul on high,
For thee sit waiting all the day,
And wear the tiresome hours away.

10 Break off my fetters, Lord, and show
The path in which my feet should go:
If snares and foes beset the road,
I flee to hide me near my God.

11 Teach me to do thy holy will,
And lead me to thy heavenly hill:
Let the good spirit of thy love
Conduct me to thy courts above.

12 Then shall my soul no more complain,
The tempter then shall rage in vain;
And flesh that was my foe before,
Shall never vex my spirit more.

PSALM CXLIV. *First Part.* Ver. 1 2.
Assistance and Victory in the spiritual Warfare.

1 FOREVER blessed be the Lord,
My Saviour and my shield;

Y

He sends his spirit with his word,
   To arm me for the field.

2 When sin and hell their force unite,
   He makes my soul his care,
Instructs me in the heavenly fight,
   And guard me through the war.

3 A friend and helper so divine
   My fainting hope shall raise;
He makes the glorious victory mine,
   And his shall be the praise.

PSALM CXLIV. *Second Part.* Ver. 3, 4, 5, 6.

The Vanity of Man, and Condescention of God.

1 LORD, what is man, poor feeble man,
   Born of the earth at first?
His life a shadow, light and vain,
   Still hasting to the dust.

2 Oh what is feeble dying man,
   Or all his sinful race,
That God should make it his concern
   To visit him with grace?

3 That God who darts his lightnings down,
   Who shakes the worlds above,
What terrors wait his awful frown,
   How wondrous is his love?

PSALM CXLIV. *Third Part.* Ver. 12—15

Grace above Riches; or, the happy Nation.

1 HAPPY the city, where their sons
   Like pillars round a palace set,
And daughters bright as polish'd stones
   Give strength and beauty to the state.

2 Happy the land in culture dress'd,
   Whose flocks and corn have large increase;
Where men securely work or rest,
   Nor sons of plunder break their peace.

3 Happy the nation thus endow'd,
   But more divinely blest are those
On whom the all-sufficient God
   Himself with all his grace bestows.

PSALM CXLV. Long Metre.
The Greatness of God.

1 MY God, my King, thy various praise,
   Shall fill the remnant of my days;
   Thy grace employ my humble tongue
   Till death and glory raise the song.

2 The wing of every hour shall bear
   Some thankful tribute to thine ear;
   And every setting sun shall see
   New works of duty done for thee.

3 Thy truth and justice I'll proclaim;
   Thy bounty flows, an endless stream;
   Thy mercy swift; thine anger slow,
   But dreadful to the stubborn foe.

4 Thy works with sovereign glory shine;
   And speak thy Majesty divine;
   Let every realm with joy proclaim
   The sound and honour of thy name.

5 Let distant times and nations raise
   The long succession of thy praise:
   And unborn ages make my song
   The joy and triumph of their tongue.

6 But who can speak thy wondrous deeds!
   Thy greatness all our thoughts exceeds;
   Vast and unsearchable thy ways,
   Vast and immortal be thy praise.

PSALM CXLV. 1—7, 11—13. *First Part.*
The Greatness of God.

1 LONG as I live I'll bless thy name,
     My King, my God of love;
   My work and joy shall be the same,
     In the bright world above.

2 Great is the Lord, his power unknown,
     And let his praise be great;
   I'll sing the honours of thy throne,
     Thy works of grace repeat.

3 Thy grace shall dwell upon my tongue;
     And while my lips rejoice,

The men that hear my sacred song
 Shall join their cheerful voice.

4 Fathers to sons shall teach thy name,
 And children learn thy ways;
Ages to come thy truth proclaim,
 And nations sound thy praise.

5 Thy glorious deeds of antient date
 Shall through the world be known;
Thine arm of power, thy heavenly state
 With public splendor shown.

6 The world is manag'd by thy hands,
 Thy saints are rul'd by love;
And thine eternal kingdom stands,
 Tho' rocks and hills remove.

PSALM CXLV. Second Part. Ver. 7, &c.

The Goodness of God.

1 SWEET is the memory of thy grace,
 My God, my heavenly King:
Let age to age thy righteousness
 In sounds of glory sing.

2 God reigns on high, but ne'er confines
 His goodness to the skies;
Through the whole earth his bounty shines,
 And every want supplies.

3 With longing eyes thy creatures wait
 On thee for daily food,
Thy liberal hand provides their meat,
 And fills their mouths with good.

4 How kind are thy compassions Lord!
 How slow thine anger moves!
But soon he sends his pardoning word
 To cheer the souls he loves.

5 Creatures with all their endless race
 Thy power and praise proclaim;
But saints that taste thy richer grace
 Delight to bless thy name.

PSALM CXLV. 14, 17, &c. Third Part.
Mercy to Sufferers; or, God hearing Prayer.

1 LET every tongue thy goodness speak,
  Thou sovereign Lord of all;
Thy strengthening hands uphold the weak,
  And raise the poor that fall.

2 When sorrow bows the spirit down,
  Or virtue lies distrest
Beneath some proud oppressor's frown,
  Thou giv'st the mourners rest.

3 The Lord supports our sinking days
  And guides our giddy youth;
Holy and just are all his ways,
  And all his words are truth.

4 He knows the pain his servants feel,
  He hears his children cry,
And their best wishes to fulfil.
  His grace is ever nigh.

5 His mercy never shall remove
  From men of heart sincere;
He saves the souls, whose humble love
  Is join'd with holy fear.

6 [His stubborn foes his sword shall slay,
  And pierce their hearts with pain;
But none that serve the Lord shall say,
  " They sought the Lord in vain."]

7 [My lips shall dwell upon his praise,
  And spread his fame abroad;
Let all the sons of Adam raise
  The honours of their God.]

PSALM CXLVI. Long Metre.
Praise to God for his Goodness and Truth.

1 PRAISE ye the Lord, my heart shall join
  In works so pleasant, so divine;
Now while the flesh is mine abode,
And when my soul ascends to God.

2 Praise shall employ my noblest powers,
  While immortality endures;
My days of praise shall ne'er be past,
While life and thought and being last.

3 Why should I make a man my trust?
 Princes must die and turn to dust:
 Their breath departs, their pomp and power,
 And thoughts all vanish in an hour.

4 Happy the man, whose hopes rely
 On Israel's God: He made the sky,
 And earth, and seas, with all their train,
 And none shall find his promise vain.

5 His truth forever stands secure:
 He saves th' opprest, he feeds the poor;
 He sends the labouring conscience peace,
 And grants the prisoner sweet release.

6 The Lord to sight restores the blind;
 The Lord supports the sinking mind;
 He helps the stranger in distress,
 The widow and the fatherless.

7 He loves the saints, he knows them well,
 But turns the wicked down to hell:
 Thy God, O Zion, ever reigns;
 Praise him in everlasting strains.

PSALM CXLVI. As the 113th Psalm.
Praise to God for his Goodness and Truth.

1 I'LL praise my Maker with my breath;
 And when my voice is lost in death
  Praise shall employ my nobler powers:
 My days of praise shall ne'er be past,
 While life and thought and being last,
  On immortallity endures.

2 Why should I make a man my trust?
 Princes must die and turn to dust;
  Vain is the help of flesh and blood;
 Their breath departs, their pomp and power
 And thoughts all vanish in an hour,
  Nor can they make their promise good.

3 Happy the man, whose hopes rely.
 On Israel's God; he made the sky,
  And earth and seas with all their train;
 His truth forever stands secure:
 He saves th' opprest, he feeds the poor,
  And none shall find his promise vain.

4 The Lord hath eyes to give the blind :
The Lord supports the sinking mind;
   He sends the labouring conscience peace
He helps the stranger in distress,
The widow and the fatherless,
   And grants the prisoner sweet release.

5 He loves his saints, he knows them well,
But turns the wicked down to hell ;
   Thy God, O Zion ever reigns ;
Let every tongue, let every age,
In this exalted work engage :
   Praise him in everlasting strains.

6 I'll praise him while he lends me breath,
And when my voice is lost in death
   Praise shall employ my nobler powers ;
My days of praise shall ne'er be past,
While life and thought and being last,
   Or immortality endures.

PSALM CXLVII. *First Part.*
The divine Nature, Providence, and Grace.

1 PRAISE ye the Lord; 'tis good to raise
   Our hearts and voices in his praise :
His nature and his works invite
To make this duty our delight.

2 The Lord builds up Jerusalem,
And gathers nations to his name :
His mercy melts the stubborn soul,
And makes the broken spirit whole.

3 He form'd the stars, those heavenly flames,
He counts their numbers, calls their names,
His sovereign wisdom knows no bound,
A deep where all our thoughts are drown'd.

4 Great is our Lord, and great his might ;
And all his glories infinite :
He crowns the meek, rewards the just.
And treads the wicked to the dust.

PAUSE.

5 Sing to the Lord, exalt him high,
Who spreads his clouds around the sky ;
There he prepares the fruitful rain,
Nor lets the drops descend in vain.

6 He makes the grafs the hills adorn,
   And clothes the fmiling fields with corn;
   The beafts with food his hands fupply,
   And feeds the ravens when they cry.

7 What is the creature's fkill or force?
   The vigorous man, the warlike horfe,
   The fprightly wit, the active limb.
   All are too mean delights for him.

8 But faints are lovely in his fight:
   He views his children with delight:
   He fees their hope, he knows their fear,
   And finds and loves his image there.

PSALM CXLVII. Second Part.

Summer and Winter.

1 LET Zion praife the mighty God,
   And make his honours known abroad;
   For fweet the joy, our fongs to raife,
   And glorious is the work of praife.

2 Our children live fecure and bleft;
   Our fhores have peace, our cities reft;
   He feeds our fons with fineft wheat,
   And adds his blefling to their meat.

3 The changing feafons he ordains,
   The early and the latter rains;
   His flakes of fnow like wool he fends,
   And thus the fpringing corn defcends.

4 With hoary froft he ftrews the ground:
   His hail defcends with dreadful found:
   His icy hands the rivers hold,
   And terror arms his wintry cold.

5 He bids the warmer breezes blow;
   The ice diffolves, the waters flow;
   But he hath nobler works and ways
   To call his people to his praife.

6 Thro' all our realm his laws are fhown;
   His gofpel through the nation known;
   He hath not thus reveal'd his word
   To every land: praife ye the Lord.

PSALM CXLVII. 7—9. 13—18. Common Metre.
The Seasons of the Year.

1 WITH songs and honours sounding loud,
    Address the Lord on high;
Over the heavens he spreads his cloud,
    And waters veil the sky.

2 He sends his showers of blessings down
    To cheer the plains below;
He makes the grass the mountains crown;
    And corn in valleys grow.

3 He gives the grazing ox his meat,
    He hears the ravens cry;
But man who tastes his finest wheat
    Should raise his honours high.

4 His steady counsels change the face
    Of the declinging year;
He bids the sun cut short his race,
    And wintry days appear.

5 His hoary frost, his fleecy snow
    Descend and clothe the ground;
The liquid streams forbear to flow,
    In icy fetters bound.

6 When from his dreadful stores on high
    He pours the sounding hail,
The wretch that dares his God defy
    Shall find his courage fail.

7 He sends his word and melts the snow,
    The fields no longer mourn;
He calls the warmer gales to blow,
    And bids the spring return.

8 The changing wind, the flying cloud,
    Obey his mighty word:
With songs and honours sounding loud
    Praise ye the sovereign Lord.

PSALM CXLVIII. Proper Metre.
Praise to God for all Creatures.

1 YE tribes of Adam, join
    With heaven, and earth, and seas,
And offer notes divine
    To your Creator's praise.

  Ye holy throng
  Of angels bright,
  In worlds of light
  Begin the song.

2 Thou sun with dazzling rays,
 And moon that rule the night,
 Shine to your Maker's praise,
 With stars of twinkling light.
  His power declares,
  Ye floods on high
  And clouds that fly
  In empty air.

3 The shining worlds above
 In glorious order stand,
 Or in swift courses move,
 By his supreme command:
  He spake the word,
  And all their frame
  From nothing came
  To praise the Lord.

4 He mov'd their mighty wheels
 In unknown ages past,
 And each his word fulfils
 While time and nature last.
  In different ways
  His works proclaim
  His wondrous name,
  And speak his praise.

    PAUSE.

5 Let all the earth-born race,
 And monsters of the deep
 The fish that cleave the seas,
 Or in their bosom sleep,
  From sea and shore
  Their tribute pay,
  And still display
  Their Maker's power.

6 Ye vapours, hail and snow,
 Praise ye th' almighty Lord,
 And stormy winds that blow
 To execute his word.

When lightning shine
Or thunders roar,
Let earth adore
His hand divine.

7 Ye mountains near the skies,
With lofty cedars there,
And trees of humbler size
That fruit in plenty bear;
   Beasts wild and tame,
   Birds, flies and worms,
   In various forms
   Exalt his name.

8 Ye kings and judges, fear
The Lord the sovereign King;
And while you rule us here,
His heavenly wonders sing:
   Nor let the dream
   Of power and state
   Make you forget
   His power supreme.

9 Virgins and youths engage
To sound his praise divine,
While infancy and age
Their feeble voices join:
   Wide as he reigns
   His name be sung
   By every tongue
   In endless strains.

10 Let all the nations fear
The God that rules above;
He brings his people near,
And makes them taste his love:
   While earth and sky
   Attempt his praise
   His saints shall raise
   His honours high.

PSALM CXLVIII. *Paraphrased* in Long Metre.
Universal Praise to God.

1 LOUD hallelujahs to the Lord
From distant worlds where creature dwell:
Let heaven begin the solemn word,
And sound it dreadful down to hell.

PSALM CXLVIII.

Note. This Pfalm may be fung to the Tune of the old 112th or 127th Pfalm if thefe two lines be added to every Stanza, (viz.)
Each of his works his name difplays.
But they can ne'er complete the praife.
Otherwife it muft be fung to the ufual Tunes of the Long Metre.

2 The Lord, how abfolute he reigns,
Let every angel bend the knee;
Sing of his love in heavenly ftrains,
And fpeak how fierce his terrors be.

3 High on a throne his glories dwell,
An awful throne of fhining blifs:
Fly through the world, O fun and tell
How dark thy beams compar'd to his.

4 Awake ye tempefts and his fame
In founds of dreadful praife declare;
Let the fweet whifper of his name
Fill every gentler breeze of air.

5 Let clouds, and winds, and waves agree
To join their praife with blazing fire;
Let the firm earth and rolling fea
In this eternal fong confpire.

6 Ye flowery plains, proclaim his fkill;
Ye vallies fink before his eye;
And let his praife from every hill
Rife tuneful to the neighbouring fky.

7 Ye ftubborn oaks, and ftately pines,
Bend your high branches and adore:
Praife him, ye beafts, in different ftrains;
The lamb muft beat, the lion roar.

8 Ye birds, his praife muft be your theme,
Who form'd to fong your tuneful voice;
While the dumb fifh that cut the ftream
In his protecting care rejoice.

9 Mortals, can you refrain your tongue,
When nature all around you fings?
Oh for a fhout from old and young,
From humble fwains and lofty kings?

10 Wide as his vast dominion lies,
   Make the Creator's name be known;
   Loud as his thunder shout his praise,
   And sound it lofty as his throne.

11 Jehovah! 'tis a glorious word!
   Oh may it dwell on every tongue!
   But saints who best have known the Lord
   Are bound to raise the noblest song.

12 Speak of the wonders of that love
   Which Gabriel plays on every chord:
   From all below and all above,
   Loud Hallelujahs to the Lord.

PSALM CXLVIII. Short Metre.
Universal Praise.

1 LET every creature join
     To praise th' eternal God;
   Ye heavenly hosts, the song begin,
     And sound his name abroad.

2 Thou sun with golden beams,
     And moon with paler rays,
   Ye starry lights, ye twinkling flames,
     Shine to your Maker's praise.

3 He built those worlds above,
     And fix'd their wondrous frame;
   By his command they stand or move,
     And ever speak his name.

4 Ye vapours, when ye rise,
     Or fall in showers or snow,
   Ye thunders murmuring round the skies,
     His power and glory show.

5 Wind, hail, and flashing fire,
     Agree to praise the Lord,
   When ye in dreadful storms conspire
     To execute his word.

6 By all his works above
     His honours be exprest;
   But saints that taste his saving love
     Should sing his praises best.

Z

PAUSE I.

7 Let earth and ocean know
    They owe their Maker praise;
Praise him, ye watery worlds below.
    And monsters of the seas.

8 From mountains near the sky
    Let his high praise resound,
From humble shrubs and cedars high,
    And vales and fields around.

9 Ye lions of the wood,
    And tamer beasts that graze,
Ye live upon his daily food,
    And he expects your praise.

10 Ye birds of lofty wing,
    On high his praises bear;
Or sit on flowery boughs and sing
    Your Maker's glory there.

11 Ye reptile myriads join,
    'T' exalt his glorious name,
And flies in beauteous forms that shine,
    His wondrous skill proclaim.

12 By all the earth-born race,
    His honours be exprest,
But saints that know his heavenly grace,
    Should learn to praise him best.

PAUSE II.

13 Monarchs of wide command,
    Praise ye th' eternal King,
Judges, adore that sovereign hand,
    Whence all your honours spring.

14 Let vigorous youth engage
    To sound his praises high;
While growing babes and withering age
    Their feeble voices try.

15 United zeal be shown
    His wondrous fame to raise;
God is the Lord; his name alone
    Deserves our endless praise.

16 Let nature join with art,
    And all pronounce him blest,

But saints that dwell so near his heart
Should sing his praises best.

PSALM CXLIX.

Praise God, all his Saints; or, the Saints judging the World.

1 ALL ye that love the Lord, rejoice,
And let your songs be new;
Amidst the church with cheerful voice
His latter wonders shew.

2 The Jews the people of his grace,
Shall their Redeemer sing;
And Gentile nations join the praise
While Zion owns her king

3 The Lord takes pleasure in the just,
Whom sinners treat with scorn:
The meek that lie dispis'd in dust
Salvation shall adorn.

4 Saints should be joyful in their king
E'en on a dying bed:
And like the souls in glory sing,
For God shall raise the dead.

5 Then his high praise shall fill their tongues,
Their hand shall wield the sword:
And vengeance shall attend their songs,
The vengeance of the Lord.

6 When Christ his judgment-seat ascends,
And bids the world appear.
Thrones are prepar'd for all his friends
Who humbly lov'd him here.

7 Then shall they rule with iron rod
Nations that dar'd rebel:
And join the sentence of their God,
On tyrants doom'd to hell.

8 The royal sinners bound in chains
New triumph shall afford:
Such honour for the saints remains:
Praise ye and love the Lord.

A Song of Praise.

IN God's own house pronounce his praise,
   His grace he there reveals;
To heaven your joy and wonder raise,
   For there his glory dwells.

2 Let all your sacred passions move,
   While you rehearse his deeds;
But the great work of saving love
   Your highest praise exceeds.

3 All that have motion, life and breath,
   Proclaim your Maker blest;
Yet when my voice expires in death,
   My soul shall praise him best.

THE CHRISTIAN DOXOLOGY.

Long Metre.

TO God the Father, God the Son,
   And God the Spirit, three in one,
Be honour, praise, and glory given,
By all on earth, and all in heaven.

Common Metre.

LET God the Father, and the Son,
   And Spirit be ador'd,
Where there are works to make him known,
   Or saints to love the Lord.

Common Metre.
Where the Tune includes two Stanzas.

I.

THE God of mercy be ador'd,
   Who calls our souls from death,
Who saves by his redeeming word,
   And new-creating breath.

II.

To praise the Father, and the Son,
   And Spirit all divine,
The one in three, and three in one,
   Let saints and angels join.

Short Metre.

YE angels round the throne,
　　And saints that dwell below,
Worship the Father, praise the Son,
　　And bless the spirit too.

As the 113th Psalm.

NOW to the great and sacred three,
　　The Father, Son, and Spirit be
Eternal praise and glory given.
Through all the worlds where God is known,
By all the angels near the throne,
　　And all the saints in earth and heaven.

As the 148th Psalm.

TO God the Father's throne
　　Perpetual honours raise,
Glory to God the Son.
To God the Spirit praise:
With all our powers,
Eternal King,
Thy name we sing,
While faith adores.

END OF THE PSALMS.

OR

TABLE to find a Pfalm fuited to particular SUBJECTS or OCCASIONS.

If you find not what Word you feek in this Table feek another of the fame Signification; Or, feek it under fome of the more general Words, fuch as *God, Chrift, Church, Saints, Pfalm, Prayer, Praife, Affliction, Grace, Deliverance, Death*, &c.

ADAM the firft and fecond, their dominion 8, *Afflicted*, Pity to them, 41, 35 fupported, 55, 145, 146. their Prayer, 102, 143. Saints happy 73, 119, 14th *Part*, 94. *Afflictions*, Hope in them 42, 13, 77. Support and Profit 119, 14*th Part*. Inftruction by them 94, 119, 18th *Part*, fanctified 94, 119, 18*th Part*. Courage in them 119, 17*th Part*, removed by Prayer 34, 107. Submiffion to them 123, 131, 39. In mind and body 143. Trying our Grace 66, 119, 17*th Part*, without Rejection 89. Of Saints and Sinners different 94, gentle 103. Moderated 125. very great 102, 143, 77. *Aged* Saint's Reflection and Hope 71. *All-feeing God* 139. *Angels*, Guardian, 34, 91, all fubject to Chrift 89, 97. Praife the Lord 103, prefent in Churches 138. *Appeal* to God againft Perfecutors 7 concerning our Sincerity 139 Humility 131. *Afcenfion* of Chrift 24 68, 47, 110. *Affiftance* from God 144, 133. *Atheifm* practical 14, 36, 12, punifhed 10. *Attributes* of God 36, 111, 145, 147. *Authority* from God 75, 82.

BACKSLIDING Soul in Diftrefs and Defertion 25, reftored 51, pardoned 78, 130. *Bleffing* of God on the Bufinefs and Comforts of Life 117. Bleffings of a Family 128, 133. of a Nation 144, 147. of the Country 65, 147, of a Perfon, 1, 32, 112. *Blood* of Chrift cleanfing from Sin 51, 69. *Book* of Nature and Scripture 19, 19, 4*th Part Brotherly* Love 133. Reproof 141. *Bufinefs* of Life bleft 127.

CARE of God over his Saints 34. *Charity* to the Poor 37, 41, 112. and Juftice 15, 112. mixed with Imprecations 35 *Children* praifing God 8. made Bleffings 127, 128. inftructed 34, 78. *Chrift* the fecond

INDEX.

Adam 8. his All-sufficiency 16, his Ascention 24, 63, 110. the Church's Foundation 118. his Coming, the Signs of it 12. his Condescention and Glorification 8. Covenant made with him 89. first and second coming 96, 97, 98. the true David 33. his Death and Resurrection 22, 16, 69. the eternal Creator, 102, exalted to the Kingdom 2, 21, 8. 72, 110, our Example 109, Faith in his Blood 51. God and Man 89. his Godhead 102. our Hope 4, 51 his Incarnation and Sacrifice 40, the King, and the Church his Spouse 45 his Kingdom among Gentiles 72, 87. 132. his Love to Enemies 109, 35. his Majesty 97, 99. his mediatorial Kingdom 89, 110. his Obedience and Death 69. his personal Glories and Government 45. Praised by Children 8. Priest and King 110. his Resurrection on the Lord's Day 118. our strength and Righteousness 71. his Sufferings and Kingdom 2, 21, 69 his Sufferings for our Salvation 69, his Zeal and Reproaches *ibid*. *Christians* Qualifications 15, 24. Church made of Jews and Gentiles 87. *Church* its Beauty 44, 48, 122. the Birth-place of Saints 87. built on Jesus Christ 118. Delight and Safety in it 27. Destruction of Enemies proceeds from thence 76. gathered and settled 132. of the Gentiles 45. 47. God fights for her 46, 10, 20. God's Presence there 132, 84. God's special Delight 37, 132. God's Garden 92. Going to it 122. the House and Care of God 135 of the Jews and Gentiles 87. its increase 67. Prayer in distress 80. Restored by Prayer 85, 102, 107. is the Safety and Honour of a Nation 48. the Spouse of Christ 45 its Worship and Order 48. *Colonies planted* 107. *Comfort* Holiness and Pardon, 4, 32, 119 11th and 12th *Parts*, and Support in God 94, 16, from antient Providence 77, 143. of Life blest 127, and Pardon 130 *Company* of Saints 16, 109 *Complaint* of Absence from Public Worship 42. of Sickness 6. Desertion 13, Pride. Atheism. Oppression, &c. 10, 12. of Temptation 13. general 102 of Quarrelsome Neighbours 120. of heavy Afflictions in Mind and Body 143. *Compassion* of God 103, 145, 147. *Communion* with Saints 106, 133. *Confession* of our Poverty 16. of Sin, Repentance, and Pardon 32, 51, 33, 130, 143. *Conscience* tender 119, 13*th Part*. its Guilt relieved 33, 32,

51, 130. *Contention* complained of 120. *Converse* with God 119, 2d *Part* 63. *Conversion* and Joy 126, at the Ascention of Christ 110 of Jews and Gentiles 87, 106, 96. *Corruption* of Manners general 11, 12. *Counsel* and Support from God 16, 119. *Courage* in Death 16, 17, 71. in Persecution 119, 17th *Part*. *Covenant* made with Christ 89 of *Grace* unchangeable 89, 106, *Creation* and *Providence* 135. 136, 33, 104, 147, 148. *Creatures* no Trust in them 62, 33. 146. vain, and God all-sufficient 33. *Praising* God 143.

DAILY Devotion 45, 139. *Day* of Humiliation for Disappointments in War 60. *Death* and Resurrection of Christ 16, 69, of Saints and Sinners 17, 37, 49. and Sufferings of Christ 22, 65. Deliverance From it 31. and Pride 49 and the Resurrection 49, 71, 89, Courage in it 16, 17, 23. the Effect of Sin 90. *Defence* in God 3, 121. and Salvation in God 18, 61. *Delaying* Sinners warned 95. *Delight* and Safety in the Church 48, 21, 84. in the Law of God 119, 5th 8th and 18th *Parts*, in God 63, 42, 73, 84, 18. *Deliverance* begun and perfected 85, from *Despair* 18, from deep *Distress* 34, 40. from *Death* 31, 118. from *Oppression* and Falshood 56. from *Persecution* 53, 94. by *Prayer* 34, 40, 15, 126, from *Shipwreck* 107, from *Slander* 31. *Surprising* 126. *Desertion* and Distress of Soul 25, 13, 38 143. *Desire* of Knowledge 119, 9th *Part*. of Holiness 119. 11th *Part*. of Comfort and Deliverance 119. 12th. *Part*. of quickening Grace 119, 16th *Part*. *Desolations*, the Church's Safety in them 46. *Despair* and Hope in Death 17, 49. *Deliverance* from it 18, 130. *Devotion* daily 54, 134, 141. on a sick Bed 39, 6. *Direction* and Pardon 25. and Defence prayed for 5. and Hope 42. *Distress* of Soul 25. relieved 51 130. *Dominion* of Man over the Creatures 8. *Doubts* and fears suppressed 3, 31, 143. *Drunkard* and Glutton 107. *Duty* to God and Man 15, 24. *Dwelling* with God, see Heaven, Church, &c.

EDucation, Religious 34, 78. *Egypt*'s Plagues 105. *End* of Righteous and Wicked 1, 37. *Enemies* overcome 18. prayed for 35, 109. destroyed 12, 76, 43. *Envy* and unbelief cured 37, 49. *Equity* and Wisdom of Providence 9. *Evening* Psalm 4, 139, 141. *Evi-*

dences of Grace, 26. of Sincerity 18, 19, 139. *Evil* Times 12. Neighbours 120. Magistrates 11, 58, 82. *Exaltation* of Christ to the Kingdom, 2, 21, 22, 69, 72, 110. *Examination* 26, 139. *Exhortations* to Peace and Holiness 34.

F*AITH* and Prayer of persecuted Saints 35. in the Blood of Christ 51, 32. in divine Grace and Power 62, 130. *Faithfulness* of God 89, 105, 111, 145, 146, of Man 15, 141. *Falshood*, Blasphemy, &c. 12. and Oppression 12, 56. *Family* Government 101. Love and Worship 133. Blessings 128. *Fears* and Doubts suppressed 3, 34, 31. in the Worship of God 89, 99, of God 119, 13th *Part. Flattery* and deceit complained of 12, 36. *Formal* Worship 50. *Frailty* of Man 89, 90, 144. *Fretfulness* discouraged 37. *Friendship* its Blessings 133. *Funeral* Psalm 89, 90.

G*ENTILES* given to Christ 2, 22, 72. Church 45, 65, 72, 87. Owning the true God 96, 98, 47. *Glorification* of Christ 8, 45, *Glory* of God in our Salvation 69, and Grace promised 84, 97, 89 *Glutton* 78. and Drunkard 107. *God* all in all 127. *All-sufficient* 16, 33. his *Being* Attributes and Providence 36, 65 147. his *Care* of Saints 7, 34. his *Creation* and *Providence* 33, 104. &c. our Defence and Salvation 3, 61, 33, 115. *Eternal* and Sovereign and Holy 93. *Eternal* and *Man* mortal 90, 102. *Faithfulness* 105, 111. 89. *Glorified* and Sinners saved 69. *Goodness* and Mercy 145, 103. *Goodness* and Truth 145. 146. *Governing* Power and Goodness 66. *Great* and Good 144, 68, 145, 147. *Judge* 9, 50, 97. *Kind* to his People 145, 146, his *Majesty* 97, and Condescension 113, 114 *Mercy* and Truth 36, 103, 135, 89, 145. Made *Man* 8. of *Nature* and Grace, 65, his *Perfections* 111, 36, 145, 147. our *Portion* and *Christ* our Hope 4. our *Portion* here and hereafter 73. his *Power* and Majesty 68, 89, 93, 96. *Praised* by Children 8. our *Preserver* 121, 138. present in his *Churches* 84, 46. our *Shepherd* 23. his *Sovereignty* and Goodness to *Man* 8, 113, 144. our *Support* and Comfort 94. *Supreme* Governor 82, 93, 75. His *Vengeance* and Compassion 68, 97, *Unchangable* 89, 111. his *Universal* Dominion 103. his *Wisdom* in his Works 111, 129. *Worthy* of all Praise 145, 146,

150. *Good* Works 15, 24; 112. profit Man, not G d 16, *Goodness* of God 8, 103. 111, 145, 146 *Gospel* its Glory and Succefs 19, 45, 110. Joyful Sound 89, 98. Worship and Order 48. *Government* of Chrift 45. from God 75. *Grace* its Evidences, or Self Examination 26, 139. above Riches 144. without Merit, 16, 32. of Chrift 45, 72. and Providence 33. 36, 135. 136, 147. Preferving and reftoring 138. Truth and Protection 57. Tryed by Affliction 17, 66, 125. and Glory 84, 97. Pardoning 130 *Guilt* of Confcience relieved 38, 32, 51, 130.

HARVEST 65, 126. 147 *Health*, Sicknefs, and Recovery 6, 30, 31. Prayed for 6, 38. 39. *Heart* known to God 139. *Hearing* of Prayer and Salvation 4, 10, 66, 102. *Heaven* of feparate Souls 17, the Saint's Dwelling-place 24. *Holinefs*, Pardon and Comfort 4 Defired 119, 11th *Part. Hope* in Darknefs 13, 77, 143. of Refurrection 16, 71. and Defpair in Death 17, 49. and Prayer 27. for Victory 20. and Direction 42. *Hofanna* of the Children 8. for the Lord's Day 118. *Humiliation* Day 10, 60. *Humility* and Submiffion 131, 139. *Hypocrites* and Hypocrify 12. 50.

IDOLATRY reproved 115, 135. *Jehovah* 68, 83. reigns 93, 96, 97. *Jews* fee Ifrael. *Imprecations* and Charity 35. *Incarnation* 96, 97. 98. and Sacrifice of Chrift 40. *Infants* 139. fee Children. *Inftruction* from God 25. from Scripture 119, 4th and 7th *Parts*. in Piety 34. *Inftructive* Afflictions 94 *Intemperance* punifhed 78. & pardoned 107. *Joy of Converfion* 126. *Ifrael* faved from the Affyrians 76, faved from *Egypt* & brought to *Canaan* 135, 136, 77, 105, 107 Rebellion & Punifhment 78. punifhed and pardoned 106, 107. Travels in the Wildernefs 107, 114 *Judgment* and Mercy 9, 68. Day 1, 50, 96, 97, 98, 149. Seat of God 9. *Juftice* of Providence 9. and Truth towards Men 15. *Juftification* free 32. 130.

KNOWLEDGE defired 19, 119, 9th *Part*.

LAW of God, Delight in it 119. *Liberality* rewarded 41, 112. *Life* and Riches their Vanity 49. fhort and feeble 89, 10, 144. *Longing* after God 63, 42 *Lord's Day* Pfalm 29, 118. Morning 5, 19.

INDEX.

63. *Love* to our Neghbour 15. of Chrift to Sinners 35. of God better than Life 63. of God unchangable 106, 89. to Enemies 109, 35 Brotherly 133. *Luxury* punifhed 78. and pardoned 107.

M*Agefirates* warned 58, 82. Qualifications 101. raifed and depofed 75. *Majefty* of God 68. fee *God* Man his Vanity as mortal 39, 89, 90, 144. Dominion over creatures 8 mortal and Chrift eternal 102. Wonderful Formation, 139. *Marriage* myftical 45. *Mafter* of a family 101. *Melancholy* reproved 42. and Hope 77. removed 126. *Mercies* common and fpecial 68, 103. Spiritual and Temporal 103. Innumerable 139. Everlafting 136. Recorded 107. and Truth of God 55, 103, 89, 136, 145, 146 *Merit* difclaimed 16. *Midnight* Thoughts 63, 139 119, 5th and 6th *Parts*. *Minifters* ordained 131. *Miracles* in the Wildernefs 114. *Morning* Pfalm 3, 141 of a Sabbath 5, 19, 63. *Mortality* of Man 39, 49, 90. and Hope 89. and God's Eternity 90, 102.

N*ATION*'s Safety is the Church 48. Profperity 67, 144. Bleft and punifhed 107. *National* Deliverance 67, 75, 76, 124, 126. Defolations, the Church's Safety and triumph in them 46. *Nature* of Man 139.

O*Bedience* fincere 32, 18, 139. better than Sacrifice 50 *Ole Age*, Death 90. and Refurrection 17, 89.

P*ARDON*, Holinefs and Comfort 4. of Backfliding 78. and Direction 25. and Repentance prayed for 38. and Confeffion 32. of original and actual Sin 51. *Patience* under afflictions 39. under Perfecutions 37, 44. In Darknefs 77, 130, 131. *Peace* and Holinefs encouraged 34. with Men defired 120. *Perfections* of God 111, 145, 147, 36. *Perfecuted* Saints, 35, 44, 74, 80, 83. *Perfecution*, Deliverance from it 7, 53. 94. Courage in it 119, 17th *Part*. *Perfecutors* punifhed 7, 129, 140. Their Folly 14. complained of 35, 44, 74, 80, 83. Deliverance from them 94, 9, 10. *Perfeverance* 138. in Trials 119, 17th *Part*. *Peftilence*, Prefervation in 91. *Piety* Inftructions therein 34. *Pity* to the afflicted 41. fee Charity, God. *Pleading* without repining 39, 123. the Promifes 119. 10th *Part*. *Poor* Charity to them 15, 37, 41, 112. *Portion* of Saints and Sinners 11, 17, 37. *Poverty* confessed 16. *Practical* Atheism 14, 36. *Praise* to God from Children 8, for Creation and Providence 33, 104. to our Creator 100. from all Creatures 148. for Eminent Deliverances 34, 118 General 86, 145, 150, for the Gospel 98. for Health restored 30, 116. for Hearing Prayer 66, 102. to Jesus Christ 45. from all Nations 117. and Prayer public 65. for Protection, Grace and Truth, 57. for Providence and Grace 36, for Rain 65, 147. from the Saints 149, 150. for Temporal Blessings 68, 147. *Prayer* heard 4, 34, 65, 66, in time of War 20. and Hope of Victory 20. Praise public 65. and Hope 27. in Church's Distress 80 Heard and Zion restored 102. and Praise for Deliverance 34. *Preserving* Grace 138. *Preservation* in Public Dangers 46, 91, 112. Daily 121 *Pride* and Atheism, and Oppression punished 10, 12. and Death 49. *Priesthood* of Christ 51, 110. *Princes* vain 91, 146. *Profession* of Sincerity and Repentance, &c. 119, 3d *part* 139. False 50. *Promises* and Threatenings 81. pleaded 119. 10th *part. Prosperity* dangerous 55, 73. *Prosperous* Sinners cursed 37, 49, 73. *Protection*, Truth and Grace 57. by Day and Night 121. *Providence,* its Wisdom and Equity 9, and Creation 33, 115, 136. and Grace 36, 147. and Perfection of God 36. its Mystery unfolded 73. recorded 77, 78, 107. in Air Earth and Sea 35, 65, 89, 104, 107, 147. *Psalm* for Soldiers 18, 60. for old Age 71. for Husbandman 65. for a Funeral 89, 90. for the Lord's Day 92. before Prayer 95. before Sermons *ibid.* for Magistrates 101 for Housholders 101. for Mariners 107. for Gluttons and Drunkards. 107. *Public* Praise for private Mercies 116, 118. for Deliverance 124 Worship attended on 122. Prayer and Praise 65, 84. *Punishment* of Sinners 1, 11, 37.

Q*Ualifications* of a Christian 15, 24. *Quickening* Grace 119, 16th *part.*

R*AIN* from Heaven 135. 65, 147. *Recovery* from Sickness 6, 30, 116. *Relative* Duties 15, 133. *Religion* and Justice 15. in Words and Deed 37. *Religious* Education 34, 78. *Remembrance* of former Deliverances 77, 143. *Repentance,* Confession and Pardon 32. and Faith in the Blood of Christ 51 *Reproach*

INDEX.

removed 31. 37. *Resignation* 39, 123, 131. *Resolutions* holy 119, 15th *part*. *Restoring* Grace 138, 23. *Resurrection* and Death of Christ 2, 16. of the Saints 16, 17, 49, 71. and Death 59, 71, 89. *Reverence* in Worship 89, 99. *Riches* their Vanity 49. compared with Grace 144. *Righteousness* from Christ 71.

Sacrifice 40, 51, 69. Incarnation of Christ 40 *Safety* in public Dangers 91. in God 61, and Delight in the Church 27. *Saints* happy and Sinners cursed, 1, 11, 119, 1st *part*. the best Company 16. characterised 15, 24. dwell in Heaven 15, 24. punished and saved 78, 106. God's care of them 34. Reward at last 50, 92. Patience and World's hatred 37 chastised and Sinners destroyed 94. die, but Christ lives 102. punished and pardoned 106. 107. conducted to Heaven 106, 137. Afflictions moderated 135. judging the World 149. *Salvation* of Saints 10. and Triumph 18. and Defence in God 62. by Christ 69, 85. *Sanctified* Afflictions 119. *last part*, 94. *Satan* Subdued 3, 6, 13. *Scripture* compared with Nature 19, 119, 7th *part*. Instruction from it 119, 4th *part*. Delight in it 119, 5th and 18th *part*. Holiness and Comfort from it 119, 6th *part*. Variety and excellency 119, 8th *part*. *Seasons* of the Year 65, 147. *Seamon's* Song 107. *Secret* Devotion 119, 2d *part*, 34. *Seeking* God 63, 27 *Self-Examination*, or Evidences of Grace 26, 139. *Separate* Souls, Heaven 17. *Sick-Bed* Devotion 6, 38, 39, 116. *Sickness* healed 6, 116. *Signs* of Christ's coming 12, 96, &c. *Sin* of Nature 14. Original and actual, confessed and pardoned 51. Universal 14 *Sincerity* 19, 26, 32, 139. Proved and rewarded 18. professed 119, 3d *part Sins* of Tongue 12, 34, 50. *Slander*, Deliverance from it 31, 120. *Souls* in Separate State 17, 146, 150. *Spirit* given at Christ's Ascension 68. His Teaching desired 119, 9th *part*, 51. *Spiritual* Enemies overcome 3, 18, 144. Blessings and Punishment 31. *Spring* of the Year 65 and Summer 65. 104. and Winter 14. *Storm* and Thunder 29, 135, 148. *Strength*, Repentance and Pardon prayed for 38. of Grace 138 *Submission* 123. 131. to Christ 2. to Sickness 39. *Suffering* and Death of Christ 22 and Kingdom of Christ 2

69 110. *Support* and Counsel from God 16. for the Afflicted and tempted 55. and Comfort in God 94, 119, 14th *part.*

TEmpt*ations* overcome 3, 18. in Sickness 6. *Thanks* public for private Mercies 116, 118, *Threatning,* promises 81. *Thunder* and Storm 19, 135. 136, 148. *Times* evil 11, 12. *Tongues* governed 34, 39. *Trust* in the Creatures vain 62, 146.

VANITY of Man as mortal 39, 89, 144. of Life and Riches 40. *Vengeance* and Compassion 68. against the Enemies of the Church 76, 249. *Vineyard* of God wasted 80. *Unbelief* and Envy cured 37. punished 95. *Unchangeable* God 89, 111. *Vows* paid in the Church 116. of Holiness 119, 15th *part.*

WAR, Prayer in Time of it 20. Disappointments therein 60. Victory 18. Spiritual 18, 144. *Warning* of God to his People 81. *Watchfulness* 19, 141. Over the Tongue 39. *Weather* 65, 107, 135, 147, 148. *Wickedness* of Man 14, 36, 51. *Winter* and Summer 147. *Wisdom* and Equity of Providence 9, of God in his Works 111. *Works* of Creation and Providence 104 147, 48, and Grace 19, 33, 111, 135, 136. Good profit Men not God 16. *World's* Hatred and Saints Patience 37. *Worship* and Order of the Gospel 48. Delight in it 84. with Reverence 89, 99. Daily 55, 134, 141. in a Family 133. Public 63, 84, 122, 132. Absence from it 63. *Wrath* and Mercy from the Judgment-Seat 9.

ZEAL and Prudence 93. *Zion,* itss Citizen 15.

A TABLE to find any PSALM by the first Line of it.

	Page
ALMIGHTY Ruler of the skies	17
Are sinners now so senseless grown	25
Are all the foes of *Sion* fools	98
Among th' assemblies of the great	142
Among the princes, earthly gods	149
Awake, my soul, to sound his praise	104
Awake ye saints; To praise your King	239
Almighty God appear and save	22
Arise, my gracious God	30
And will the God of grace	143
Amidst thy wrath, remember love	69
All ye that love the Lord, rejoice	267
Along the banks where Babel's current flows	249
BLEST is the man who shuns the place	4
Blest are the undefil'd in heart	210
Blest are the sons of peace	237
Blest is the nation where the Lord	58
Blest is the man, whose breast can move	74
Blest are the souls who hear and know	153
Blest is the man, forever blest	56
Bless, O my soul, the living God	179
Behold the morning sun	36
Behold the love, the generous love	63
Behold us Lord, and let our cry	98
Behold, O God, what cruel foes,	140
Behold the sure foundation stone	207
Behold thy waiting servant, Lord	216
Behold the lofty sky	35
Before Jehovah's awful throne	174
CHildren, in years and knowledge young	61
Come, children, learn to fear the Lord	62
Come, sound his praise abroad	167
Come let our voices join to raise	168
Consider all my sorrows, Lord	219
DAVID rejoic'd in God his strength	40
Deep in our hearts let us record	121
EARLY my God, without delay	106
Exalt the Lord our God	173

FAR as thy name is known	84
Father, I bless thy gentle hand	222
Father, I sing thy wondrous grace	121
Firm and unmov'd are they	229
Firm was my health, my day was bright	53
Fools in their hearts believe and say	24
Forever blessed be the Lord	253
Forever shall my song record	151
From age to age exalt his name	190
From all that dwell below the skies	206
From deep distress and troubled thoughts	234
From foes, that round us, rise	103
GIVE thanks to God, he reigns above	189
Give thanks to God most high	241
Give thanks to God the sovereign Lord	240
Give thanks to God, invoke his name	186
Give to our God immortal praise	243
Give to the Lord, ye sons of fame	52
God in his earthly temple lays	149
God is the refuge of his saints	81
God my supporter and my hope	128
God of eternal love	188
God of my childhood, and my youth	125
God of my life, look gently down	71
God of my mercy and my praise	194
Good is the Lord, the heavenly King	113
Great God attend, while *Zion* sings	145
Great God attend to my complaint	109
Great God, how oft did Israel prove	139
Great God, indulge my humble claim	107
Great God, the heaven's well order'd frame	37
Great God, whose universal sway	126
Great is the Lord, exalted high	239
Great is the Lord; his works of might	198
Great is the Lord our God	83
Great shepherd of thine Israel	140
HAD not the God of truth and love	227
Happy is he that fears the Lord	200
Happy the city, where their sons	254
Happy the man, whose cautious feet	5
Hear me, O God, nor hide thy face	176
Hear what the Lord in vision said	153

A TABLE.

Help, Lord, for men of virtue fail	22
He reigns; the Lord, the Saviour reigns	170
He that hath made his refuge God	159
High in the heavens, eternal God	64
How blest the man to whom his God	56
How awful is thy chastening rod	138
How long wilt thou conceal thy face	23
How did my heart rejoice to hear	225
How fast their guilt and sorrows rise	27
How pleasant 'tis to see	237
How pleasant, how divinely fair	144
How pleas'd and blest was I	226
How shall the young secure their hearts	212
JEHOVAH reigns: he dwells in light	163
Jesus shall reign where-e'er the sun	126
Jesus, our Lord, ascend thy throne	196
Judge me, O Lord, and prove my ways	49
Judge me, O God, and plead my cause	76
Judges, who rule the world by laws	102
Just are thy ways and true thy word	33
Joy to the world: the Lord is come	172
If God succed not, all the cost	230
If God to build the house deny	231
I love the Lord: He heard my cries	204
I waited patient for the Lord	72
I will extol thee, Lord, on high	52
I set the Lord before my face,	29
I lift my soul to God	47
I'll speak the honours of my King	79
I'll praise my maker with my breath	258
I'll bless the Lord from day to day	61
In anger, Lord, do not chastise	13
In thee, great God, with songs of praise	40
In haste, O God, attend my call	123
In God's own house pronounce his praise	268
In all my vast concerns with thee	248
In Judah God of old was known	133
Is there ambition in my heart	234
It is the Lord our Saviour's hand	178
LET all the earth their voices raise	169
Let all the heathen writers join	214

A a 2

Let every creature join	255
Let every tongue thy goodness speak	257
Let Zion praise the mighty God	260
Let Zion, and her songs rejoice	177
Let earth, with every isle and sea	171
Let *Sion* in her King rejoice	81
Let sinners take their course	100
Let God arise in all his might	116
Let children hear the mighty deeds	137
Lord, thou hast heard thy servant cry	207
Lord, I esteem thy judgments right	214
Lord, I have made thy word my choice	215
Lord, thou has search'd and seen me thro'	246
Lord, when I count thy mercies o'er	250
Lord, what was man, when made at first	18
Lord, I am thine: but thou wilt prove	30
Lord, thou hast seen my soul sincere	32
Lord, we have heard thy works of old	77
Lord, I am vile, conceiv'd in sin	94
Lord, when thou didst ascend on high	117
Lord, what a thoughtless wretch was I	129
Lord, thou hast call'd thy grace to mind	148
Lord, thou hast scourged our guilty land	104
Lord, I will bless thee all my days	60
Lord, thou wilt hear me when I pray	11
Lord, in the morning thou shalt hear	12
Lord, I can suffer thy rebukes	13
Lord, I would spread my sore distress	95
Lord, If thine eyes survey our faults	158
Lord, what a feeble piece	159
Lord, 'tis a pleasant thing to stand	162
Lord, what is man, poor feeble man	254
Long as I live I'll bless thy name	255
Lord of the worlds above	146
Lo! what a glorious corner-stone	209
Lo! what an entertaining sight	236
Loud hallelujahs to the Lord	263
MAKER and sovereign Lord	6
Mercy and judgment are my song	175
Mine eyes and my desire	48
My trust is in my heavenly friend	14
My shepherd is the living Lord	44

A TABLE.

My shepherd will supply my need	44
My never-ceasing song shall show	151
My soul, how lovely is the place	145
My God, my everlasting hope	123
My Saviour, my almighty Friend	124
My God, permit my tongue	108
My spirit looks to God alone	105
My God, in whom are all the springs	102
My spirit sinks within me, Lord	75
My Saviour and my King	78
My heart rejoices in thy name	54
My God, the steps of pious men	63
My refuge is the God of love	21
My God, how many are my fears	9
My God, accept my early vows	251
My righteous Judge, my gracious God	252
My God, my King thy various praise	255
My God, what inward grief I feel	243
My soul lies cleaving to the dust	221
My God, consider my distress	218
My soul, repeat his praise	181
My soul, thy great Creator praise	183
NO sleep nor slumber to his eyes	236
Not to our names, thou only just and true	203
Not to ourselves, who are but dust	202
Now may the God of power and grace	39
Now from the roaring lion's rage	42
Now let our mournful songs record	43
Now be my heart inspired to sing	79
Now shall my solemn vows be paid	115
Now let our lips with holy fear	120
Now I'm convinc'd, the Lord is kind	127
O God! to whom revenge belongs	165
O all ye nations, praise the Lord	205
O thou whose grace and justice reign	227
O happy man, whose soul is fill'd	231
O Lord, how many are my foes	10
O God of grace and righteousness	11
O Lord, our heavenly King	15
O Lord, our Lord, how wondrous great	16
O blessed souls are they	55
O God of my salvation, hear	150

A TABLE.

O God, my refuge, hear my cries	99
O thou, whose justice reigns on high	101
O thou that hear'st when sinners cry	94
O God of mercy, hear my call	96
Oh that thy statutes every hour	220
Oh happy nation where the Lord	59
Oh bless the Lord, my soul	131
Oh for a shout of sacred joy	82
Oh what a stiff rebellious house	137
Oh that the Lord would guide my ways	217
Oh how I love thy holy law	215
Out of the deeps of long distress	233
Our God, our help in ages past	157
Of justice and of grace I sing	175
PROTECT us, Lord, from fatal harm	250
Preserve me, Lord, in time of need	27
Praise ye the Lord, exalt his name	235
Praise ye the Lord, my heart shall join	257
Praise ye the Lord; 'tis good to raise	259
Praise waits in Sion, Lord, for thee	112
RETURN, O God of love, return	153
Remember Lord, our mortal state	154
Rejoice, ye righteous, in the Lord	57
SWEET is the memory of thy grace	256
Save me, O Lord, from every foe	28
Save me, O God, the swelling floods	118
Shew pity, Lord, O Lord forgive	93
Shine, mighty God, on Sion, shine	115
Soon as I heard my father say	50
Salvation is forever nigh	148
Sing to the Lord aloud	142
Sing, all the nations to the Lord	114
Sing to the Lord, *Jehovah's* name	166
Sing to the Lord, ye distant lands	168
Songs of immortal praise belong	197
Sure there's a righteous God	130
See what a living stone	208
Sweet is the work, my God, my King	162
THRO' every age, eternal God,	156
To God I made my sorrows known	251
To God, the Great, the ever blest	188
To thee, most high and holy God	133

To God I cry'd with mournful voice	134
To thee, O Lord, I raise my cries	51
To thee, O God of truth and love	53
To thine almighty arm we owe	34
To thee, before the dawning light	211
To heaven I lift my waiting eyes	224
To our almighty Maker, God	172
Th' Almighty reigns exalted high	171
The Lord is come; the heavens proclaim	170
The God of glory reigns, he reigns on high	163
The Lord *Jehovah* reigns	164
The God *Jehovah* reigns	173
The Lord, how wondrous are his ways	180
The man is ever blest	5
The heavens declare thy glory, Lord	37
The Lord my shepherd is	45
The earth forever is the Lord's	46
The Lord of glory is my light	50
The wonders, Lord, thy love has wrought	73
The praise of Sion waits for thee	110
The God of our salvation hears	111
'Tis by thy strength the mountains stand	113
The Lord, the Judge his churches warns	88
The Lord, the sovereign sends his summons forth	89
The God of glory sends his summons forth	91
The Lord, the Judge, before his throne	87
The King of saints, how fair his face	80
The Lord, the sovereign King	182
The Lord appears my helper now	205
Thy name, almighty Lord,	205
Thy works of glory, mighty Lord,	192
Thy mercies fill the earth O Lord	215
Teach me the measure of my days	70
Thrice happy man who fears the Lord	199
Thus I resolv'd before the Lord	70
Thus saith the Lord, " your work is vain	72
Thus saith the Lord, " the spacious fields	87
Thus God th' eternal Father spake	195
Thus the great Lord of earth and sea	196
That man is blest who stands in awe	198
This is the day the Lord hath made	203
This spacious earth is all the Lord's	46

Thee will I love, O Lord, my strength	31
'Twas in the watches of the night	107
'Twas for our sake, eternal God	122
'Twas from thy hand, my God, I came	247
Think, mighty God, on feeble man	155
Thou God of Love, thou ever-blest	222
Thou art my portion, O my God	211
VAIN man on foolish pleasures bent	191
Up to the hills I lift mine eyes	223
Up from my youth, may Israel say	232
Upward I lift mine eyes	215
Unshaken as the sacred hill	228
WE bless the Lord, the just the good	118
We love thee, Lord, and we adore	33
When overwhelm'd with grief	105
When Israel sinn'd, the Lord reprov'd	138
When Christ to judgment shall descend	83
When man grows bold in sin	65
When God is nigh, my faith is strong	23
When the great Judge, supreme and just	19
When I with pleasing wonder stand	249
When God, provok'd with daring crimes	193
When pain and anguish seize me, Lord	221
When Israel, freed from Pharaoh's hand	202
When God restor'd our captive state	229
When God reveal'd his gracious name	230
With all my powers of heart and tongue	245
With my whole heart I'll raise my song	18
With songs and honours sounding loud	261
With reverence let the saints appear	152
With earnest longings of the mind	75
Where shall the man be found	48
Where shall we go to seek and find	235
Why should I vex my soul, and fret	66
Why do the wealthy wicked boast	67
Why did the nations join to slay	7
Why did the *Jews* proclaim their rage	8
Why should the haughty hero boast	97
Why should the mighty make their boast	97
Why do the proud insult the poor	86
Why doth the man of riches grow	84
Why doth the Lord depart so far	20

A TABLE.

Why has my God my soul forsook	41
Who shall inhabit in thy hill	25
Who shall ascend thy heavenly place	26
Who will arise and plead my right	165
Will God forever cast us off	131
While I keep silence and conceal	57
While men grow bold in wicked ways	64
Would you behold the works of God	191
What shall I render to my God	205
With my whole heart I've sought thy face	218
YE sons of pride, that hate the just	85
Ye tribes of Adam, join	261
Ye that delight to serve the Lord	200
Ye servants of th' almighty King	201
Ye sons of men, a feeble race	161
Ye nations round the earth, rejoice	174
Ye holy souls in God rejoice	59
Ye that obey th' immortal King	238
Yet (saith the Lord) if *David*'s race	154

HYMNS
AND
SPIRITUAL SONGS.

Hymn I.
A Song to the Lamb that was slain. Rev.

1 BEHOLD the glories of the Lamb,
   Amidst the Father's throne;
 Prepare new honours for his name,
   And songs before unknown.

2 While angels worship at his feet,
   And saints around him throng,
 The church on earth with joy shall meat,
   And join the heavenly song.

3 Eternal Father, who shall look
   Thro' all thy secret will?
 Who but the Son shall take the book,
   And open every seal?

4 He shall accomplish thy decrees,
   And all thy wonders tell:
 Lo! in his sovereign hand, the keys
   Of heaven, and death, and hell.

5 He hath redeem'd our souls with blood,
   Hath broke the prisoner's chain;
 Hath made us kings and priests with God,
   And we with him shall reign.

6 Now, to the Lamb, that once was slain,
   Be endless blessing paid;
 While saints and angels fill his train,
   And glories crown his head.

HYMN II.

The Nativity of Christ. Luke i. 30, &c. ii. 10.

1 BEHOLD, the grace appears!
　　The promise is fulfill'd;
Mary, the wondrous virgin, bears,
　　And Jesus is the child!

2 To bring the glorious news,
　　A heavenly form appears:
He tells the shepherds of their joys,
　　And banishes their fears.

3 *Go humble swains;* said he,
　　To David's city fly;
The promis'd infant, born to-day,
　　Doth in a manger lie.

4 *With looks and hearts serene,*
　　Go, visit Christ, your King;
And strait a flaming troop was seen;
　　The shepherds heard them sing.

5 *Glory to God on high!*
　　And heavenly peace on earth;
Good will to men, to angels joy,
　　At the Redeemer's birth!

6 In worship so divine,
　　Let saints employ their tongues;
With the celestial hosts we join,
　　And loud repeat their songs.

7 *Glory to God on high!*
　　And Heavenly peace on earth,
Good will to men, to angels joy,
　　At our Redeemer's birth.

HYMN III.

Submission to afflictive providences, Job. i. 21.

1 NAKED, as from the earth we came,
　　And rose to life at first,
We to the earth return again,
　　And mingle with our dust.

2 The dear delights we here enjoy,
　　And fondly call our own,
Are but short favours borrow'd now,
　　To be repaid anon.

HYMN IV.

3 'Tis God who lifts our comforts high,
    Or sinks them in the grave;
  He gives, and (blessed be his name!)
    He takes but what he gave.

4 Peace, all our angry passions then!
    Let each rebellious sigh,
  Be silent at his sovereign will,
    And every murmur die.

5 If smiling mercy crown our lives,
    Its praises shall be spread,
  And we'll adore the justice too,
    Which strikes our comforts dead.

HYMN IV.

The invitation of the gospel, Isa. iv. 12, &c.

1 LET every mortal ear attend,
    And every heart rejoice,
  The trumpet of the gospel sounds
    With an inviting voice.

2 Come all ye hungry starving souls,
    Who feed upon the wind,
  And vainly strive with earthly toys,
    To fill th' immortal mind.

3 Eternal wisdom has prepar'd
    A soul-reviving feast,
  And bids your longing appetites
    The rich provision taste.

4 Come, ye who pant for living streams,
    And pine away, and die;
  Here you may quench your raging thirst
    With springs that never dry.

5 Rivers of love and mercy here
    In spreading oceans join;
  Salvation in abundance flows
    Like floods of milk and wine.

6 Great God, the treasures of thy love
    Are everlasting mines,
  Deep our helpless mercies are,
    And boundless as our sins.

HYMN V.

Blessedness of gospel times. Isa. v. 2, 7, &c.

1 HOW beauteous are their feet
   Who stand on Zion's hill,
 Who brings salvation on their tongues,
   And words of peace reveal.

2 How charming is their voice!
   How sweet the tidings are!
 " Zion, behold thy Saviour king,
 " He reigns and triumphs here.

3 How happy are our ears,
   That hear thy joyful sound,
 Which kings and prophets long to know
   And sought, but never found!

4 How blest our ravish'd eyes,
   That see this heavenly light;
 Prophets and kings desir'd it long,
   But dy'd without the sight!

5 The watchmen join their voice,
   And tuneful notes employ;
 Jerusalem breaks forth in songs,
   And deserts learn the joy.

6 The Lord displays his arm
   Through all the earth abroad;
 Let every nation now behold
   Their Saviour and their God.

HYMN VI.

The triumph of Faith, Rom. viii. 33.

1 WHO shall the Lord's elect condemn,
   'Tis God who justifies their souls,
 And mercy, like a mighty stream,
   O'er all their sins divinely rolls.

2 Who shall adjudge the saints to hell?
   'Tis Christ who suffer'd in their stead;
 And, the salvation to fulfil,
   Behold him rising from the dead.

3 He lives! He lives! and sits above,
   Forever interceding there:
 Who shall divide us from his love,
   Or what shall tempt us to despair?

4 Shall persecution, or distress,
Famine, or sword or nakedness?
He who hath lov'd us, bears us through,
And makes us more than conqu'rors too.

5 Faith has an overcoming power,
It triumphs in the dying hour:
Christ is our life, our joy, our hope,
Nor can we sink with such a prop.

6 Not all that men on earth can do,
Nor powers on high, nor powers below,
Shall cause his mercy to remove,
Or wean our hearts from Christ our love.

HYMN VII.
Christ our strength. 2 Cor. XII. 7, 9, 13.

1 OH, let me hear my Saviour say,
 Thy strength be equal to thy day,
Then I'll rejoice in deep distress,
And trust secure his sovereign grace.

2 My weakness shall my glory prove,
That power may aid me from above;
When flesh is weak, my soul is strong,
Be grace my shield and Christ my song.

3 All things I do, all sufferings bear,
While God, my strength is with me here;
But, he withdrawn, temptations reign,
And pains and weakness rise again.

4 So Sampson, when his locks were lost,
First bow'd beneath Philistia's host;
Shook his vain limbs with sore surprise,
Made feeble sight, and lost his eyes.

HYMN VIII.
Hosannah to Christ. Ma. xxi. 9. Luke xix 33.

1 HOSANNA to the royal Son,
 Of David's ancient line
His natures two, his person one,
 Mysterious and divine.

2 The root of David here we find
 And offspring is the same:

  Eternity and time are join'd
   In our Emanual's name.

3 Bleſt he who comes to wretched men
  With peaceful news from heaven!
 Hoſannah in the higheſt ſtrain
  To Chriſt the Lord be given!

4 Let mortals ne'er refuſe to take
  Hoſannah on their tongues,
 Leſt rocks and ſtones ſhould riſe, and break
  Their ſilence into ſongs.

HYMN IX.
Hope of Heaven, by the Reſurrection of Christ.
1ſt Pet. 1, 3, 4, 5.

1 BLEST be the everlaſting God,
  The father of our Lord;
 Be his abounding mercy prais'd,
  His majeſty ador'd.

2 When from the dead he rais'd his Son,
  And call'd him to the ſky,
 He gave our ſouls a lively hope
  That they ſhould never die.

3 What though our ſins have doom'd our fleſh
  A while with duſt to blend,
 Yet as the Saviour riſes firſt,
  His followers ſhall aſcend.

4 There's an inheritance divine
  Reſerv'd againſt that day,
 'Tis uncorrupted, undefil'd,
  And cannot waſte away.

5 Saints by the power of God are kept,
  Till full ſalvation come:
 We walk by faith, as ſtrangers here,
  Till Chriſt ſhall call us home.

HYMN X.
Adoption, 1 John, iii. &c. Gal. vi. 6.

1 BEHOLD, what wondrous grace
  The Father has beſtowed
 On ſinners, of a mortal race,
  To call them—*ſons of God!*

2 'Tis no surprising thing
 That we should be unknown;
The Jewish world knew not their king,
 God's everlasting Son:

3 Nor can it yet appear
 How great we must be made;
But, when we see our Saviour near,
 We shall be like our head.

4 We shall no longer lie
 Like slaves, beneath the throne
Our faith shall Abba Father cry,
 And he the kindred own.

Salvation, Righteousness, and Strength in Christ,
 Isa. xlv. 21—25.

1 JEHOVAH speaks—let Israel hear!
 Let all the earth rejoice and fear;
While God's eternal Son proclaims
His sovereign honours, and his names:

2 " I am the last, and I the first,
 " The Saviour God, and God the just;
 " Look up to me, from distant lands,
 " Light, life, and heaven, are in my hands.

3 " I by my holy name have sworn,
 " Nor shall the word in vain return!
 " To me, shall all things bend the knee,
 " And every tongue shall swear to me.

4 " In me alone, shall men confess
 " Lies all their strength and righteousness;
 " But such as dare despise my name,
 " I'll clothe with everlasting shame.

5 " In me, the Lord, shall all the seed
 " Of Israel, from their sins be freed;
 " And, by their shining graces prove,
 " Their interest in my pardoning love."

HYMN XII.

Youth and Judgment. Eccl. xi.

1 YE sons of Adam, vain and young,
 Indulge your eyes, indulge your tongue,

Taste the delights your souls desire,
And give a loose to all your fire.

2 Pursue the pleasures you design,
And cheer your hearts with songs and wine:
Enjoy the day of mirth—but know
There is a day of judgment too!

3 God, from on high, beholds your thoughts,
His book records your secret faults;
The works of darkness you have done,
Must rise unveil'd before his throne.

4 The vengeance, to your follies due,
Should strike your hearts with terror through;
How will you stand before his face,
Or answer for his injur'd grace?

5 Almighty God, turn off their eyes
From works of vanity and lies;
And let the terrors of thy word
Awake their souls to fear the Lord.

HYMN XIII.
Advice to Youth, Eccl. xii, 1, 7.

1 NOW, in the heat of youthful blood,
Remember your Creator God:
Behold, the months come hastening on,
When you shall say—*my joys are gone!*

2 Behold the aged sinner goes,
Laden with guilt and heavy woes,
Down to the regions of the dead,
With endless curses on his head.

3 The dust returns to dust again;
The soul, in agonies of pain,
Ascends to God: not there to dwell,
But hears her doom, and sinks to hell.

4 Eternal king! I fear thy name:
Teach me to know—how frail I am—
And when my soul must hence remove,
Give me a mansion in thy love.

HYMN XIV.

Justification by Faith, not by Works.
Rom. iii. 19—22.

1 VAIN are the hopes, the sons of men
    On their own works have built;
Their hearts, by nature, all unclean,
    And all their actions guilt.

2 Let Jew and Gentiles stop their mouths,
    Without a murmuring word,
And all the race of Adam stand
    In guilt before the Lord.

3 In vain, we ask God's righteous law
    To justify us now;
Since—to convince, and to condemn—
    Is all the law can do.

4 Jesus, how glorious is thy grace,
    When in thy name we trust!
Our faith receives a righteousness
    Which makes the sinner just.

HYMN XV.

Regeneration, John i. 13. and iii. 3 &c.

1 NOT all the outward forms on earth,
    Nor rites which God has given,
Nor will of man, nor blood, nor birth,
    Can raise a soul to heaven.

2 The sovereign will of God, alone
    Creates us heirs of grace;
Born in the image of his Son,
    A new peculiar race.

3 The spirit, like some heavenly wind,
    Breathes on the sons of flesh;
Creates anew the carnal mind,
    And forms the man afresh.

4 Our quickned souls awake—and rise
    From the long sleep of death;
On heavenly things we fix our eyes,
    And praise employs our breath.

HYMN XVI.

Heaven invisible and holy, 1 Cor. ii. 9, 10. Rev. xxi. 27.

1 NOR eye hath seen, nor ear hath heard,
    Nor sense, nor reason known,
What joys the Father has prepar'd
    For those who love the Son.

2 But the good spirit of the Lord
    Reveals a heaven to come;
The beams of glory, in his word,
    Allure and guide us home.

3 Pure are the joys above the sky,
    And all the regions peace;
No wanton lips nor envious eye,
    Can see or taste the bliss.

4 Those holy gates forever bar
    Pollution, sin, and shame;
None shall obtain admittance there,
    But followers of the lamb.

5 He keeps the Father's book of life,
    There all the names are found;
The Hypocrite in vain shall strive
    To tread the heavenly ground.

HYMN XVII.

The Fall and recovery of Man: Or, Christ and Satan at enmity. Gen. iii. 1. 15, 17. Gal. iv. 4. Col. ii. 15.

1 DECEIV'D by subtile snare of hell,
    Adam, our head, our father, fell;
His unborn race receiv'd the wound,
And heavy curses smote the ground.

2 Thus saith the vengeance of the Lord—
But satan found a worse reward;
    " Let everlasting hatred be
    " Betwixt the woman's seed and thee.

3 " The woman's seed shall be my Son;
    " He shall destroy what thou hast done—
    " Shall break thy head—and only feel
    " Thy malice raging at his heel."

4 He spake—and bade four thousand years
   Roll on—at length his Son appears;
Angels, with joy descend to earth,
   And sing the blest Redeemer's birth.

5 Lo, by the sons of hell he dies!
   But, as he hung 'twixt earth and skies,
He gave their prince a fatal blow,
   And triumph'd o'er the powers below.

HYMN XVIII.
Conviction of sin by the law, Ro. vii, 8. &c.

1 LORD, how secure my conscience lay,
   And felt no inward dread;
I liv'd a while without the law,
   And thought my sins were dead.

2 My hopes of heaven were firm and bright,
   But since the precept came
I stand convicted by its light,
   And find how vile I am.

3 I'm like a helpless captive sold,
   Beneath the power of sin;
I cannot do the good I would,
   Nor keep my conscience clean.

4 My God, I'll cry with every breath,
   For some kind power to save,
To break the yoke of sin and death,
   And thus redeem the slave.

HYMN XIX.
Love to God and our Neighbours. Mat. xxii.

1 THUS saith the first, the great, command,
   Let all thy powers unite,
To love thy Maker and thy God,
   With vigour and delight.

2 Then shall thy neighbour, next in place,
   Thy warm affections prove;
And be thy kindness to thyself
   The measures of thy love.

3 This Moses and the prophet spoke,
   And Jesus from above;
For want of this the law is broke,
   And all the law is love.

4 But oh, how base our passions are!
   How cold our blinded zeal!
Lord, fill our hearts with warm desires,
   To learn and do thy will.

HYMN XX.
Election, sovereign and free. Ro. ix. 21.

1 THE potter moulds the pliant clay,
      And forms to various shapes with ease;
Such is our God, and such are we,
The subjects of his high decrees.

2 May not the sovereign Lord on high
Dispense his favours as he will,
Choose some to life, while others die,
And yet be just and gracious still?

3 Shall man reply against the Lord,
And call his Maker's ways unjust,
The thunder of whose dreadful word
Can crush a thousand worlds to dust?

4 But, O my soul, if truth so bright
Should dazzle and confound thy sight,
Yet still his written will obey,
And wait the great decisive day.

5 Then shall he make his justice known,
And the whole world, before his throne,
With joy or terror, shall confess
His sovereign power and pardoning grace.

HYMN XXI.
Moses and Christ; or, *sin against the law and gospel,*
   Joh. i. 17. He. iii. 3, 5, 6. 2. 28.

1 THE law by Moses came,
      But peace, and truth, and love,
Were brought by Christ (a nobler name)
   Descending from above.

2 Amidst the house of God
      Their different works were done;
Moses a faithful servant stood,
   But Christ—*a faithful son.*—

3 Then to his new command
      Be strict obedience paid;

O'er all his Father's house he stands
    The sovereign and the head.

4 The man who durst despise
    The law which Moses brought,
Behold! how terribly he dies
    For his presumptuous fault:

5 But sorer vengeance falls
    On that rebellious race,
Who hate to hear when Jesus calls
    And dare resist his grace.

HYMN XXII.

The different Success of the Gospel.
1 Cor. i. 13, 24. 2 Cor. ii. 16. 1 Cor. iii. 6, 7.

1 CHRIST and his cross are all our themes;
    The myst'ries which we speak,
Are scandal in the Jews esteem,
    And folly to the Greek:

2 But souls, enlightened from above,
    With joy receive the word;
They see what wisdom, power, and love,
    Shine in their dying Lord.

3 The vital savor of his name
    Restores their fainting breath;
But unbelief perverts the same
    To guilt, despair, and death.

4 'Till God diffuse his graces down,
    Like showers of heavenly rain,
In vain Apollos sows the ground,
    And Paul may plant in vain.

HYMN XXIII.

Children devoted to God. Gen. xvii. 7, 10, Acts xvi. 14, 15, 33.
(For those who practice Infant Baptism)

1 THUS saith the mercy of the Lord,
    " I'll be a God to thee;
" I'll bless thy numerous race—and they
    " Shall prove a seed for me."

2 Abra'm believ'd the promis'd grace,
   And gave his sons to God;
But water seals the blessing now,
   Which once was seal'd with blood.

3 Thus Lydia sanctify'd her house,
   When she receiv'd the word;
Thus the believing jailor gave
   His houshold to the Lord.

4 Thus later saints, eternal king,
   Thine ancient truth embrace;
To thee their infant offspring bring,
   And humbly claim the grace.

HYMN XXIV.

Christ's *Compassion to the Weak and the Tempted*, Heb. iv 15, 10. & v. 9. Mat. xii. 20.

1 WITH joy we meditate the grace
   Of our High Priest, above;
His heart is made of tenderness,
   His bowels melt with love.

2 Touch'd with a sympathy within,
   He knows our feeble frame,
He knows what sore temptations mean,
   For he has felt the same.

3 But spotless, innocent, and pure,
   The great Redeemer stood;
While satan's fiery darts he bore,
   And did resist to blood.

4 He, in the days of feeble flesh,
   Pour'd out his cries and tears;
And, in his measure, feels afresh
   What every member bears.

5 Then let our humble faith address
   His mercy and his power;
We shall obtain delivering grace
   In the distressing hour.

Hymn XXV.

Submission and Deliverance. Gen. xxii. 6.

1 SAINTS, at your heavenly Father's word,
Give up your honours to the Lord;
He shall restore what you resign,
Or grant you blessings *more divine.*

2 So Abra'm with obedient hand
Led forth his son at God's command;
The wood, the fire, the knife he took,
His arm prepar'd the dreadful stroke.

3 " Abra'm, forbear, the angel cry'd,
" Thy faith is known, thy love is try'd;
" Thy son shall live—and in thy race
" Shall all the nations learn my grace."

4 Just in the last distressing hour
The Lord displays delivering power;
The mount of danger is the place,
Where we shall see surprising grace.

Hymn XXVI.

Pharisee and Publican, Luke xviii. 10.

1 BEHOLD how sinners disagree,
The Publican and Pharisee!
One doth his righteousness proclaim,
The other owns his guilt and shame.

2 *This* man at humble distance stands,
And cries for grace with lifted hands;
That boldly rises near the throne,
And talks of duties he has done.

3 The Lord their different Language knows,
And different answers he bestows:
The humble soul, with grace he crowns,
While on the proud his anger frowns.

4 Dear Father, let me never be
Join'd with the boasting Pharisee;
I have no merits of my own,
But plead the Sufferings of thy son.

HYMN XXVII.

Holiness and Grace, Tit. ii 10—13.

1 SO let our lips and lives express
    The holy gospel we profess:
So let our works and virtues shine
To prove the doctrine ALL DIVINE.

2 Thus shall we best proclaim abroad
The honours of our Saviour God;
When the salvation reigns within
And grace subdues the power of sin.

3 Our flesh and sense must be deny'd,
Passion and envy, lust and pride!
While justice, temperance, truth, and love,
Our inward piety approve.

4 Religion bears our spirits up,
While we expect that blessed hope,
The bright appearance of the Lord,
And faith stands leaning on his word.

HYMN XXVIII.

Love and Charity, 1 Cor. xiii. 2—7.

1 LET Pharisees, of high esteem,
    Their faith and zeal declare;
All their religion is a dream,
    If love be wanting there.

2 Love suffers long with patient eye,
    Nor is provok'd in haste:
She lets the present inj'ry die,
    And long forgets the past.

3 She lays her own advantage by
    To seek her neighbour's good;
So God's own Son came down to die,
    And bought our lives with blood.

4 Love is the grace which keeps her power,
    In realms of light above;
There faith and hope are known no more,
    But saints forever love.

HYMN XXIX.

Religion vain without Love, 1 Cor. xiii. 1, 2, 3.

1 HAD I the tongues of Greeks and Jews,
    And nobler speech than angels use,
  If love be absent, I am found
  Like tinkling brass, an empty sound.

2 Were I inspired to preach and tell
  All that is done in heaven and hell;
  Or could my faith the world remove,
  Still I am nothing, without love.

3 Should I distribute all my store
  To feed the bowels of the poor,
  Or give my body to the flame,
  To gain a martyr's glorious name—

4 If love to God, and love to men
  Be absent—*all my hopes are vain:*—
  Nor tongues, nor gifts, nor fiery zeal,
  The work of love can e'er fulfil.

HYMN XXX.
The Death of a Sinner.

1 MY thoughts on awful subjects roll,
    Damnation and the dead;
  What horrors seize the guilty soul
    Upon a dying bed.

2 Lingering about these mortal shores,
    She makes a long delay;
  'Till, like a flood with rapid force,
    Death sweeps the wretch away!

3 Then, swift and dreadful she descends
    Down to the fiery coast;
  Among abominable fiends,
    Herself a frightful ghost.

4 There endless crouds of sinners lie,
    And darkness makes their chains;
  Tortur'd with keen despairs they cry,
    Yet wait for fiercer pains.

5 Not all their anguish, and their blood,
    For their own guilt attones;

Nor the compaſſion of a God
  Shall hearken to their groans.

6 Amazing grace, which kept my breath,
  Nor bid my ſoul remove
'Till I had learn'd my Saviour's death,
  And well inſur'd his love!

HYMN XXXI.
The Death and burial of a Saint.

1 WHY ſhould we mourn departing friends?
    Or ſhake at death's alarms?
  'Tis but the voice which Jeſus ſends
    To call them to his arms.

2 Are we not tending upward too
    As faſt as time can move?
  Nor would we with the hours more ſlow
    To keep us from our love.

3 Why ſhould we tremble to convey
    Their bodies to the tomb?
  There the dear fleſh of Jeſus lay,
    And left a long perfume.

4 The graves of all his ſaints be bleſt,
    And ſoftened every bed:
  Where ſhould the dying members reſt,
    But with the dying head?

5 Thence he aroſe, aſcending high,
    And ſhow'd our feet the way:
  Up to the Lord our ſouls ſhall fly,
    And hail the riſing day.

6 Then let the laſt loud trumpet ſound,
    And bid our kindred riſe;
  Awake ye nations, from the ground,
    Ye ſaints, aſcend the ſkies.

HYMN XXXII.
A Morning Song.

1 ONCE more, my ſoul, the riſing day
    Salutes the waking eyes;
  Once more, my voice, thy tribute pay
    To him who rools the ſkies.

2 Night unto night his name repeats,
   The day renews the sound,
Wide as the heaven, on which he sits
   To turn the seasons round.

3 'Tis he supports my mortal frame,
   My tongue shall speak his praise;
My sins would rouze his wrath to flame—
   And yet his wrath delays!

4 A thousand wretched souls are fled
   Since the last setting sun;
And yet thou lengthenest out my thread,
   And yet my moments run.

5 Dear God, let all my hours be thine,
   While I enjoy the light;
Then shall my sun in smiles decline,
   And bring a pleasing night.

HYMN XXXIII.
An Evening Song.

1 DREAD Sovereign, let my evening song
   Like holy incense rise:
Assist the offerings of my tongue
   To reach the lofty skies.

2 Through all the dangers of the day
   Thy hand was still my guard;
And still to drive my wants away,
   Thy mercy stood prepared.

3 Perpetual blessings from above
   Incompass me around,
But Oh, how few returns of love
   Hath my Creator found!

4 What have I done for him who dy'd
   To save my wretched soul!
How are my follies multiply'd,
   Fast as my minutes roll!

5 Lord, with this guilty heart of mine,
   To thy dear cross I flee;
And to thy grace my soul resign,
   To be renew'd by thee.

6 Sprinkled afresh with pardoning blood,
   I'd lay me down to rest;

As in th' embraces of my God,
  Or on my Saviour's breast.

HYMN XXXIV.
Lord's Day; or, Delight in Ordinances.

1 WELCOME, sweet day of rest,
    Which saw the Lord arise:
Welcome, to this reviving breast,
    And these rejoicing eyes!

2 The King himself comes near,
    And feasts his saints to-day;
Here we may sit, and see him here,
    And love, and praise, and pray.

3 One day amidst the place
    Where heavenly glories shine,
Is sweeter than ten thousand days
    In all the joys of sin.

4 My willing soul would stay
    In such a frame as this;
And sit, and sing herself away
    To everlasting bliss.

HYMN XXXV.
Death and Eternity.

1 STOOP down, my thoughts, which use to rise,
    Converse a while with death:
Think how a gasping mortal lies,
    And pants away his breath.

2 His quivering lips hang feebly down,
    His pulses faint and few;
Then speechless, with a doleful groan,
    He bids the world adieu.

3 But Oh, the soul, which never dies!
    At once it leaves the clay!
Ye thoughts, pursue it where it flies,
    And trace its wondrous way.

4 Up to the courts where angels dwell,
    It mounts triumphing there;
Or devils plunge it down to hell,
    In terror and despair!

5 And must my body faint and die!
  And must this soul remove?
 Oh, for some guardain angel nigh,
  To bear it safe above.

6 Almighty Saviour, to thy hand,
  My naked soul I trust:
 My flesh shall wait thy kind command,
  To mingle with the dust.

HYMN XXXVI.
Frailty and Folly.

1 HOW short and hasty is our life!
   How vast our souls affairs!
 Yet senseless mortals vainly strive
   To lavish out their years.

2 Our days run thoughtlesly along
   Without a moment's stay;
 Just like a story or a song,
   We pass our lives away.

3 God from on high, invites us home,
   But we march heedless on;
 And, ever hasting to the tomb,
   Stoop downward as we run.

4 How we deserve the deepest hell,
   Who slight the joys above!
 What chains of vengeance should we feel,
   Who break such cords of love!

5 Draw us, O God, with sovereign grace
   And lift our thoughts on high,
 That we may end this mortal race,
   And see salvation nigh.

HYMN XXXVII.
Breathing after the holy Spirit.

1 COME, holy Spirit, heavenly Dove,
   With all thy quickening powers,
 Kindle a flame of sacred love
   In these cold hearts of ours.

2 Behold us groveling here below,
   Engag'd in trifling toys!
 Our souls can neither fly, nor go,
   To reach eternal joys.

3 In vain we tune our formal songs,
   In vain, we strive to rise;
Hosannah's languish on our tongues,
   And but devotion dies.

4 Dear Lord! and shall we still remain
   In this declinging state?
Our love so faint, so cold to thee,
   And thine to us so great?

5 Come, holy Spirit, heavenly Dove,
   With all thy quickening powers;
Come, shed abroad a Saviour's love,
   And that shall kindle ours.

HYMN XXXVIII.
Christ's *Intercession*.

1 THE great Redeemer's gone
      To stand before our God,
   To sprinkle o'er the flaming throne
      With his attoning blood.

2 No firey vengeance now,
      No burning wrath comes down:
   If justice calls for sinners blood,
      The saviour shews his own.

3 Before his Father's eye
      Our humble suit he moves;
   The Father lays his thunder by,
      And looks, and smiles, and loves.

4 Now may our joyful tongues
      Our Maker's honour sing;
   Jesus, the priest, receives our songs,
      And bears them to the king.

5 "On earth thy mercy reigns,
   "And triumphs all above;
  "But, Lord, how weak our mortal strains
   "To speak immortal love!

HYMN XXXIX.
Hell; or, *Vengeance of God.*—

1 WITH holy fear, and humble song,
      The dreadful God our souls adore;

HYMN XL.

Reverence and awe become the tongue
Which speaks the terrors of his power.

2 Far, in the deep, where darkness dwells,
The land of horror and despair,
Justice has built a dismal hell,
And laid her stores of vengeance there.

3 There satan the first sinner lies;
And roars, and bites his iron bands;
In vain the rebel strives to rise,
Crush'd with the weight of heavenly hands.

4 There guilty ghosts, of Adam's race,
Shriek out, and howl beneath thy rod;
Once they could scorn a Saviour's grace,
And so incens'd a dreadful God.

5 Tremble, my soul, and kiss the Son—
Sinner, obey thy Saviour's call;
Else your damnation hastens on,
And opening hell awaits your fall.

HYMN XL.
Love to the Creatures is dangerous.

1 HOW vain are all things here below!
   How false and yet how fair!
Each pleasure hath its poison too,
   And ev'ry sweet—a snare.

2 The brightest things below the sky
   Give but a flattering light;
We should suspect some danger nigh,
   Where we possess delight.

3 Our dearest joys, and nearest friends,
   The partners of our blood,
How they divide our wavering minds,
   And leave but half for God!

4 The fondness of a creature's love,
   Allures the flattering sense!
Thither the warm affections move,
   Nor can we call them thence.

5 Dear Saviour, let thy beauties be
   My soul's eternal food;

And grace command my heart away
From all created good.

HYMN XLI.
Shortness of Life, and goodness of God.

1 TIME, what an empty vapour 'tis!
And days, how swift they are!
Swift as a feather'd arrow flies,
Or like a shooting star.

2 Our life is ever on the wing,
And death is ever nigh;
The moment when our lives begin,
We all begin to die.

3 Yet mighty God! our fleeting days
Thy lasting favours share;
And still the bounties of thy grace,
Enrich the rolling years.

4 'Tis sovereign mercy finds us food,
And we are cloth'd by love:
While grace stands pointing out the road,
That leads our souls above.

5 Thus we began the lasting song;
And when we close our eyes,
Let ages down thy praise prolong,
'Till time and nature dies.

HYMN XLII.
God the Thunderer:—or, the last Judgment, and Hell.[*]

1 SING to the Lord ye heavenly hosts,
And let the earth, adore:
Let death and hell, thro' all their coasts,
Stand trembling at his power.

2 His sounding chariot shakes the sky,
He makes the cloud his throne;
There all his stores of lightning lie,
'Till vengeance darts them down.

3 Before him rolls a fiery stream—
And from his awful tongue
A sovereign voice divides the flame,
And thunder roars along!

[*] Made in a great Storm of Thunder, August 20th, 1697.

4 Think, O my soul, the dreadful day
  When this incensed God
Shall rend the sky, and burn the sea,
  And send his wrath abroad!

5 What shall the wretch, the sinner do?
  He once defy'd the Lord:
But he shall dread the thunderer now,
  And sink beneath his word.

6 Tempests of angry fire shall roll
  To blast the rebel worm;
And beat upon his naked soul
  In one eternal storm.

HYMN XLIII.
A Funeral Thought.

1 HARK from the tombs, a doleful sound,
    Mine ears attend the cry—
  "Ye living men, come, view the ground
  "Where you must shortly lie.

2 "Princes this clay must be your bed,
  "In spite of all your towers;
  "The tall, the wise, the reverend head
  "Must lie as low as our's.

3 Great God, is this our certain doom?
    And are we still secure!
  Still walking downwards to the tomb,
    And yet prepar'd no more!

4 Grant us the powers of quickening grace,
    To fit our souls to fly;
  Then, when we drop this dying flesh,
    We'll rise above the sky.

HYMN XLIV.
The Lord's Day; or, *The Resurrection of* Christ.

1 BLEST morning, whose young dawning rays,
    Behold our rising God;
  Which saw him triumph o'er the dust,
    And leave his dark abode!

2 In the cold prison of a tomb
    The dear Redeemer lay;

D d

'Till the revolving skies had brought
   The third, th' appointed day.

3 Hell, and the grave unite their force
   To hold our God in vain;
   The sleeping Conquerer arose,
   And burst their feeble chain.

4 To thy great name, almighty Lord,
   These sacred hours we pay;
   And loud Hosannas shall proclaim
   The triumph of the day.

HYMN XLV.
The Christian Warfare.

1 STAND up, my soul, shake off thy fears,
    And gird the gospel-armour on;
   March to the gates of endless joy,
   Where Jesus went and claim'd his throne.

2 Hell, and thy sins resist thy course;
   But hell and sin are vanquish'd foes;
   Thy Jesus nail'd them to the cross,
   And sung the triumph when he rose.

3 Then let my soul march boldly on,
   Press forward to the heavenly gate;
   There peace and joy eternal reign,
   And glittering robes for conquerers wait.

4 There shall I wear a starry crown,
   And triumph in almighty grace;
   While all the armies of the skies
   Join in my glorious Leader's praise.

HYMN XLVI.
Salvation.

1 SALVATION! Oh, the joyful sound!
    'Tis pleasure to our ears;
   A sovereign balm for every wound,
   A cordial for our fears.

2 Bury'd in sorrow, and in sin,
   At hell's dark door we lay;
   But we arise, by grace divine,
   To see a heavenly day.

3 Salvation! let the echo fly
  The spacious earth around,
While all the armies of the sky
  Conspire to raise the sound.

HYMN XLVII.
Look on him who they pierced and mourn.

1 INFINITE grief! amazing woe!
    Behold my bleeding Lord!
  Hell and the Jews conspire his death,
    And use the Roman sword.

2 Oh! the sharp pangs of smarting pain
    My dear redeemer bore,
  When knotty whips, and ragged thorns,
    His sacred body tore!

3 But knotty whips, and ragged thorns,
    In vain do I accuse;
  In vain I blame the Roman bands,
    And more insulting Jews:

4 'Twere you, my sins, my cruel sins,
    His chief tormentors were;
  Each of my crimes became a nail;
    And unbelief—the spear.

5 'Twere you that pull'd the vengeance down
    Upon his guiltless head:
  Break, break, my heart—Oh, burst mine eyes,
    And let my sorrows bleed!

6 Strike, mighty grace, my flinty soul,
    Till melting waters flow;
  And deep repentance drown mine eyes
    In undissembled woe!

HYMN XLVIII.
The Book of God's Decrees.

1 LET all the race of creatures lie
    Abas'd before their God:
  Whate'er his sovereign voice has form'd
    He governs with a nod.

2 Ten thousand ages ere the skies
    Were into motion brought;
  All the long years and worlds to come
    Stood present to his thought.

3 If light attend the course I run,
   'Tis he provides the rays;
And 'tis his hand which hides my sun,
   If darkness cloud my days.

4 Yet I would not too far enquire,
   Nor vainly long to see
In volumes of his deep decrees,
   What lines are mark'd for me.

5 When he reveals the book of life,
   Oh, may I read my name
Among the chosen of his love,
   The followers of the Lamb.

HYMN XLIX.

The World's Three chief Temptations.

1 WHEN, in the light of faith divine,
   We look on things below,
Honour, and gold, and sensual joy,
   How vain and dangerous too.

2 Honour's a puff of noisy breath;
   Yet men expose their blood,
And venture everlasting death,
   To gain that airy good.

3 Whilst others starve the nobler mind,
   And feed on shining dust;
They rob the serpent of his food,
   T' indulge a sordid lust.

4 The pleasure which allures the sense,
   Are dangerous snares to souls;
There's but a drop of flattering sweet,
   And dash'd with bitter bowls.

5 God is mine all-sufficient good,
   My portion, and my choice;
In him my vast desires are fill'd,
   And all my powers rejoice.

6 In vain the world accosts my ear,
   And tempts my heart anew;
I cannot buy your bliss so dear,
   Nor part with heaven for you.

HYMN L.
Christ's Commission. John iii. 16, 17.

1 COME, happy souls, approach your God,
    With new melodious songs;
  Come, tender to almighty grace
    The tribute of your tongues.

2 So strange, so boundless was the love
    Which pity'd dying men,
  The Father sent his equal Son
    To give them life again.

3 Thy hands, my Saviour, were not arm'd
    With a revenging rod;
  Nor had commission to perform
    The vengeance of a God.

4 But all was mercy—all was love
    And wrath forsook the throne;
  When Christ descended from above,
    And brought salvation down.

HYMN LI.
God glorified in the Gospel.

1 THE Lord, descending from above,
    Invites his children near;
  While power and truth, and boundless love
    Display their glories here.

2 Here in the gospel's wondrous frame,
    Fresh wisdom we may view
  A thousand angels learn thy name,
    Beyond whate'r they knew.

3 Thy name is writ in fairest lines,
    Thy wonders here we trace,
  Wisdom thro' all the mystery shines,
    It shines in Jesus' face.

4 The law its best obedience owes
    To our incarnate God;
  And thy revenging justice shows
    Its honours in his blood.

5 But still the lustre of thy grace
    Our warmer thoughts employs;

Gilds the whole scene with brighter rays,
And more exalts our joys.

HYMN LII.
Circumcision and Baptism.
(Written only for those who practice the Baptism of Infants.)

1 ONCE did the sons of Abra'm pass
   Beneath the bloody seal of grace;
The young disciples bore the yoke,
'Till Christ the painful bondage broke.

2 By milder ways doth Jesus prove
His Father's covenant, and his love;
He seals, to saints his glorious grace,
And kindly owns their infant race.

3 Their seed is sprinkled with his blood,
Their children set a-part from God;
His spirit on their offspring's shed,
Like water pour'd upon the head.

4 Let every saint, with cheerful voice,
In this large covenant rejoice;
Young children, in their early days,
Shall give the God of Abra'm praise.

HYMN LIII.
The example of Christ.

1 MY dear Redeemer, and my Lord,
   I read my duty in thy word:
But in thy life thy law is best
In living characters exprest.

2 Such was thy truth, and such thy zeal—
Such deference to thy Father's will—
Such love, and meekness, so divine,
I would transcribe, and make them mine.

3 Could mountains, and the midnight air,
Witness'd the fervor of thy prayer;
The desert thy temptations knew,
Thy conflict, and thy victory too.

4 Be thou my pattern—make me bear
More of thy gracious image here;
Then God, the Judge, shall own my name
Among the followers of the Lamb.

HYMN LIV.
The Deceitfulness of Sin.

1 SIN has a thousand treacherous arts
　To practice on the mind;
With flattering looks she tempts our hearts,
　But leaves a sting behind.

2 With names of virtues she deceives
　The aged and the young;
And, while the heedless wretch believes,
　She makes his fetters strong.

3 She pleads for all the joys she brings,
　And gives a fair pretence;
But cheats the soul of heavenly things,
　And chains it down to sense.

4 So, on a tree divinely fair,
　Grew the forbidden food;
Our mother took the poison there,
　And tainted all her brood.

HYMN LV.
Christian Virtues.

1 STRAIT is the way, the door is strait,
　Which leads to joys on high;
'Tis but a few who find the gate,
　While crouds mistake, and die.

2 Beloved *self* must be deny'd,
　The mind and will renew'd,
Passion suppres'd, and patience try'd,
　And vain desires subdu'd.

3 The love of gold be banished hence,
　(That vile idolatry)
And every member, every sense
　In sweet subjection lie.

4 The tongue, that most unruly power,
　Requires a strong restraint:
We must be watchful every hour,
　And pray, but never faint.

5 Lord! can a feeble helpless worm

Thy grace must all my work perform,
And give the free reward.

HYMN LVI.

Communion with Christ *and with Saints.*
1 Cor. x. 16, 17.

1. JESUS invites his saints
   To meet around his board;
Here pardon'd rebels sit and hold
   Communion with their Lord.

2. For food he gives his flesh:
   He bids us drink his blood:
Amazing favour! matchless grace,
   Of our descending God!

3. This holy bread and wine,
   Maintain our fainting breath,
By union with our living Lord,
   And interest in his death.

4. Our heavenly Father calls
   Christ and his members one;
We the young children of his love,
   And he the first-born Son.

5. Let all our powers be join'd
   His glorious name to raise:
Pleasure and love fill every mind,
   And every voice be praise.

HYMN LVII.

The Memorial of our absent Lord, John xvi. 16.
Luke xxii. 19. John xiv. 3.

1. THE Lord ascends above the skies,
      Where our weak senses reach him not;
And carnal objects court our eyes,
   To turn the Saviour from our thought.

2. He knows what wand'ring hearts we have,
   That lose the memory of his face;
And, to refresh our minds, he gave
   These kind memorials of his grace.

3. The Lord of life this table spread
   With his own flesh and dying blood,

HYMN LIX.

 We on the rich provision feed,
 And taste the wine, and bless our God.

4 Let sinful sweets be all forgot,
 And earth grow less in our esteem;
 Christ and his love fill every thought,
 And faith and hope be fix'd on him.

5 Whilst he is absent from our sight,
 'Tis to prepare our souls a place:
 That we may live in heavenly light,
 And dwell forever near his face.

HYMN LVIII.

Christ Crucify'd; the Wisdom and Power of God.

1 NATURE with open volume stands,
 To spread her Maker's praise abroad;
 And every labour of his hands
 Displays the wisdom of a God:

2 But in the grace which rescu'd man,
 His brightest form of glory shines;
 Here, on the cross, 'tis fairest drawn
 In precious blood, and crimson lines.

3 Here I behold his inmost heart,
 Where grace and vengeance strangely join;
 Piercing his Son with sharpest smart,
 To make the purchas'd pleasures mine.

4 Oh! the sweet wonders of that cross,
 Where God, the Saviour, lov'd and dy'd!
 Her noblest life my spirit draws
 From his dear wounds, and bleeding side.

5 I would forever speak his name
 In sounds to mortal ears unknown,
 With angels join to praise the Lamb,
 And worship at his Father's throne.

HYMN LIX.

The Gospel Feast. Luke xiv. 16, &c.——

1 HOW rich are thy provisions, Lord!
 Thy table furnish'd from above!
 The fruits of life o'erspread the board,
 The cup o'erflows with heavenly love.

2 Thine ancient family, the Jews,
　Were first invited to the feast:
　We humbly take what they refuse
　And Gentiles thy salvation taste.

3 We are the poor, the blind, the lame;
　And help was far, and death was nigh!
　But at the gospel call, we came,
　And every want receiv'd supply.

4 From the high way which leads to hell,
　From paths of darkness and despair,
　Lord, we are come with thee to dwell,
　And feel thy gladsome presence here.

5 Our everlasting love shall flow,
　To him who left his blest abode,
　And sought these darksome realms below,
　To bring us wanderers back to God.

HYMN LX.
Our Lord Jesus at his own Table.

1 THE memory of our dying Lord
　　Awakes a thankful tongue:
　How rich he spread his royal board,
　　And bless'd the food, and sung.

2 Happy the man who eat this bread,
　　But doubly-bless'd was he
　Who gently bow'd his loving head,
　　And lean'd it, Lord, on thee.

3 By faith the same delights we taste
　　As that great favourite did,
　And sit and lean on Jesus' breast,
　　And take the sacred bread.

4 Down from the palace of the skies;
　　The King of grace descends!
　" Come my beloved, eat (he cries)
　" And drink salvation friends."

5 Hosannah to his bounteous love,
　　For such a feast below!
　And yet he feeds his saints above
　　With nobler blessing too.

5 Come the dear day, the glorious hour,
    That brings our souls to God,
  Then we shall need these types no more,
    But taste the heavenly food.

HYMN LXI.
Grace and Glory by the Death of Christ.

1 WHILE sitting round our father's board,
    We raise our tuneful breath;
  Our faith beholds our dying Lord,
    And dooms our sins to death.

2 We see the blood of Jesus shed,
    Whence all our pardons rise,
  The sinner views th' atonement made,
    And loves the sacrifice.

3 Thy cruel thorns thy shameful cross;
    Procure us heavenly crowns;
  Our gain arises from thy loss;
    Our healing, from thy wounds.

4 Not all the race of mortals here,
    Who dwell in feeble clay,
  For thee can equal sufferings bear
    Or equal thanks repay.

HYMN LXII.
Divine Glories and Graces.

1 HOW fair thy glories here display'd,
    Great God, how bright they shine;
  While at thy word we break the bread,
    And pour the flowing wine!

2 Here thy revenging justice stands,
    And pleads its dreadful cause:
  Here saving mercy spreads her hands,
    Like Jesus on the cross.

3 Thy saints attend with every grace
    On this great sacrifice,
  And love appears with cheerful face,
    And faith with lifted eyes.

4 Our cheerful hope that waiting sits,
    To heaven directs her sight;

Here every warmer passion meets,
And stronger powers unite.'

5 Zeal and revenge perform their part,
And rising sin destroy;
Repentance comes with aching heart,
Yet ne'er forbids the joy.

6 Dear saviour, change our faith to sight,
Let sin forever die;
Then shall our souls be all delight,
And every tear be dry.

HYMN LXIII.

Our Saviour present at his Table.

1 COME let us join the sacred song
To our ascending Lord;
Ye saints and angels round his throne,
And we around his board.

2 Tho' rais'd beyond the worlds of light,
His brighter glories shine,
Where purer souls enjoy the sight
And presence more divine.

3 Yet here, unseen by mortal eyes,
The boundless God resides,
Renews the atoning sacrifice
And o'er the feast presides.

4 Let every hand that shares the food
And every heart with fear,
Feel the full presence of the God,
That spreads his bounties here.

5 But Oh, the love, the wondrous love
The bleeding Lord displays,
Shall earth's united songs improve,
And heaven's eternal praise.

HYMN LXIV.

Invitation to the gospel feast.

1 THE King of heaven his table spreads,
And dainties crown the board;
Not paradise with all its joys
Could such delight afford.

2 Lo, in the blood that Jesus shed,
　　To raise the soul to heaven,
　Pardon and peace for dying men,
　　And endless life is given.

3 Ye hungry poor that long have starv'd
　　In sin's dark mazes, come:
　Come from the hedges and highways,
　　And grace shall find you room.

4 Millions of souls, in glory now,
　　Were fed and feasted here,
　And millions more, still on their way,
　　Around the board appear.

5 All things are ready, come away,
　　Nor weak excuses frame;
　Assume your places at the feast,
　　And bless the founder's name.

HYMN LXV.

Innumerable mercies acknowledged.

1 IN glad amazement, Lord, I stand,
　　Amidst the bounties of thy hand;
　How numberless those bounties are!
　How rich, how various and how fair!

2 But oh, what poor returns I bring!
　What lifeless songs of praise I sing!
　Lord, I confess, with humble shame,
　My offerings scarce deserve the name.

3 Fain would my labouring heart devise
　Some nobler gift and sacrifice;
　It sinks beneath the mighty load
　That I should render to my God.

4 To him I consecrate my praise,
　And vow the remnant of my days;
　Enlarge my soul with grace divine,
　And make it worthier to be thine.

5 Give me at length an angel's tongue,
　To sound thro' heaven the grateful song;
　A theme so great my voice shall raise,
　And crown eternity with praise.

HYMN LXVI.

For a vacant Congregation.

1 O God of heaven, whose gentle rays
    Illumes the worlds of light,
Thy wisdom rules the realms of day,
    And leads the host of night.

2 Behold thy waiting servants stand,
    And claim with feeble cries,
Some skilful guide with gentle hand
    To lead us to the skies.

3 While absent from thy temple, Lord
    Like wandering flocks we stray
We lose the memory of thy word
    And waste the sacred day.

4 And when, within these walls of thine
    We find our wonted place;
How faint our feeble voices join
    To seek thy pardoning grace.

5 Almighty Saviour, hear our prayer,
    Some chosen servant raise,
For us the bread of life to share
    And help our lips to praise.

6 Then in thy house, with joy unknown
    We'll raise a nobler song
Till we shall meet around thy throne,
    And join the heavenly throng.

HYMN LXVII.

For a New-Year's Day.

1 ETERNAL Source of every joy,
    Thy praise shall every voice employ,
While we within thy courts appear,
    And sing the bounties of the year.

2 As worlds of glory round thee roll,
    Thy hand supports the steadfast pole,
Directs the sun what hour to rise,
    And darkness when to veil the skies.

HYMN LXVIII.

3 The flowery Spring at thy command
   Embalms the air, and paints the land;
   The blazing beams of Summer shine
   To raise the corn and cheer the vine.

4 Thy hand in Autumn richly pours
   The copious fruits along the shores,
   While wintry storms direct our eyes
   With fear and wonder to the skies.

5 Seasons, and months, and weeks, and days
   Demand returning songs of praise;
   The opening light and evening shade
   Shall see the cheerful homage paid.

6 And Oh, may our harmonies tongues
   In words unknown pursue the songs;
   And in those brighter courts adore,
   Where days and years revolve no more.

HYMN LXVIII.
A Hymn for Marriage.

1 GREAT God, who form'd for social joys,
       Our natures by thy power and grace,
   And join'd in blest connubial ties,
       The parents of our favour'd race.

2 Our Saviour, our ascended Lord,
       In Canan once a heavenly guest,
   Whose bounty cheer'd the friendly board
       Whose presence grac'd the nuptial feast.

3 Attend with smiles of heavenly love,
       The pair thy sacred laws combine;
   Their union bless, their vows approve,
       And crown the rites with grace divine.

4 Let love assist their mutual toils,
       And every social bliss bestow;
   Increase each joy with friendly smiles,
       And share and soften every woe.

5 While each a kindly aid imparts,
       To run secure the heavenly race;
   And make their dwelling and their hearts,
       Perpetual temples of thy praise.

6 When death dissolves these sacred ties,
    May each to happier realms remove;
    There meet and range the peaceful skies,
    In bands of everlasting love.

HYMN LXIX.

Christ's Ascension.

1 HAIL the day that sees him rise,
    Ravish'd from our wishful eyes;
Christ awhile to mortals given,
Re-ascends his native heaven;
There the pompous triumph waits,
Lift your heads, eternal gates;
Wide unfold the radiant scene,
Take the King of glory in.

2 Him tho' highest heaven receives,
Still he loves the earth he leaves;
Though returning to his throne,
Still he calls mankind his own;
Still for us he intercedes,
Prevalent his death he pleads,
Next himself prepares a place,
Harbinger of human race.

3 Master, may we ever say,
Tak'n from our world away,
See thy faithful servants, see,
Ever gazing up to thee;
Grant, though parted from our sight,
High above yon azure height,
Grant our souls may thither rise,
Follow thee beyond the skies.

4 Ever upward let us move,
Wafted on the wings of love;
Looking when our Lord shall come,
Longing for a happier home;
There we shall with thee remain,
Partners of thine endless reign;
There thy face unclouded see,
Find a heaven of heavens in thee.

HYMN LXX.

The Pilgrim's Song.

1 RISE, my soul, and stretch thy wings,
　　Thy better portion trace;
Rise from transitory things,
　　Tow'rds heaven thy native place:
Sun, and moon, and stars, decay,
　　Time shall soon this earth remove;
Rise, my soul, and haste away
　　To seats prepar'd above.

2 Rivers to the ocean run,
　　Nor stay in all their course,
Fires ascending seek the sun,
　　Both speed them to their source;
So a soul, that's born of God,
　　Pants to view his glorious face;
Upward tends to his abode,
　　To rest in his embrace.

3 Fly me, riches; fly me, cares,
　　While I that coast explore;
Flattering world, with all thy snares,
　　Solicit me no more
Pilgrims fix not here their home,
　　Strangers tarry but a night;
When the last dear morn is come,
　　They'll rise to joyful light.

4 Cease, ye pilgrims cease to mourn,
　　Press onward to the prize;
Soon the Saviour will return,
　　Triumphant in the skies;
Yet a season, and you know
　　Happy entrance will be given,
All our sorrows left below,
　　And earth exchang'd for heaven.

End of the HYMNS.

ANTHEM, From Job, VII.

IS *there* not an appointed time to man upon earth? *Are not* his days also as the days of an hireling? I'm made to possess months of vanity, and wearisome nights are appointed to me. When I lie down, I say, When shall I arise, and the night be gone? I'm full of tossings to and fro, unto the dawning of the day. My flesh is cloth'd with worms, and clods of dust; my skin is broken, and become loathsome, I loath *it*, I would not live always: let me alone, for my days *are* vanity. My days are swifter than a weaver's shuttle, and are spent without hope. O remember that my life is wind! mine eye shall no more see good. As the cloud is consumed, and vanisheth away: so he who goeth down to the grave, shall come up no *more*: for now shall I sleep in the dust, and thou shalt seek me in the morning, but I *shall* not *be*.

ANTHEM, From Sundry Scriptures.

ARISE, shine, O Zion, for thy light is come, and the glory of the Lord is risen upon thee: and the gentiles shall come to thy light, and King's to the brightness of thy rising. Sing, sing, O Heavens, and be joyful, O earth, for behold I bring you glad tidings of great joy, which shall be to all people. For unto you is born this day in the city of David, a Saviour, who is Christ the Lord. Glory be to God on high, and on earth peace good will towards men. For unto us a Child is born, unto us a son is given; and his name shall be called Wonderful, Counsellor, the Mighty God, the everlasting Father, the Prince of Peace. Amen. Hallelujah. Amen.

ANTHEM. From Psalm CXXIV.

IF the Lord himself had not been on our side—now may Israel say; if the Lord himself had not been on our side, when men rose up against us; they had swallowed us up quick; yea, the waters had drown'd us; and the stream had gone over our soul. But praised be the Lord, our soul is escaped, even as a bird out of the snare of the fowler; the snare is broken, and we are delivered. Our help standeth in the name of the Lord, who made heaven and earth.

ANTHEM. From LUKE II.

BEHOLD I bring you glad-tidings of joy, which shall be to all people. For unto you is born this day, in the city of David, a Saviour who is Christ the Lord. And this shall be a sign unto you. You shall find the Babe wrapt in swadling clothes, lying in a manger. And suddenly there was with the angel a multitude of the heevenly host, praising God and saying, Glory to God in the highest, and on earth peace, good will towards men. Hallelujah!

ANTHEM. From ISAIAH XLIV.

SING, sing O ye Heavens; for the Lord hath done it: Shout, shout, ye lower parts of the earth: For the Lord hath redeem'd Jacob, and glorified himself in Israel. Break forth into singing, ye mountains, O forest, and ev'ry tree therein: For the Lord hath redeemed Jacob, and glorified himself in Israel. Glory be to the Father, Son, and Holy Ghost, as it was in the beginning, is now, and ever shall be, world without end. Amen.

ANTHEM. From PSALM CIV.

PRAISE the Lord, O my soul! O Lord, my God, thou art become exceeding glorious! Thou art clothed with majesty and honour. Hallelujah Amen. Thou deckest thyself with light, as it were with a garment, and spreadest out the Heavens like a curtain. Who layeth the beams of his chambers in the waters, and maketh the clouds his chariot and walketh upon the wings of the wind: He maketh his angels spirits, and his ministers a flaming fire: He laid the foundations of the earth, that it never be removed. O Lord, how manifold are thy works! In wisdom hast thou made them all. The earth is full of thy riches. The glorious majesty of the Lord shall endure forever. The Lord shall rejoice in his works. Hallelujah—Amen.

not in Gath, publish it not in the streats of Askelon: Let the daughters of the Philistines should rejoice, and the daughters of the uncircumcised should triumph.—Ye mountains of Gilboa, let there be no dew, neither rain upon you; for ther the shield of the Mighty is vilely cast away. Saul and Jonathan were lovely and pleasant in their lives, and in their deaths they were not divided.—Ye daughters of Israel, weep, weep over Saul, who clothed you in scarlet with other delights; who put ornaments of gold upon your apparel. How are the mighty fallen in the midst of the battle!—O Jonathan! thou wast slain upon *thine* high places: I am distressed for thee, O my brother Jonathan! very pleasant hast thou been unto me, thy love to me was wonderful, passing the love of women.—How are the mighty fallen, and the weapons of war perished.

ANTHEM. FROM PSALM VIII.

O LORD, our Governor, how excellent is thy name in all the world: Thou hast set thy glory above the heavens! Out of the mouth of babes and sucklings thou hast ordained strength that thou mightest still the enemy and the avenger. I will consider the heavens the works of thy fingers: the moon and stars which thou hast ordained. What is man, that thou art mindful of him? and the son of man, that thou visitest him? Thou madest him lower than the angels, to crown him with glory and worship, O Lord, our Governor, how excellent is thy name in all the world.

THE END.

SEE the Lord of glory, dying,
See him gasping, hear him crying,
  See his burden'd bosom heave;
Look, ye sinners, ye who hung him,
Look, how deep your sins have stung him,
  Dying sinners, look and live.

See the rocks and mountains shaking;
Earth unto her centre quaking,
  Nature's groans awake the dead;
Look on Phœbus, struck with wonder,
While the peals of legal thunder
  Smite the blest Redeemer's head.

Heaven's bright melodious legions,
Chanting to the tuneful regions,
  Cease to trill the quiv'ring string;
Songs seraphic, all suspended,
Till the mighty war is ended
  By the all victorious King.

Hell and all the powers infernal,
Vanquish'd by the King eternal,
  When he pour'd the vital flood;
By his groans, which shook creation,
Lo! we sound the proclamation,
  Peace and pardon through his blood.

Shout, ye saints, with admiration,
Fill with songs the wide creation,
  Since he's risen from the grave;
Shout with joy and acclamation,
To the Rock of your salvation,
  Who alone has power to save.

6 Bear with patience tribulation,
　Overcoming all temptation,
　　Till the glorious jubilee;
　Soon he'll come with bursts of thunde
　Then shall we adore and wonder,
　　Singing on the highest key.

7 See the blissful scene before us,
　Join the universal chorus,
　　Bid the flowing numbers rise;
　Songs immortal sweetly sounding,
　Notes angelic, loud rebounding,
　　Trembling round the vocal skies.

www.ingramcontent.com/pod-product-compliance
Lightning Source LLC
Chambersburg PA
CBHW030001240426
43672CB00007B/779